FULL
ON

IVAN
YATES
FULL
ON

A Memoir

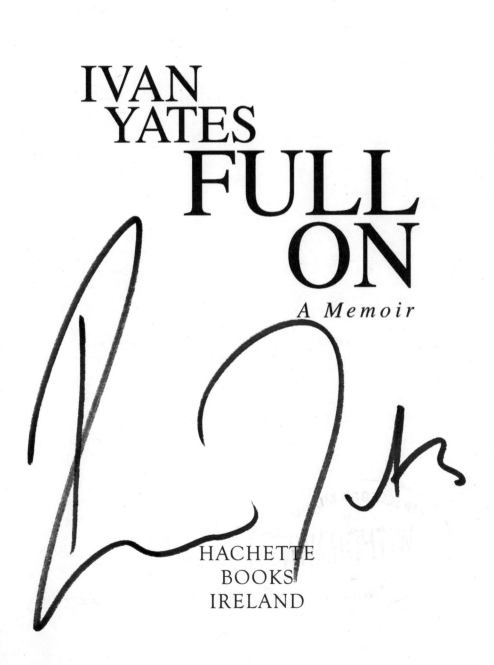

HACHETTE
BOOKS
IRELAND

First published in 2014 by
HACHETTE BOOKS IRELAND

A CIP catalogue record for this book is available from the British Library.

ISBN 978 1444 79873 9

Typeset in Garamond by redrattledesign.com

Printed and bound by Clays Ltd, St Ives plc

Hachette Books Ireland policy is to use papers that are natural, renewable and recyclable products and made from wood grown in sustainable forests. The logging and manufacturing processes are expected to conform to the environmental regulations of the country of origin.

The publishers would like to thank the following for permission to reproduce photographs in the book: Patrick J Browne & People Papers, The Department of Agriculture, *The Irish Times* and Newstalk FM.

Hachette Books Ireland
8 Castlecourt Centre
Castleknock
Dublin 15, Ireland

A division of Hachette UK Ltd.
338 Euston Road
London NW1 3BH

*This book is dedicated to two remarkable women in my life,
both of whom have been an unstinting source of support
and loyalty, inspiration and strength:*

Mary Yates and Deirdre Yates.

Contents

Preface

Why a book? My time in politics, business and media has been a rollercoaster ride – unbelievable highs and lows. I am not sufficiently up my own ass to think that any of these careers were important enough to justify a memoir. My main motivation for writing the book was primarily to thank all those who said 'yes' to me. Whether it was a vote at a selection convention or at the ballot box; punters choosing Celtic Bookmakers; being offered a media column or broadcast show or many other great opportunities: while I expressed gratitude, I was always in such a rush on to the next project that I never really thanked properly all those people who had belief in me. This autobiography has been written for those countless characters who gave me the green light. It is my payback in appreciation.

Along my journey I have encountered success and endured failure. Getting elected to the Dáil at twenty-one years, without any political pedigree; reaching cabinet office; building up, from scratch, a business with revenues of almost €200 million and multiplying radio listenership must have meant that I got some things right along the way. Similarly, in retrospect, I have gained experience into what works and what doesn't. Therefore, a primary purpose of this book is to provide my insights and tips on how to attain your ambitions and avoid hazardous pitfalls. You may not always agree, but I hope it may make you reflect on how best to go about climbing your own mountains.

My circumstances during 2012/13 – life in bankruptcy – meant that I was effectively prohibited from any economic or business activity. Living in Swansea has been like no other period in my life. I was no longer thrusting forward, chasing my latest pioneering plan. The illustrious local poet Dylan Thomas once wrote 'he who seeks rest finds boredom, he who seeks work finds rest'. With so much time on my hands, I felt that if I didn't write a book now, I never would. Hopefully, by getting my past off my chest I will be able to close those chapters in order to allow me to make a fresh start.

I need to make an advance apology to the many people who should have read their names in this book on the basis of their impact on my life or my valued friendship with them. For reasons of brevity and to protect people's privacy, I deliberately erred on the side of minimising reference to individuals.

In contract negotiations there is a term, 'best endeavours', which covers obligations on each party where future circumstances are unpredictable. Throughout this book I have described detailed conversations over the years. These quotes are based on my 'best recollections' and reflections of my take on events. For those involved, forgive me if these are not verbatim accounts – they are as accurate as possible in retrospect.

I hope you enjoy the ride.

Ivan Yates
September 2014

1: Lost Innocence

My ancestors provided me with a heritage rich in alcohol, entrepreneurship and bankruptcy. This I know, courtesy of RTÉ television's *Who Do You Think You Are?* When, five years ago, the programme-makers surfaced, wanting to make an edition about my ancestors, I told them I was going to cause their researchers endless trouble: I had spent my time plunging forward through life and never bothered to find out anything about my background. I was a blank canvas.

Off they went to delve deep into the past of my forebears, every now and again coming back to me with a new revelation. Like that my great-great-great-great-grandfather was none other than John Jameson. Knowing you descend from one of the founders of the Irish whiskey firm carries a bit of a charge.

John, a Scottish lawyer by trade, married into alcohol. His wife, Margaret Haig, belonged to the Scottish whisky-distilling family. The two of them came to Ireland in the late eighteenth century, established the Bow Street Distillery in Dublin and achieved sufficient social prominence to ensure that their portraits, painted by Sir Henry Raeburn, hang in the National Gallery of Ireland. The Bow Street Distillery is a key part of what is today the global multinational conglomerate Irish Distillers, owned by Pernod Ricard.

Margaret and John's son Andrew moved to Fairfield, outside Enniscorthy, County Wexford where he set up a small distillery, which might have been as successful as his father's except for timing. Andrew launched his business straight into the teeth of a virulent anti-alcohol campaign led by the temperance reformer Father Mathew. Father Mathew won.

Then, since 'sorrows come not single spies but in battalions', Annie, one of his two daughters, compounded his miseries by eloping with an Italian, ending up in her new husband's home country and giving birth to a son, named after his father: Guglielmo Marconi. Annie's lad converted electromagnetic waves into electricity, the bedrock technology for broadcasting and communication. The original Marconi Corporation was put together in London during 1897 by Henry Jameson Davis, his first cousin. He procured the investment finance to lay cable and start experimental transmissions across the Atlantic, thus providing Andrew Jameson, back in Wexford, with that worst of fates: personal failure culminating in bankruptcy, complicated by the success of most of the rest of his family.

The stay-at-home daughter, Helen Jameson, married Abraham Grub Davis, my great-grandfather on my mother's side, thereby ensuring that he got drummed out of the Quakers. They did not approve of mixed marriages and they approved even less of bankruptcy.

Abandoning alcohol as an income source, Abraham, with his brother Samuel, established one of the most technologically modern flour mills in the country at St John's, Enniscorthy. For more than a hundred years, this was one of the principal local employers. Their respective son and daughter, first cousins Francis Davis and Anne Davis, married. One of their children was my grandmother, Helen Davis. She married a clergyman, Alfred Forbes, who became the Dean of Ferns. They had four children, one of whom was my mother, Mary.

RTÉ also traced my father's predecessors back to the nineteenth century, where they found John Yates, a member of the Royal Irish

Constabulary. His son, John F. Yates, born in 1862, pitched up as an adult at Templeshannon Quay in Enniscorthy to establish a grain, coal and timber business. He imported stock using boats on the river Slaney. To this day, the top of a large four-storey warehouse has a memorial stone accredited to him, dated in the year of construction, 1884. He was my great-grandfather and a hugely successful businessman. In 1890, he bought our current family home and farm at Blackstoops, just outside Enniscorthy. We still have the estate agent's advertising blurb from the time. It was a prized residence overlooking the town with a panoramic view of the Slaney. When John F. Yates, my great-grandfather, died in 1922, his estate was valued at £85,486, making him a multimillionaire in today's terms. He owned property around Enniscorthy and had a large family, including a son named Ivan Yates, who took over the business, farm and house. By 1934, local people would have perceived Ivan Yates as a merchant prince in the 'big house'. He was part of the local Protestant community who opposed Éamon de Valera's monocultural view of Gaelic Ireland. When Dev's Minister for Education, Thomas Derrig, issued an order that all primary-school education be principally taught in the Irish language, Ivan sent his daughter Hazel (my aunt) to a small private school that did not conform; he was fined one shilling in the District Court under the School Attendance Act. Appealing the judgement to the Circuit Court, he won a landmark case against the government, thus ensuring that his daughter would be allowed to continue her education in English.

The underlying point of my family tree is that for more than 150 years it shows nothing other than a 100 per cent Protestant heritage, in a country that was 90 per cent Catholic. Throughout the era of Irish independence and the evolution of the new state, this strand of Irishness was predicated and sustained on being insular, independent and financially secure. Most Protestant families were not dependent on public services. They ran their own self-reliant enterprises and kept to themselves socially and in marriage. It wasn't until the 1950s that a generation, which included my parents John F. Yates and Mary Forbes, became fully integrated into the local community.

My parents were not West Brit or Anglo-Irish: they were just Protestants, Church of Ireland, both of them. They were as Irish as anyone else. And tough. Toughness defined my father, perhaps because, after his mother died when he was four years old, he went to boarding school: Aravon in Bray, followed by Campbell College in Northern Ireland. He was thirty-two and my mother was twenty-one when they married in 1953. That year, his father made him a partner in the business, vacating the house at Blackstoops for him and my mother. In October 1959, I was brought up there as the third child in the family, my two Christian names, Alfred Ivan, taken from my grandfathers.

I hate to admit it, but I was born with privilege and every advantage in life. No six-in-the-bed, arses-out-of-trousers hunger. Rather the opposite. We had a live-in housekeeper, other occasional domestic staff and a full-time gardener. In the early 1950s eight people worked on the farm, some living in cottages scattered throughout the estate, one family in the gate lodge. The farm was renowned for rearing pedigree Jersey, Angus and Hereford cattle. Elaborate farm sheds, cement yards, stables and a cow byre occupied space within about a hundred acres of land. Owing to other business expansion, the farm was rented out from my childhood onwards.

Eventually we were a family of four. The oldest was my brother John, called Junior by us all to avoid confusion with my father's name. Christine and Valentine are my two sisters, one older than me by two years, one younger by about two years. By all accounts, I was a good baby and slept a lot. Other than a passion for Farley's rusks and once having a dead mouse on my pillow, my infant years were uneventful and I remember little about them. I have a generalised sense of happy times. Maggie, the housekeeper, served our main meal in the dining room at lunchtime, when my father would come in from work. I adored her. Looking back, I realise I was as close to her as I was to my mother at that time – for completely selfish reasons. Each day she would make delicious steamed puddings, and I loved to lick the spoon and bowl. Maggie had her own bedroom. In later years, I would lie with her on the bed and watch telly. She cooked, cleaned and cared for our every need. She suffered terribly with varicose veins in her legs, which bled a lot and required bandages. I was her pet. There was nothing she wouldn't do willingly for me. Maggie was, for me, a member of my family, not an employee.

We were an ordinary Protestant family, attending church and Sunday school, enduring sermons every weekend. We were all enrolled in St Mary's national school in Enniscorthy. Miss Betty Patton, with a strong Donegal accent, taught us through infant classes up to second class. I was good at spelling and knew my multiplication tables off by heart.

My mother was the religious one, her father and grandfather being clergymen. My father, in sharp contrast, rarely went to church, was not remotely religious and never got involved in any organisation like the Freemasons. But, then, my father rarely got involved in anything. I do not recall him ever bringing me to a match – rugby, football or Gaelic – although he had been a successful member of the rugby Towns Cup winning team for Enniscorthy in the 1950s. His motivating force was the family business. He did not take summer holidays or weekends off. He was dedicated to making money and not going broke. I suspect he thought about business even when he went rod fishing on the Slaney where, every spring, he would catch large quantities of salmon. The other constant factor was his forty cigarettes a day – the strongest brand: Major. He regularly suffered severe bronchitis.

My father expanded the solid fuel business, sending a delivery lorry around Enniscorthy with coal, turf and logs. In 1959 he opened a drapery shop in the town, mostly selling menswear. Eventually it had a sports department, including fishing tackle, a ladieswear section and, upstairs, a large toyshop. Each Christmas, we used to work behind the counter selling toys and making sure that our cash takings tallied at the end of the day. Our gardener, Con – who talked to himself, smoked a pipe, wore a sack over his shoulders in the rain and put up with us sneaking up behind him to give him a fright – always played Santa Claus in the shop, with blue parcels for boys and pink for girls. It was magical but, most importantly, profitable, except when the Slaney flooded in 1966 and shop stocks were destroyed.

None of these enterprises was anything like as important as the main business: wool. How he got into it and how he developed the marvellous expertise he had is one of those mysteries I never got to explore with my Father. All I know is that from Dingle to Portumna, from Down to Arklow, he had a network of small merchants, guys with a pub and an undertaker's business, who would buy wool from farmers for him and he in turn bought it from them. In May, when tens of thousands of sheep were shorn, he'd sort the fleeces into all the different types: there'd be Blackface, Suffolk, Cheviot and Border Leicester, among others. Once it was sorted, it would be packed in bales with metal bands around it and sent off for spinning to places like Bradford, the principal export market. He used to get the *Yorkshire Post* to keep abreast of price fluctuations. He employed about twenty people and sold wool as far afield as China and Switzerland.

We couldn't watch television at night because our father was always on the phone, for hours on end, to the agents who worked for him across the country, buying wool on commission. Wool is a commodity business and subject to risky price rises and falls. If he overpaid farmers and agents, he ran the risk of severe losses. This meant that he was fearful and tight about money. He took pride in employing local families and believed that he treated them well, but he expected everybody to work as hard as he did, and few could or would. Each season brought its own challenge. The grain harvest in August was busy, because John F. Yates & Son Ltd did a big trade in renting out sacks to farmers. In wet weather the sacks had to be dried out. A team of local women mended torn ones.

My father was in charge of everything. His entire life hinged on frugality and a strict work ethic. He used to have expressions like 'working to the scrunt', meaning hardship. 'Gramps' meant basics in food and drink. In other households, the conversations might have been about politics, religion, entertainment or the arts. In our household, they were nearly always about the state of the business – and they weren't conversations. They were a constant recounting by my father of that day's highs and lows. He was thinking aloud for our benefit. And we listened attentively, respectfully, quietly.

My mother looked after us. She did not spoil us, but we lacked nothing. Which didn't stop me wanting more than I was entitled to. When we went shopping in Earle's grocery in Enniscorthy, she would always allow us one treat apiece from the confectionery counter. I got a squared-off brown carton of Smarties. Jimmy, the man serving us, was tall, with a distinguished Roman nose, a brown coat and hair combed back with Brylcreem. One day, when his back was turned, I grabbed a bar of Fry's Chocolate Cream, its navy wrapping promising the delicious blend of dark chocolate with white fondant on the inside. In the back of Mummy's green A40 car, I proudly produced my ill-gotten gains. There was a hushed silence. My mother was outraged. My siblings revelled in my deep humiliation. I was frogmarched back into the shop to apologise to Jimmy and my pocket money was removed for several weeks as a fine. That permanently stifled any aspirations I had for a career as a thief.

Looking back, most of my childhood seems to have happened out of doors, where we were surrounded by animals. My dad was great pals with Gerry Connors, the local King of the Travellers. He used to buy donkeys from him and we were expected to ride the animals bareback. We would yoke up a cart, with elaborate tackle, to the donkey with long reins and take off on local trips. Invariably it turned into a nightmare because the stubborn animal would not go in the direction we wanted.

On one occasion, my mother, reading a book in the front porch of the house, was startled and puzzled to see a donkey galloping wildly up the avenue on its own. It was followed, a few minutes later, by her four disconsolate youngsters, red in the face from the effort of pushing the cart that had briefly been attached to the donkey. I was carrying the donkey's broken tackle. Our first attempt to ride ponies also ended in failure because we couldn't control them.

In later years, on a fly-fishing trip to Lough Mask with his closest friend and solicitor Des McEvoy, my father bought a rundown cottage for five hundred pounds in Tourmakeady, where we spent part of the summer holidays each year after 1970. The only other family holidays I remember involved our granny bringing us for a few days to the Salthill Hotel beside the sea in Dún Laoghaire.

Because my dad was busiest in the summer, the best he could manage was irregular weekend visits to join us. On rare Sundays, he might bring us to Blackwater beach, but that was it. My mother looked after trips to the circus, children's parties and the annual county show.

We mostly entertained ourselves. On our bikes, we raced around pretending to be show-jumpers Eddie Macken, David Broome or Harvey Smith. We would head off to a stream for picnics, and light fires to roast dead birds, apples and spuds. We converted an outhouse into our own room called the 'bar'. Val and I played together mostly, despite her bossiness.

Home for me has always been Enniscorthy and the Model County of Wexford. I have a deep affinity with Blackstoops, which undoubtedly stiffened my spine when fighting with the banks in recent years to try to retain it in Yates family ownership.

Everywhere you go in Enniscorthy, you rub up against history. The town is famous for Vinegar Hill, where the 1798 rebellion was defeated. Enniscorthy is a medium-sized market town with a population of about five thousand and a hinterland stretching to the sea on the east, the Blackstairs mountains to the west. It's a beautiful scenic area, with the river Slaney passing through. Local features I love are the Castle Museum, the greyhound track and Showgrounds, the Pugin cathedral, and the adjoining coastline with its endless sandy beaches. And everywhere people of genuine decency, warmth, sincerity, who aren't impressed by fame, money, triumph or disaster and would wind you up just for the craic.

That's the way I remember it – a golden wash of happiness over my childhood from the first memory onward. It took therapy – after a bout of nervous exhaustion when I was in my thirties – to thin out that golden gloss and let me see some of the bad times, like the year when I was eight years of age, in third class in the national school. Third class was under the direction of the school principal, Jack Hayton. Jack and my father had been close friends for many years. His son, Alan, used to come to my house to play and I would go to his house. In my house, we played with my precious toy farm animals, until the day Alan cut the tails off all of them. I was mystified.

It was the first of a series of frightening incidents, many of which happened in the classroom, where Alan's admittedly mischievous tendencies would provoke in his father a response well out of proportion to the behaviour. Coming from a house where neither affection nor aggression was ever on crude display, I found this strange and deeply frightening.

It was this response that ruined the schooldays of many of the classmates. To see his father shouting at Alan, hitting him across the head and beating him with a ruler provided us all with a free sample of raw anger none of us needed to witness. We never understood the underlying reason for the fury, so we were never sure that we would not get sucked into this terror.

I would come home each day ashen-faced, sullen and upset. My parents became increasingly worried. They decided in January 1968, in the middle of the academic year, to take me out of the situation and send me to a preparatory boarding school in Bray – Aravon (on the Novara Road, spelled backwards). My brother John was in his last year there, before he went on to Portora Royal School in Enniskillen.

On the face of it, my time in Aravon was golden. In my final year I was head boy and captain of the hockey team. I did well in my studies and was set eventually to go to college. That was how I remembered it, until therapy peeled away the misery at the heart of my secondary schooldays.

In my first year at Aravon, 1968, I was the youngest of about sixty boys in the school. I was number 33 (tacked on to my shoes), with name tapes on all my clothes. The smallest boys were put in a dormitory wing. I wasn't used to the total darkness – I would always have a light on at home during the night. Terror mixed with homesickness meant that I cried myself to sleep, night after night, hopelessly missing Maggie and all the family.

I would wake up in the morning to find myself in an icily saturated and stinking bed. During the night I would have wet it, deliberately, Matron Moore clearly believed. Or it had happened, she decided, because I was too lazy to get out of bed and go to the toilet. Matron Moore seemed to be permanently furious with me. A rubber blanket was put under the sheet, partly to protect the mattress but also, it seemed, as a punishment for my evil bedwetting. I desperately wanted to overcome this shameful problem, but nothing worked. Not fear, not shame, not even the hot rubber beneath me, its presence branding me, like a mark on my forehead or a great capital letter worn on my chest. Hot tears when the lights went out. Cold urine when they came back on.

The ethos of the school and its treatment of small boys seems incredible by today's standards. Every morning we had to take a bath or shower so shockingly cold that it made us breathless. If we accidentally spilled a glass of milk or water, we had to eat standing at the Pig's Table in the corner. In winter, we were made to wear short trousers so we were constantly frozen and caught the flu. Only older boys could wear long trousers. One of the teachers, Miss Armstrong, was always kind to the smaller boys, and when our legs were raw and painfully chapped, she would give us Vaseline to rub on them.

On some Saturday nights we got to watch a film in the gym. I can vividly recall the first few scenes of *Where Eagles Dare* but have not the slightest idea what happens afterwards because I felt ill in the middle and was immediately sent to the sickbay, which consisted of two beds in a top-floor room, situated above where Matron Moore slept. I was there for two days with an awful dose of flu, feeling rotten, desperately homesick, hiccuping through my sobs. 'Grow up, you big baby,' Matron would yell at me.

Today, if she were alive, I would ask her how the hell she could be so lacking in compassion for a frightened, isolated and sick child. I would want to know where her callousness came from, and why she thought any bright child – which I demonstrably was – would want to draw down daily shame on himself by wetting his bed, or would continue to sob when it was inescapably doing him no good at all.

I learned to cry quietly, hugging myself to stop the sobs being heard. I wept as I wrote letters home to Maggie and my parents. The worst night was Sunday, during evensong, when every minor key in the hymns added to my sadness.

The worst aspect of it was the constant fear. Charles Mansfield, headmaster and owner of the school, flattered himself that he was a disciplinarian. In fact, he was a sadist, liberally administering corporal punishment for any infringement of a forest of rules. Beatings were meted out with a slipper or a hairbrush on bare buttocks.

In my second year, I was in a dormitory adjacent to the headmaster's office. If we were caught talking at night or early in the morning, he would come in and beat us. It became a familiar ritual. When he came round to each bed, we would turn over, pull down our pyjamas and receive our beating, faces in our pillows, counting the blows. Some boys got punished much worse than I did. One boy was black and blue from constant thrashings.

At eight and nine years old, I was out of my depth. I wasn't perfect. Far from it. On one occasion I was cheeky to a cleaner, who reported me for it, and staff asked my brother John to talk sense into me. He told me that I needed to toughen up in order to survive. It must have seemed like good advice, from his point of view. It even sounded like good advice from my point of view. I just didn't know how to do it.

It was unremitting torture. We got home only at Christmas, Easter and for the summer holidays, because the exeats (when pupils were allowed out on one Sunday a month) were too short to drive down to Enniscorthy and back. The older, bigger boys felt they were entitled to payback time, since they had been on the receiving end, so beatings came from them too. Fortunately, I wasn't too regular a victim, but realised early on that a few boys suffered dreadfully because some inchoate aspect of their personality or appearance marked them out for bullying. You couldn't report it or you would be called a sneak.

In fairness to Aravon, I have to acknowledge a culture change when Mr Freddie Cooper, a millionaire from Jersey, took over ownership of the school around 1971/72. He was sensitive. Also around that time, a new housemaster, Mr Terry O'Malley, and his wife, Patti, treated me kindly, inviting me to their eldest daughter Kate's christening. Freddie used to bring us on Sunday nights to the Gaiety Theatre for orchestral concerts, with a hot dog on the way home. Corporal punishment continued, however. He used a large plastic ruler, but you could tell he didn't take any pleasure from it. He would sweat profusely and be out of breath when he felt he had to chastise students.

My favourite, even though he could be strict, was Mr Brian Studdert, who taught me English. He would train us to read the lesson in St Paul's Church in Bray, where the services were sometimes broadcast on RTÉ radio, including the carols at Christmas. He had a game in his class called 'scooper's club', which meant you had to keep talking and answering questions on a given topic without stopping. The winner was the person who talked their way out of trouble. I frequently won, gaining self-confidence in being able to think and talk spontaneously.

We were banned from going outside the grounds to the local shop or the sea front. Breaches led to beatings.

As I grew up, I remembered the beatings, but not the overwhelming sadness. It took therapy to put me front and centre in a misery from which I learned nothing at the time, just as it took therapy for me to recall the day, when I was about eleven, when Mr Mansfield asked me to come and see him in the French room. This was situated in the building away from the main block at the school, called Newlands. When I arrived, he was in the room, alone, standing by a table in the corner, away from the blackboard and the pupils' desks. He asked me to pull up a chair and sit down in front of him, explaining that as part of his sex education duties, he had individual consultations with the boys. He needed to see that we were developing properly. He asked me to take down my trousers and pants, so that he could examine me. I vividly recall that we were standing so close together that I could see the tiny blood vessels on his cheeks and could smell him. I did as I was told.

He put on his glasses and duly examined me. I queried whether everything was all right. He said it was fine. I felt so self-conscious, awkward and embarrassed. I didn't know any better, didn't think this was wrong at the time and didn't dare question why.

On the Richter scale of abuse, it didn't amount to much. He did not touch me and there was no overt sexual activity. Puberty didn't knock on my door for another few years, so the incident meant little to me other than that I was ashamed and felt guilty. I don't know if a similar event happened to any other boy, because I didn't tell anyone about it. I just kept my head down and survived. The one thing I was sure of was that no child of mine was ever going to a preparatory boarding school. I do not accept the tradition that justifies cruelty to one generation on the basis that an earlier generation endured much worse.

The original plan was for me, as I moved into my early teens, to follow in my brother's and father's footsteps by attending secondary boarding school in Northern Ireland. The troubles there in the early 1970s militated against that. Instead, my two sisters and I went to St Columba's College adjacent to the Dublin mountains overlooking the city. It was like something out of a Harry Potter movie. Pupils wore black gowns that covered them to their knees.

Each morning began with a service in the college chapel at 8.25, called matins. On Sundays we wore a white surplice, like that of an altar boy or priest. Many of the pupils – it was boys only until the senior cycle – were sons of clergymen or from Northern Ireland Protestant families. The curriculum and examination structure were the same as they were at every other school, except that O levels were substituted for the Intermediate Certificate in the third form/year.

This was and is the most expensive secondary school in Ireland. My parents made enormous sacrifices to ensure that all four of their children went to boarding schools. At that time the annual fees were several thousand pounds. This had to be paid out of after-tax income. The school, at that time, had about two hundred students, with seventeen teachers. The average class size was twelve pupils. The backbone of the school was ceremonial tradition. Boarders were accommodated in four houses: Stackallan, Grange, Gwyn and Glen. Each had a different colour tie.

I was in Glen, with a green tie. Bud McMullan, the housemaster, was an easy-going family man who taught biology and loved coaching the senior rugby team. Freedom and latitude were more on offer than they had been at Aravon, even though my first year saw me back on the bottom rung of the ladder. New students were called 'punks' and expected to do fagging duties for their house captains or prefects. You kept out of the way of all the heavy guys, who wouldn't hesitate to beat you up if you annoyed them.

Academically, I did fine. I was in the top three in the class in most subjects and even won form prizes in my second and third years. But my greatest achievement was in a public-speaking competition held in front of an assembly of the entire school. You had to speak for up to ten minutes on a chosen topic, with authority, humour and fluency. In the preceding weeks, each night in the dormitory, I would practise and rehearse my speech on why the world should be vegetarian – so that there would be enough food for the entire global population. I prepared all my facts and figures for a convincing notional case.

Adam Clayton, subsequently of U2 fame, was in the adjoining bed. I recall he was learning the guitar at the time, but with limited success . . . Another dormitory inmate, John Leslie, was a really good guitarist and was teaching Adam. That had to stop when I was rehearsing my speech. I insisted that Adam listen to my whispered orations and pass judgement. He didn't think much of either content or delivery, but I didn't let that discourage me. Despite nerves, and being much more junior than the other competitors, I pulled it off. It went down a treat. They laughed in the right places and clapped at the end. Talk about a high. I got a huge buzz out of winning and went on to participate in inter-school debating competitions held in Trinity College.

The greatest gift St Columba's gave me was self-confidence to the point of cockiness. I loved English classes with my teachers John Fanagan and Colin Polden, who allowed us to debate literary subjects in their classes. History was my other favourite subject, taught by a stern-faced Ninian Faulkner.

Regime change occurred after my first year. An elderly clergyman named Argyll was school principal (or 'Warden') when I started. He retired in 1974, to be replaced by David Gibbs, who had served in India when it was part of the British Empire; within days the easy-going culture of the school had been transformed into one of strict discipline. Caning of students became a far more regular occurrence, and it provoked mutterings of mutiny among us. One anonymous boy daubed 'Brits Out' on the front walls. In the prep school, just a few years earlier, Gibbs's obsession with discipline would have been another brick in the Wailing Wall built around my pre-teens. However, now that I was a little older and a lot more confident, I found his rigid discipline tiresome and unnecessary and kept clear of him at all costs.

My special treat for the four exeats per term was to get on the Taney bus into town and meet up with John or Christine, my siblings, who were both then in Trinity as undergraduates studying modern languages, French and German. They would bring me to the cinema, followed by a burger at Captain America's in Grafton

Street. On the bus home, I always felt grown-up and cool. I never had to put aside thoughts of the terrified, humiliated little prep-school boy I had been, because such thoughts never entered my head. That was another country and everything to do with it was covered with today's activities and tomorrow's possibilities.

2: Dungarees and Donkey Coat

I was always entrepreneurial, but my first foray into agri-business met with disaster. At nine, studying the small ads in the *Farmers Journal*, spotting advertisements for day-old chicks, I got the notion that I could rear the hens and sell the eggs. Thirteen Golden Comet chickens duly arrived in a wooden box at Enniscorthy railway station. We bought an infrared lamp and put them in an outhouse in an enclosed circle.

After a number of months they grew into pullets, ready to lay their eggs. I had read in a book that, to maximise their output, they should be fed garlic. As I returned to boarding school, my poor mother had strict instructions to buy garlic pearls (capsules) from a specialist shop in Dublin. These had to be melted with hot water into the feed. They were free-range hens, so sometimes they wouldn't lay in the nest boxes provided, which meant that when the eggs were found, they were rotten.

The enterprise was showing a small profit until the hens stopped laying. I was told that it would be months before they could lay again. This did not stop them continuing to eat the costly meal, wiping out all my savings. I enquired about their value for slaughter. The local meat agent would pay only three shillings each. I was in a no-win situation until my sister Val offered to buy them for five shillings each. I should have suspected foul play. A day after the transaction, she resold them for ten bob apiece to Kathleen at the gate lodge. Val had assured her that they would be laying again soon and were a guaranteed money-spinner. My sister made more in one day than I did in the entire year.

My next venture came during the summer holidays when I was twelve. Val and I trooped up on our bicycles to the mart, one of the largest in the country, which adjoined our farm. On Mondays, they sold sheep in three different auction rings. I'd had a brainwave that I might buy a few breeding ewes, then let them run with the sheep flock and a ram belonging to a neighbour.

I was dressed in a most garish bright red Manchester United jersey (I got sense since) as I sat in the front row of the sales arena. The prices seemed to be very cheap, around three pounds per ewe, which I could afford. I duly lifted my finger and started bidding. Before I knew it, a pen of three sheep was knocked down to me for three pounds ten shillings. I gave my name and address to the sales clerk and cycled home excitedly to contact my father in order to arrange collection of my prized new animals.

At that time Daddy drove a blue Vauxhall Victor station wagon. The back seats could be let down and the sheep loaded into the boot. Off we set together and I stayed in the car while he went around the back of the building. He emerged with a face like thunder. To my horror, he told me he had ascertained that the sheep I had bought were from the cast ewe ring, which meant they were fit only for mutton and could not breed. One had a broken belly and the other two were wrong in their udders (no milk for lambs from previous mastitis). If I had set out to embarrass myself, I couldn't have done it so comprehensively.

Daddy contacted a local sheep dealer named Charlie Byrne to resell the sheep to a local butcher and buy three proper breeding ewes. He paid the balance of the extra cost. After my initial mortification, I was back in business. Unfortunately, one of the ewes died and the other was a complete mad yoke – she must have had scrapie – always running round in circles. But the last was a gem. She had a lovely white Border Leicester face, was a brilliant mother and duly produced two lambs each year for sale.

Because I loved everything to do with farming, when I went to St Columba's I spent every afternoon working on the farm there, learning to handle animals and become proficient in farm work. Instead of sport each afternoon, when other students might be playing hockey or rugby, I was one of a handful involved in the Young Farmers Club. We worked as helpers to David Pullman, the tenant on the farm at the school. This taught me the rudimentary features of animal husbandry: feeding and dosing cattle; castrating and dehorning calves; driving a tractor badly; making silage and doing general chores. The best bit was Mrs Pullman's tea and hot fresh scones at the end of the sessions.

My parents decided that I would finish my school year, do my O levels, then go to Gurteen Agricultural College for a one-year course leading to a National Certificate in Agriculture. I swotted like never before and passed with flying colours the only academic exams I would ever sit. In common with many who are forced to, or choose to, get out of education before the 'proper' time, I was reasonably sanguine: escaping a situation where my every move was circumscribed and where people were always called by their surname had its upside. (To this day, surname-calling is a pet hate of mine. I always call everybody by their first name.)

I might have gone to Trinity College, after school, rather than Gurteen, were it not for a letter from my mother when I was fourteen to tell me my father was very ill. He had lung cancer, she said, and Professor Shaw in Baggot Street would operate to remove one lung while the other was subjected to radiation. He was determined, however, that I would reactivate the farm. It had been run by a previous generation of Yateses, but my father had leased most of the land to a friend of his, Billy Oakes; he let the rest to Tom Byrne. That had allowed him to open the shop that sold sporting goods and toys, then concentrate on his wool business. He was an expert in wool, that I know. He loved the business, that I know, too. And it was a good business, albeit a tough and demanding one. What I don't know is whether or not, as his health worsened, he realised that the wool trade was dying. That's the tragedy of not knowing him fully: I cannot know how prescient he was. I suspect he knew the business was dying because his ambition for me was that I would be a farmer, rather than a wool merchant, and farm-related business was where my entrepreneurial instincts lay.

During my father's long dying, he sold off the wool business and put the money into doing up all the farm buildings – he employed some of his former wool workers to get the job done – and setting up as a farm again. It was an astonishing project for a man so near death because, in essence, he wasn't re-creating a farm, he was creating one from scratch. The land had no water, no electricity, no stock, no tractor, no nothing.

Meanwhile, I was in Gurteen, which, from my first day in September 1976, knocked hell out of boarding school. Boarding school had had its points, but Gurteen offered wonderful possibilities in extra-curricular activities. I got a formal farming education, too, and loved every minute of it. The college was located in the middle of nowhere on the border between Counties Offaly and Tipperary. I was only sixteen, among sixty-eight students, some of whom were adults in their thirties, looking to pursue farming as a late career. I was younger than the youngest of them and less mature than any.

The college was run by the Methodists, but there was very little emphasis on religion or discipline. All students lived in the college. The young housemaster, Michael Hanna, just asked us to respect each other and the facilities. This relaxed attitude was a fantastic release from the strictness I'd been used to.

I had a ball. Before Gurteen I hadn't done much drinking, never smoked and was a virgin. All that was to change. I lost my virginity in the girls' dormitory, despite the distraction that there was no lock on the door. Drinking happened on weekends in the Glue Pot pub in the nearby village of Ballingarry – a walk of more than three miles back in the dark, pissed, because none of us had a car. Between games of pool we learned to down a pint in four seconds. I started smoking Silk Cut cigarettes, although I suffered from asthma, and my father's lung cancer should have served as a deterrent. I never smoked in front of my parents. My hair grew down to my shoulders. Life was looking good.

Daily lectures were interesting and relevant to all aspects of livestock and plant production, farm machinery, veterinary science and agricultural economics. Afternoons involved practical group work on the college's farm, which included a dairy herd, sheep, cattle, pigs and poultry and a full range of tillage crops. Killing the turkeys at Christmas (we had to wring their necks with a broom handle) was a battle. When cleaning the hen-house, we had power-hose water fights in which the battery-caged birds were collateral casualties. Along the way, I learned to castrate pigs with razor blades.

I liked everything about Gurteen: the company, the learning, the food. The buildings, too, although a bunch of us very nearly did away with one when we were ringing in the New Year in one of the staff rooms with no one else around. For the craic, one of the lads, messing with a cigarette lighter, set fire to the Christmas streamers hanging from the ceiling. We managed to extinguish the resultant blaze, but it caused damage that couldn't be concealed. We were summoned by the principal, an elderly man named Oscar Loane. Fortunately, forgiveness rates highly with the Methodists and we were spared suspension.

My biggest problem for the year was lack of cash. My parents didn't seem to appreciate the depth of my need for spending money to cover drink, cigarettes, women and the other pastime I had learned to love: gambling. Pleas for funds fell on deaf ears. I had no choice but to get a job with a local farmer on Saturdays. Mr Stanley was a tough taskmaster. I would spend nine-hour days picking stones for ten pounds. Then I would go to the hotel in Roscrea that night and blow the lot in one round of drinks.

We also socialised in Birr. My hormones were in overdrive, so I took part in the local pantomime, *Cinderella*. Some of the girls were hot, which meant I was willing to attend endless rehearsals, although it quickly emerged that I was too young for most, while my acting and singing limited me to the chorus line or being a tree.

In between the craic and the socialising, I learned much of what I was supposed to learn, like the difference between ringworm and roundworms; how to take an animal's temperature; how to tell the age of sheep and cattle by counting their teeth; the importance of vaccinating against liver fluke; the significance of soil-testing, determining the need to raise the pH, nitrogen and potassium levels on the land to increase output yields and fertility. I duly passed the National Certificate in Agriculture examination and headed home, ready to take charge. We bought 250 sheep, ewes and rams, and set about rearing the subsequent lambs, which meant running around after the ewes with a torch in the middle of the night when we'd spotted two legs sticking out of their rear end, which meant they were in distress while lambing. I quickly learned how to help, and deployed everything, from bottles to infrared lamps, to save the lambs.

My greatest anxieties on coming home to work centred on my capability to re-establish the farm enterprise successfully, and how best to deal with my father. The parent–child relationship alters when your father or mother is also your employer. I wanted to please my father, yet I resented his stubbornness. There was a fear factor in our relationship: I was the raw recruit and apprentice flush with Gurteen theory, which he sniffed at as unrealistic, while he had fixed views from his experience, which I knew to be outdated, going back, as it did, to his farming days in the 1950s. For example, he maintained for months that we could not afford to buy a tractor, so, instead, we had to adhere to the 'old ways' of donkeys and horses. I was too young to understand irony, which meant I was slow to discern when he was joking and when he was in earnest. In the case of the tractor, we eventually bought an old Massey Ferguson 135 for two thousand pounds.

The farm required significant investment. The previous tenants, Billy Oakes and Tom Byrne, had rented the land relatively cheaply on an annual conacre basis, so they didn't reinvest in upgrading any aspect of it. Why would they? But that meant, among other things, that the soil on the 160 acres that made up our holding was of poor quality. An army was needed to accomplish all the work but, as far as my father was concerned, I was to farm without a full-time assistant. We set about building new lean-to sheds, sheep-handling facilities and a cattle crush; we had water piped into troughs in every field, installed electrical wiring and bought basic farm machinery. We applied lime and fertilisers to transform land fertility. My father continually complained about the costs.

Sheep were the farm's main enterprise and the most time-consuming. Every Saturday, my part-time helper Bobby 'Baa' Wildes, who had worked for my father in the wool business, and I would round up the sheep with the help of our untrained and fairly useless (but adorable) sheepdog, Jackie, pare their feet and put on a disinfectant purple spray. They also had to be dosed regularly for worms and vaccinated. Sheep-dipping was essential to keep away serious maggot infestations in the summer months.

Each ewe had an ear-tag number. When we put the rams with them for breeding, they would wear a leather harness, called a raddle, that contained a thick crayon. We would change the colour every two weeks and kept a record of when the sheep went in lamb and were due to yean (give birth) so that we could house them at the right time; it also showed the non-performers, which were culled. Some ewes were all the colours of the rainbow – they must have been more interested in sex than in getting pregnant.

The most difficult time was lambing, usually in January and February, when the weather was at its worst. I had to go around the fields at night, wearing a navy donkey jacket and faded dungarees over my jeans, carrying a flashlight to spot any unexpected new-born lambs. The birthing process was hazardous. I learned the tell-tale signs: ewes grinding their teeth, going off on their own, walking round in circles, and then the water bag would appear. Sometimes the lambs would come the wrong way, with the tail instead of the front feet protruding. Other times the lamb's head would be caught in the womb. In such cases I had to act as midwife, inserting my hand and manoeuvring the lamb out. It was vital that the mother immediately took to the lamb, licking it, eating the afterbirth and ensuring that it suckled. Hogget ewes (maiden one-year-olds) were a nightmare of maternal irresponsibility.

The work was subject to constant setbacks and disappointments. Because we lived so close to Enniscorthy, marauding stray dogs attacked and killed dozens of our sheep. I laid poison and bought a shotgun. I would follow the dogs back to their homes and pursue their owners for recompense, an option that wasn't open to me when foxes and mink killed small lambs at night. Sheep were constantly vulnerable. If they rolled over on their back, the weight of the fleece made it impossible for them to get up, so they could die unless helped to their feet. Orphaned lambs, raised in our house, invariably had a poor immune system and died. It was better to try to foster them on another ewe that had a single or no lamb. Losses through mortality were unavoidable.

I did well to produce 1.5 lambs per ewe each year. Finally, having reared them, I would try to have them ready in time for the

Easter lamb trade. We would weigh them very early on Monday mornings, to select the best lambs (those around forty kilos) and bring them up to the mart. The cost of the ewes was then sixty to seventy pounds. Good lambs made roughly forty, so I would try to get them to pay for themselves in a year. The commercial farm objective was to make a hundred pounds per acre annually, based on a stocking rate of four ewes per acre.

Our type of farm would be called dry stock and tillage (no cows). We had a calf-to-beef system for the grassland areas. I would buy very young calves in the mart and teach them to drink by putting my fingers into their mouths, which they would suck, and then insert my hand into the bucket of milk so they got the hang of it. We would keep them until they were more than two years old, reared on summer grassland and wintered in sheds. Additionally, we would, with the help of a local cattle dealer, Mike Nolan, buy twenty bullocks for summer grazing from April until October. This was a speculative venture, because the price of store cattle could be too high in the spring.

Since the cost of a plough, rotavator, harrow and combine harvester was so high, we set the most suitable fields for tillage to Billy Ashmore and his son Niall from 1978 onwards. They were excellent professional farmers, who took out a lot of conacre for malting barley and sugar beet each year. This ensured a cash return on those fields. We kept the straw to feed to the older cattle during the winter. The Ashmores also grew fodder beet for us as a winter feed crop for both cattle and sheep.

I relied on the local Teagasc adviser, Tom Power, for technical support. Through him, I enrolled in the local course for young farmers. Our farm was selected as a model pilot project and each student had to draw up a possible development plan as part of the course. The general conclusion, among the more witty participants, was that I should consider fish farming because the farm was so run down. Gradually and eventually I got the whole enterprise operational and profitable, albeit at the cost of blood, sweat and tears.

I would claim only to be an average farmer – a jack of all trades and master of none. You can tell master farmers by their attention to detail: how neat, tidy and clean their yards are; how well they exhibit their livestock for sale; their fluency with all forms of machinery. I could just about reverse the trailer, hitch the shaft to work the Vicon fertiliser spreader and concrete mixer, operate the front-end loader with the bucket and fork attached. Making silage, ploughing and cutting corn were beyond me.

My agricultural experience taught me that profitability could often be low, even though Ireland had now entered the European Economic Community, with Common Agriculture Policy benefits. The most we ever made was £18,000 in one year, but some years we only broke even, owing to high costs. Dairying and sugar beet (as distinct from fodder beet) were always the most lucrative sectors. What are the benefits of being a farmer? You are your own boss; it's a healthy outdoor life; rearing animals is profoundly satisfying; you are close to nature and all its fascinations, dependent on the seasons for growth and rebirth.

Meanwhile, my relationship with my father continued to be difficult. He was dictatorial at the best of times, and these were not, for him, the best of times. We clashed constantly, in many instances my own naïveté contributing to rows that erupted, then simmered under the surface. Our domestic water supply depended on an antiquated pump-house that worked on a gravity flow system from a local pond and stream. It was an engineering masterpiece in its day, but leaves or a small eel caught in its filter stopped it from working, and each time that happened, it took hours to get it going again. The water was undrinkable. I wanted to hook up to the mains supply, which was already on the farm. My father said no, so that was that.

His health continued to deteriorate. The gruelling bouts of radium treatment in hospital achieved no improvement that I could see. The cancer spread throughout his body, putting him to bed from late 1978 onwards. He was on heavy pain medication, which led to him gaining a lot of weight. He required a cylinder of oxygen at his bedside to help him breathe. He had no quality of life, but his adamant desire was not to go to hospital: he wanted to be cared for at home. My mother was constantly at his bedside, still devoting her life to him. They celebrated their twenty-fifth wedding anniversary in December 1978.

I observed all this, yet never acknowledged the terminal reality.

'He'll never get out of that bed alive,' my brother John told me one evening in the sitting room, in the tone he used to confirm a shared understanding. But I was astounded, in denial, and didn't believe him. I just kept doing what I had to, reporting to my father as he required me to do, sitting quietly with him as a morphine dose took effect.

Then one evening I was sitting beside the fire in his bedroom, giving it the odd half-hearted poke. Just the two of us. My father started to cry. This had never happened before and I didn't know what to do. Between his sobs, he talked. He realised he was dying. He was deeply upset at having his life cut short, not being able to help me on the farm. He seemed full of regrets. To see such vulnerability and despair in a man who had always been so self-reliant, so strong, was terrifying and confusing. All my life, he had been the definition of potency. Now he was not only powerless, but swamped in misery. I felt acutely sorry for him, but was useless at any true comfort or reassurance.

We rarely, if ever, had had an adult conversation about anything other than work. That generation of parents, particularly fathers, did not believe in telling their children that they loved them. They were reared to conceal feelings. They followed traditional patterns of sending their children too early to boarding school. They sought to maintain Protestant lineage by controlling whom their children socialised with, and they bitterly opposed marriages to Catholics. Damn them. They were wrong and misguided. I came to resent their unquestioning acceptance and loyalty to narrowness. I was determined to act differently if I ever became a dad.

By mid-February 1979, my father's deterioration grew more rapid. One Wednesday the local clergyman, Archdeacon Kenneth Wilkinson, visited. Daddy told me afterwards that he had never been a committed religious believer and it would be dishonest to start now. Above all else, he insisted on being as straight as a die to the bitter end. Des McEvoy, his solicitor and closest confidant, met him to explain that there would be a serious capital acquisitions tax liability unless he changed his will. Instead of everything being transferred to his wife, only £250,000 worth could be done tax-free. The two of them set up a discretionary trust to hold all the other assets in his estate. The farm was to be legally divided, with one half to be owned by my mother and the rest put in the trust.

My father was slipping in and out of consciousness, requiring ever-heavier doses of morphine. He spoke about people from his childhood. There was no sense to it – just a rambling visit to his half-remembered past.

On Saturday, 24 February, I had done my morning chores on the farm and was looking forward to watching the horseracing from Leopardstown on the television. The Scalp Hurdle was the feature event, with top horses, that afternoon. Mummy called me up to the bedroom to ask me to help raise Daddy in the bed so that he could breathe more easily. We each grasped an arm and a shoulder. As we did so, his blue eyes rolled up and he died in our arms. My mother was the first to realise what had happened. She let him sink back into the pillows and slid to her knees beside the bed, her hands over her face as she began to pray. It had a practised economy, that movement. She told me afterwards that, for months, she had regularly knelt at their bedside, as he slept, to pray to God to take him because he was in such acute and chronic pain.

The essence of numbness is that you can't feel it, and I was numb with shock, even though intellectually I had known my father was dying. Unjustified shock. I had been a daily witness to his journey towards death, but it had never become one of the realities of my life. It was just a possibility, a concept, denied and glossed over. Now denial was done for, but I stood as still as a statue while my mother made phone calls. I could hear her as if from a great distance as she phoned Tom Browne, the local undertaker, then our closest relatives and friends. Within an hour, Tom and his main man, John Joe, were in the room. They asked me to help them dress my father and prepare him for the coffin. I nodded dumbly. Tom gave me instructions that got me moving. I had never touched a dead body before. My father was laid out within a few hours.

Arrangements were made for the funeral, with the traditional Protestant unvarnished oak coffin. The house was 'private', with all blinds down. Although my father's death had been inevitable, I couldn't believe it. I would sneak up to the room to touch his cold body and talk to him, apologising for all my inadequacies. There was so much unsaid between us. The most influential person in my life no longer existed, yet I would spend the rest of my days trying to please him, seeking his approval, always suspecting or grimly certain that I had let him down.

I knew my father's politics. I knew the business he had been in. I knew what had killed him. But in some ways I didn't know him at all. That was because I'd gone away to boarding school when I was eight, and he died when I was nineteen, leaving a lifetime of questions unanswered. It's in your twenties that you begin to find your father interesting, begin to trawl through his life and attitudes by asking questions to discover the explanations for your own life.

In the brief years in the late 1970s when I came home, he constantly berated me about life principles. His *modus operandi* was honesty in all dealings. He would say, 'Lies have legs: if you tell one, you will have to tell another to cover up the first.' He drilled into me the need for a strict work ethic. 'At the end of the day, all you'll ever make [meaning money] is through hard work.'

In the decades that followed his death, I was to leave farming and become a politician, a bookmaker, a broadcaster and a bankrupt: almost everything he disregarded or despised. And yet my father runs through the essence of who I am. I have lived to work, rather than worked to live. His frugality has become an ingrained characteristic in me: I always drive a clapped-out old banger, dress in cheap casuals, never take holidays and order house wine with a meal. He made me feel guilty about any luxury or opulence. While he was a risk-taker, particularly in the wool business, he had a horror of debt. Bills had to be paid on time. His good credit reputation mattered to him.

Some of what he was surfaces in my own habits. He always advised me, in dealing with any problem, to ask everybody's opinion, then do your own thing. Somewhere along the line, almost by osmosis, that habit of his became mine too.

Nevertheless, in some cases my instinct ran directly against his. When he was still mobile and the two of us were in the mart one day, a beautiful pen of ten breeding ewes was up for sale. I really wanted to buy them. He agreed and we bid up to seventy-two pounds each for them, becoming the unsuccessful under-bidder. I was disappointed and annoyed. Later on we saw the farmer who had bought the animals.

'Fuck him anyway,' I muttered to my father, who stopped and looked at me. 'Fuck him for paying over the odds for those lovely ewes,' I said, thinking he might not have heard me the first time. 'I really wanted them.'

My father took me by the elbow and pulled me into a corner where we couldn't be overheard. 'Don't ever talk like that again,' he said, fiercely quiet. 'Never. No begrudgery. You go over to him and wish him good luck.' When I didn't move, he didn't say, '*Now!*' but he might as well have done. I moved. When I came back, teeth gritted, after the task, he nodded. 'That way you'll get on better in life,' he said.

Our linked lives, like the lives of too many fathers and sons, were threaded through with misunderstanding, longing and failure. The sad benefit of his early death was that he was not to see me fail in his constantly expressed determination to pass on the family farm to the next generation. And therein lies a double guilt for me, knowing that I didn't measure up to a father who so deeply revered family tradition, who was so conscious of his obligations in the progress of his family, who felt so deeply grateful to his own father and grandfather, and was so resolute that I would secure the family name by having children of my own, and ensure the Yates succession in the Blackstoops home and farm.

'The first generation makes it. The second generation keeps it,' he would say, 'and the third generation spends it.' In the immediate aftermath of his death, immaturity collided in me with obligation. On the one hand, I would go to the solitude of the farm outhouses and cry my eyes out at my enormous loss and isolation; on the other, I had to step up and be an adult, taking full responsibility for my mother and the farm. On the one hand, I was lost without his advice and experience; on the other, I had a guilty sense of release and freedom. I was off the leash: I could live my own life as I saw fit.

My father's death allowed me to emerge as a man in my own right, ready, willing and more than able to make my own mistakes.

Within a few months, I would begin to create my own narrative as an adult. I was no longer shackled by his opposition to any interest of mine that he felt would take me away from my farming obligations. I could and did embark on entirely new and uncharted adventures. Marriage – and politics.

3: Life Support

'Who's that? Over there, navy jumper, arms folded – do you know who she is?'

It was an October Friday night in 1979 and Adrian Rothwell, my pal from Gurteen, was standing beside me at the social in Bunclody.

'Brown hair. Where I'm nodding towards.'

This hadn't happened before, so Adrian was a bit slow on the uptake. At the end of the week, he would pick me up in his red Austin 1100 and off we'd go to local pubs, followed by alcohol-free dances organised by Protestant parishes as far away as Carlow and Kildare. Adrian's nickname from his days in Kilkenny College was Rusty, for his red hair. Rusty had a steady girlfriend. At the end of each night, after the pubs and socials, he would bring her home up a mountain lane. I would have to wait in the cold car until they had finished their courting. I was the ultimate gooseberry. He would then give me a lift home and chat at our kitchen table into the small hours about life's woes and working for our fathers.

'Oh, *that* one,' he said now, trying not to stare at the girl. 'I think she's Roger's sister, one of the Boyds from around Tinahely.'

'Jesus,' I said to myself. 'I'd love a bit of that now.'

'Class swot. Brainy,' Adrian said. 'She's doing the Leaving Cert through Irish.'

I was already working on shifting her – trying to establish eye contact by staring at her, so that when her eyes accidentally met mine I would look for a while, then do a casual half-smile.

'She's a bit young for you,' Adrian said.

I left him where he was, headed over and asked the stunner to dance. She brushed me off as if I was dandruff. Deirdre Boyd might have been only sixteen, but she was cocky and self-assured when it came to rejecting guys with casual half-smiles.

'Oh, come on, you'd like to dance,' I said.

'No thanks.'

'I didn't think you were with anybody. Why not? Ah, go on, I won't bite. It's just a dance. My name is Ivan Yates, and I think you're beautiful. Where's the harm in one dance?'

She looked up at me as if she'd seen a dozen of my kind before and was ineffably bored. I did my casual half-smile again.

'Okay,' she said. 'Just the one.'

Just the one. Terms and conditions apply. When I tried to talk, she just shook her head, gesticulating that she couldn't hear me over the loud music. At the end of the set, she was done with me. Courteously done with me, but done with me nonetheless. Or so she thought. I thought otherwise. I had no idea just how resistant one small dark teenager could be.

On St Stephen's night each year, a similar social attracted a good crowd to the Church Institute building opposite St Mary's in Enniscorthy. I had heard Roger Boyd – who had gone to Gurteen Agricultural College in the same year as Rusty and me – was planning to bring his sisters in his car. I was determined to make a better impression than I had in October.

Suitably tanked up, I greeted her as if she was a long-lost friend. The payoff was poor. She was distantly polite, asking me to remind her who I was and where we had met before.

'Oh,' she said when I'd finished, and agreed to dance in a dutiful way. The minute the dance was over, I hustled her into the room where they sold Coke and tea and bombarded her with questions. Was she going out with anyone? Why had she left Newtown School in Waterford to go to Coláiste Moibhí in Rathmines? How did she feel about boyfriends? What did she want to do with her life? These were interspersed with compliments about how attractive she was. She seemed mildly irritated that I knew so much about her.

The object of the interrogation was to get her phone number, agreement to meet sometime, somewhere, or even go to a car for a court right now, although that last one was a bit of a stretch. Any small chink of light would have satisfied me, but none was forthcoming. No phone number, no second dance. (I never got as far as making the car suggestion.) She declined all requests, direct and indirect. While disappointed, I was neither dismayed nor deterred. To me, Deirdre was more than a female conquest. I wanted her for the long term. If patience was required, so be it. She was only a teenager and I was twenty. My persistence would be rewarded eventually, I was sure of it. If I want something, I really go for it, and I really wanted Deirdre. From then on, I chased her. Met her at parties, met her at dances. She would maybe give me a couple of dances, then the familiar brush-off. If I saw her drinking with friends, I'd be over like a shot.

'Would you like a drink?'

She'd take a drink, all right, and listen to me talking, and I'd decide this was the breakthrough night for chancing my arm.

'Would you like me to take you home?'

'No.'

Always no. And for reasons such as she was sort of going out with this guy. 'This guy,' she would say vaguely, played under-eighteen rugby for Ireland.

'Well, I'm not a complete loser either,' I would respond.

As we moved into the 1980s, I was still smitten and in pursuit, but beginning to wonder was I a complete eejit. In the meantime, what had my best mate Adrian Rothwell gone and done? Got off with her sister Gillian and they were inseparable. I somewhat resented his progress compared to my failure, while at the same time I was getting the inside information on Deirdre's whereabouts and life. Each rejection would be more embarrassing and emphatic.

The lowest point was in the early summer of 1981, when Rusty and I went as usual to Courtown Harbour one Sunday night. In the upstairs lounge, Deirdre was sitting with a group of friends. As usual, I went over to chat her up. She allowed me to buy her a gin and tonic. I was getting fed up with pussyfooting around and asked straight out if I could bring her home. I wasn't prepared for the response.

'You just don't get it, do you? No. I don't want to go out with you. Please go away.'

I apologised and left with my tail firmly between my legs, thinking, Feck her, stuck-up cow. See if I care.

Not too long after that humiliation – as I'll shortly explain – I became a Dáil deputy. Back at the same hotel with TD attached to my name, I found people knew who I was, wanted to shake my hand, congratulate me and be in my company. My self-confidence was growing. I was gregarious and congenial. I spotted Deirdre with her friends. Would I face more pain? Would I hell! I smiled and turned my back on her. To my utter shock, she came over to me and suggested I might join her group.

'You hurt me the last time we met,' I told her. 'I got the message and I've moved on.' Nonetheless, I joined in the general chat of the group until it was time to go home. As we began to gather our coats for departure, I found her beside me.

'Are you not going to bring me home then?'

Wow. I wasn't expecting that.

'Of course. My car is outside in the car park. Let's go.'

After chasing Deirdre so hard for so long, I was hoping not to be just a chauffeur for the night. I told her I wanted to kiss her and asked her to name a quiet concealed place where I could pull in the car. She knew just the spot at a lay-by near the Togher crossroads. It seemed it wasn't the first time she had been in this situation. At that stage I was still driving my granny's battered old Ford Escort.

'Do the seats go back?' she asked, when I turned off the engine.

'Let me lean over and push back this lever.'

The seat bucketed back about six inches – so suddenly it nearly gave her whiplash. She looked astonished and I realised that what she had meant to ask was, how did the seat*back* recline? Recline? A reclining seat in an old Escort?

'No, it does not, and I don't know what you're used to,' I told her, acting shocked but allowing myself to get over it and have a wonderful court with her. I could not believe my luck. I was falling in love. I brought her home, but didn't go inside. I got a phone number and said I would call to arrange a date during the coming week. I'd come down from Dublin to collect her at home because she was on her summer holidays.

The following Wednesday, I duly arrived at Ballinglen House, this time in my mother's bigger, modern red Renault (complete with plush reclining seats – just the job for later). Instead of Deirdre opening the back door, her mother appeared. Once Betty Boyd heard that her beloved daughter was seeing a TD, she immediately assumed he was a married man, looking for a bit on the side, and she was determined to check out my credentials before this went any further. I gingerly introduced myself and shook hands. When she saw that I was only a little older than her daughter – far too young to be married already – her concern visibly evaporated.

From then on, Deirdre and I saw each other twice a week, usually me driving over to Tinahely. There seemed to be no question of my staying overnight at her house. I was angling to push forward on the agenda of sleeping together, without much success. Manipulative hoor that I am, I made this an issue of mutual commitment. I needed to bring matters to a head. We agreed to go on holidays together to the Rose of Tralee Festival, mostly because horseracing was a big part of the week and I was already heavily into betting. Her parents reluctantly allowed her to go.

We stayed at a bed-and-breakfast, and action was there none. It dawned on me that this girl was not as experienced, streetwise and adult as I'd thought. In fact, she knew little about the real world. She was way too innocent and naïve for an ambitious hustler and opportunist like me. She had little interest in politics or horseracing. On the face of it, we were ideally suited by virtue of our respectable Protestant farming backgrounds. In reality, she was eighteen and I was twenty-one going on thirty-five. I broke it off. Time passed.

The next contact was from a teenager who was very clear on what she wanted, right down to telling me that she had been to the Well Woman Clinic because an unplanned pregnancy wasn't acceptable for either of us. She wanted our love affair to resume and it did. The best decision in my life Deirdre made for me.

Over the next four years we shuffled our respective routines to overlap. She was an undergraduate at the Church of Ireland College of Education in Rathmines, training as a primary-school teacher. Initially she would stay with me in the various hotel bedrooms I frequented while overnighting in Dublin on Dáil business, hopping into a taxi at four in the morning. When she worked as a teacher, living in various flats around Dublin with other girls, I stayed at her place. We always holidayed together in the summer, usually staying in our family cottage at Gortmore in Mayo.

I was crazy about her. She was a sensitive, caring, loving, beautiful girl – and she was mine. There was never any doubt that we would get married.

The Galway racing festival is an unmissable week for me. A particularly good run of winners in the summer of 1985 meant that I was flush with cash. In the cottage, overlooking Lough Mask, I was studying the racing pages of the newspaper. I looked up at Deirdre, who was standing on a chair in the small kitchen. She was changing a light bulb – always the 'handy Andy' of us.

'I was thinking,' I said. 'You know the way we've been together for four years now? Maybe we should get married. Like getting engaged … Is now a good time? I think it is. Let's do it.'

'Are you asking me to marry you?'

'Yeah, why not? Now is the right time to settle down. I got planning permission for a dormer bungalow at Blackstoops and am ready to start the building. We could have it finished by Christmas and move in. I don't believe in long engagements. I want to have lots of kids, boys and girls. It'll be such an adventure.'

'Okay, but where's the ring?'

We spent the next ten days in and out of every jewellery shop in Galway city and Dublin. Finally, she settled on a sapphire with two diamonds. All my cash was gone. But first I had to ask her father, Cam, for permission. On our return from the holiday, I nervously asked to see him privately. One of life's gentlemen – quiet-spoken, thoughtful, sincere, reserved, whose whole life had been dedicated to his family and dairy farm – Cam couldn't have made it easier.

'That would be very nice. Congratulations. Betty and I hope you'll be very happy together.'

Job done. Fantastic.

We chose the shortest day of the year, 21 December 1985, as our wedding day because I could take the honeymoon over the Dáil's Christmas recess and not miss out on any of my commitments at work.

The day itself was disastrous, starting with a final check that all was okay with our new bungalow for us to move in after the honeymoon. All was not. Pools of water lay in two rooms, owing to leaks in the dormer windows. I freaked on the phone to the builder and my solicitor, demanding that it be sorted immediately.

The three o'clock ceremony was conducted by Deirdre's local clergyman. We had agreed that 'honour and obey' would be deleted. He forgot this, so she had to recite the unacceptable words. He called Deirdre by her sister's name, Gillian, whom he had recently married to Adrian. As we held hands at the altar, Deirdre's fingernails cut into me, such was her rage. After the service we came out of the small country church in Preban, County Wicklow, into virtual darkness, to be greeted by media photographers, family and friends.

Matters didn't improve at our modest reception in the Seven Oaks Hotel, Carlow. The ratio of her guests to mine was six to one, because if I invited any political colleagues, I would offend dozens of others. So I invited nobody connected with politics. (Instead, the local Fine Gael organisation held a series of celebratory dinner dances beforehand.) Then, according to Deirdre, the candles on the wedding cake were hideous. The photographer irritated her. Throughout the day she was moody, anxious and cross.

'Get used to it,' Adrian, my best man, told me.

Eventually, after all rituals were observed, we scarpered to the Burlington Hotel in Dublin, and the following day took off on our fantastic winter honeymoon in sunny Cyprus.

'If you want to know me, come live with me.' It's true, that one. Marriage has a lot going for it, but it's a whole new experience, starting with poverty. All our money is paid into a joint bank account my wife controls. She deals with the household bills. I discovered early on that I now had responsibilities that superseded the need to have cash in my pocket. My wife also makes all decisions about interior decor and domestic routine. I soon learned to accept all this: it avoided needless arguments and I saved my energy for the battles in my work.

Men and women are programmed differently. Leave aside women's frequent lack of interest in sport. Ignore the way they carry so much gear in their handbags that they can't find anything. Pay no attention to them bringing so much luggage on holiday they could be moving house permanently. Overlook the reality that going out requires hours of preparation, that shopping means touring every shop and ending up making a purchase in the first. These minor shortcomings are more than offset by all they achieve for everyone else.

Deirdre made our house into a home, bought all my clothes to dress me properly, ensured proper personal hygiene, turned groceries into meals and made me remember birthdays and anniversaries. Marriage is about the answers to mundane questions. Pork chops or lamb chops for dinner? Who puts out the wheelie bin? It is also about making ordinary things wonderful because you're doing them together.

An additional bonus can be the in-laws. In my case, the Boyds are a genuine, fiercely loyal, sizeable tribe. There is nothing they wouldn't do for you, including electioneering. Over three decades, they have unflinchingly supported our every exploit.

For me, correctly or not, the higher biological objective of life is procreation. Like all animals, we're put here to live and die with the prospect of reproduction. I believe that you repay to your own children the immense debt you owe to your parents, so the human cycle goes on. Parenting requires incredible energy. There is a conspiracy not to tell first-time mothers and fathers precisely the extent to which their life will be turned upside-down by the new arrival. Your own life becomes secondary to rearing them. Ignorant of this, Deirdre and I wanted lots of kids. So it was that a Saturday in early January 1988 found us in Wexford General Hospital's maternity ward. Originally, she had been determined to have a natural birth, but the fact that she was a few days overdue changed that. I was at her bedside throughout the evening as the waves of pain intensified to the point at which she readily agreed to breathe in gas and air, which made her the equivalent of drunk. The midwives were on top of the situation and administered an epidural drip as the pain became more acute.

The minutes turned into hours of no progress. The consultant obstetrician appeared. To my horror, he procured these enormous metal tongs called forceps. These were inserted into Deirdre and clamped around the baby's head. The scene was truly gruesome. Deirdre was in a semi-conscious state of exhaustion when the final delivery happened. Blood, umbilical cord and tears. Then this tiny baby boy appeared, shrieking for life. After the trauma, we were reassured that everything was fine. We were in seventh heaven for the next week.

I played the same song on my car cassette player over and over again: Serge Gainsbourg's international hit, 'Je t'aime . . . moi non plus'. The ecstasy was a confused lightheaded sense of unconditional love for the new-born, a glimpse of immortality through the next generation and a scary uncertainty of how to cope with this life-changing event.

Amid the elation on the return home of our son, Andrew, we began to worry about the care of this tiny baby, who had no neck muscles to prop up his head. Breastfeeding, painful mastitis, milk bottles, Moses basket, nappies, sleepless nights, winding and Babygros took up all our attention. Your first child is so vulnerable and you are so inexperienced that you always fear the worst. The marvel of watching your kid grow, gurgle, smile, stare and utter a first few words compensates for the hard work of full-time care. Night feeds and consequent sleep loss were the worst aspects for Deirdre: I pretended to be fast asleep. In truth, we didn't know what we were doing; just got on with what was required.

Ciara arrived a year later, in January 1989. Fortunately, Deirdre had few problems, loved being pregnant and was positively radiant throughout. Ciara had to be induced (she was nearly two weeks overdue) but from the moment she was born, she was the least trouble – a cute blonde baby girl. The routine was now becoming familiar. But a second child, just a year apart from the first, meant that Deirdre felt she should give up teaching to become a full-time mum.

When Sarah smoothly arrived in July 1991, my mother suggested that we swap houses. She was rattling around in the big old house on her own, while we were overcrowded in the bungalow, which was much more suited to her needs. Our homes were only fifty yards apart. We did so, investing heavily to modernise the big house. Now we had space for what I had always wanted: two boys and two girls at a minimum. That was exactly the quota we got when John arrived in November 1994. His birth coincided with a critical period in my political career. I was Fine Gael director of elections in one of the two Cork by-elections being held at that time. I lived for three weeks in the Imperial Hotel in the city centre, leading an intense campaign. Deirdre was overdue and wanted me at the birth.

'Keep your legs crossed,' I'd tell her in our nightly phone calls. 'You have to defer the birth until after polling day.' I doubt if this instruction meant much to her or to the birth process, but the minute political circumstances changed, I altered my instructions. 'This baby now has to be induced immediately,' I told her. 'We may be going into government.'

And he was, the following Monday.

The most pleasurable years of parenthood were when the kids were aged from about four to ten. Once they were able to feed themselves, walk, talk and play on their own, they became a source of enormous joy. Their curiosity and innocence were so endearing and they were unashamedly affectionate, sitting on our laps, wanting hugs and kisses. The youngest in nearly all families is usually the most spoiled because they will always be the baby, and you relax. John learned this early and well.

'Daddy, I love you the first,' he would whisper into my ear. Moments later, he would furtively repeat a slightly amended version of these treasured words to his mother, extracting maximum returns.

Our children's most vivid memories related to external financial or other pressures we were under at various times. Their memory of my dismissive refrain 'I'm busy', when they asked me to play with them, reflects my own regret that I always gave priority to my job over recreation with them. From the late 1980s to 2001, I was simply never at home from Monday to Friday, while weekends involved work commitments. Even at home, my mind was miles away. Deirdre, to a great extent, was a lone parent. Annual holidays were either package sun destinations with Deirdre or periods in the Mayo cottage, where – they falsely allege – I would cheat at family board games, such as Careers. According to them, I always had to beat them at everything, including hurling, cricket, table tennis and Monopoly. I couldn't argue with that.

I was loud and condemning as a father, and completely disregarded. When they annoyed me – for example, when they counted out money from the piggybank incorrectly – I would call them 'fucking gombeens'. They thought this was hilarious. It never bothered me that most of the time they had a playful disrespect for me. Eventually they dominated the TV remote control; Deirdre and I became guests in our own house. At least Deirdre was a posh guest – sometimes even hamming it up as Hyacinth Bucket from the television series *Keeping Up Appearances*. She's the only person I ever met who sampled wine and sent back the bottle. I would never have the nerve and was always in sharp contrast to Deirdre, with my chav mentality and disregard for appearances. My theory was that this engendered in the children the notion that you can have dignity without being showy.

We placed the highest personal priority on education at the local Church of Ireland national school in Enniscorthy, followed by Newtown School in Waterford, Deirdre's *alma mater*. It was run by Quakers, who tried to produce rounded, balanced individuals while charging an arm and a leg in annual fees. I used to get more upset than the kids at each initial enrolment and departure from home, a throwback, methinks, to my boarding-school misery.

Academic *laissez-faire* was fine for the girls, who matured quicker and therefore took their exams really seriously, studying in earnest. The lads tended to bring their school books home and leave them on the hall floor for the weekend. Any distraction took precedence over homework. This was reflected in their exam results.

I was determined, as a father, never to hit any of my children, believing that this would engender a misguided respect for violence. My worst punishment would be to shout threats at them and send them to their rooms. Much more importantly, I wanted them to know every day how much I loved them. To this day, I end every conversation or encounter by telling them so. It may seem superficial, but that's better than the silence and impervious lack of or controlled emotion of yesteryear's family life. Why leave it to assumptions, presumptions and guesswork?

Apart from one incident on holidays in the west of Ireland, when John got a bad gash on his face, we were fortunate that none of our children experienced any disability or serious illness. Which was just as well, given that when John's wound was being sewn up, it generated so much blood that Deirdre fainted in the doctor's surgery, so we had two patients for the price of one. I realise how lucky we have been in our own family of six people and one black Labrador, Ben, to grow up together in health and reasonable harmony.

I left it to Deirdre to deal with sex education – who wants to talk to their dad about that? The two of us did our best to be facilitators, rather than trying to live our lives through our children or using them to pursue our own unfulfilled dreams. Life is full of disappointments, setbacks and hard knocks, from which nobody can be shielded. All you can do is try to teach your kids to accept and adapt, and try to prevent them turning into permanent students, travelling the world in gap years at their parents' expense, getting their first job (making the coffee) at the age of thirty. I believe in the approach taken by seagulls as parents: when they're ready, they push the young off a cliff to fly away or swim.

Happy-ever-after marital bliss is not a slam-dunk. The lifestyle and work circumstances of a Dáil deputy, away from home regularly overnight, are not conducive to idyllic fidelity. Intense work pressures require the antidote of relaxation. These circumstances can lead to bad habits of late-night drinking with mates in pubs and clubs. Alcohol tends to have the effect of allowing your morals and self-control to take the night off. Marriage had a high attrition rate among many of my closest political friends, with whom I regularly socialised in Dublin.

Attitude changes from the 1970s onwards meant greater promiscuity: lots of horny women didn't have an issue about sex with a married man. Life is short and for living to the max. It's reckoned 50 per cent of all future marriages in the UK and US will fail. Perhaps 100 per cent monogamy in perpetuity is for swans, not for men and women. Surveys suggest as many as 60 per cent of adults cheat on their partner at some stage. Many of the partners never find out.

Our marriage nearly hit the rocks in the spring of 2006 when I had proven to be immature, selfish and reckless. The details are for Deirdre and me, nobody else, ever. All I will say is that, although I never stopped loving Deirdre, I was cavalier in pursuit of gratuitous fun. I was in the wrong, and when I realised how much in the wrong, I sincerely apologised, begged forgiveness and genuinely said I had learned the harshest lesson of my life. Anyone would say that, but I truly meant it.

After a ropy few days of staring into the abyss of life without each other, we realised that it would be absurd and wrong to part because we wanted to be together. The opposite of separation happened. We set out to earn each other's enduring trust and, as a result, our relationship matured and deepened, with a renewed commitment to each other. We vowed never to let circumstances undermine the most important thing in our lives – each other. It would be easier and more comfortable to sweep such things under the carpet, but the most generous act of love is forgiveness.

'Most marriages, even the most durable and long-lasting, nearly always have some breaking point when it could have pivoted either way,' my mother said, when I told her we were going to continue as a couple, having earlier confided my fear that we might break up. 'That's life. Just be thankful your marriage survived.'

In more recent years, we faced deepening despair as our business became insolvent, resulting in my having to file for bankruptcy abroad, while Deirdre resumed her teaching career in Dublin. Living apart and alone was and is horrible. I cannot describe how our relationship provided me with the life-support mechanism to survive, akin to oxygen for a patient with emphysema. I have needed Deirdre as my lifeline more in recent years than either of us would have wanted.

I believe that in any relationship there is a 'lover' and a 'loved'. I was always very happy to be the lover, as the greatest pleasure is in giving. While I publicly slag off our marriage and Deirdre as the 'ball and chain', I would be completely lost without her. I have learned that no funeral hearse has a trailer of worldly goods behind it. All that matters is what cannot be bought. Relationships and love, rather than power or money, are the keys to happiness. Although we have been a couple for more than thirty years, I would never, now, take her for granted. In my darkest times, she has been by my side when I needed her, and she is more attractive to me now than ever.

Wives are sexier. That's all there is to it. When I stare at her in the evening – relaxing, doing her knitting, preparing schoolwork, on the iPad scanning the news, whatever – I find her as alluring as ever. We are as likely now to hold hands and touch as in the first flush of passionate rapture. The bond is continually reinvented as we get older. Wrinkles and gravity take their toll; body hair replaces normal hair; reading glasses are a necessity; metabolism worsens and delivers weight gain. (Let's not even consider future, grimmer, prospects like losing teeth, prostate cancer and erectile dysfunction.) My future hope? I will predecease Deirdre. The price and flip side of love is loss. Both our mothers are widows living alone.

If I could blush, I would blush at the memory of the drive from Dublin airport back to Enniscorthy, on our return from our honeymoon. 'You do realise,' I was saying to her, all clear and ruthless, 'I don't carry any passengers. It will mean a lot of hard work and effort ahead for both of us. It may not be easy, but it'll be one heck of an exciting ride. You'll need to fasten your seatbelt.'

She nodded silently. I had no idea what she was thinking. I know, however, that if I said that today, she wouldn't be silent. 'Ah, get over yourself,' I'd be told, and I'd climb down from grandiosity. Being grandiose is fine – for fun – behind a microphone, but between husband and wife it makes no sense.

As events were to unfold, though, I wasn't exaggerating. Everything I said that night turned out to be true.

4: Right Place, Right Time

When I was seventeen, politics suddenly became exciting, with Dr Garret FitzGerald taking the reins in Fine Gael and infusing the party with a new openness, a new sense of possibility. I was enthralled. My father, who was Fianna Fáil, had reservations about my growing interest: he was afraid that if I became actively involved in politics, it would reduce my commitment to the farm.

Politics struck me first as a way to have social interaction at weekends that involved more than drinking and craic, although they had a lot going for them. I decided I must join a political party, in the way normal teenagers join a sports or a youth club.

The largest and most successful party was Fianna Fáil, then in government under Jack Lynch. Wexford was a Fianna Fáil stronghold, dominated by the Browne family. Even if I had not fallen under Garret's spell, I felt Fianna Fáil wouldn't want me. My Protestant background didn't seem to resonate with their republican ethos.

'Where was your grandfather in 1916?' That was one of the classic questions asked at the time. If I ran into it, it would be obvious that neither of my grandfathers was anywhere near the GPO and I would immediately be suspect. Moreover, I did not believe in a republicanism that had as its central tenet the absorption of the six counties of Northern Ireland into an all-Ireland unitary state –

52

whether a million Unionists liked it or not. I didn't agree with the narrow viewpoint that partition was the problem. So, Fianna Fáil and I seemed mutually incompatible.

If Irish politics was Fianna Fáil versus the rest, I was with the rest. Up to a point: since I was self-employed, wanted my hard work rewarded and believed passionately in profit (even if I wasn't making much of it), the Labour Party was never going to be my natural home. Fine Gael, on the other hand, had a leader in FitzGerald who radiated idealism about his new political philosophy. This involved moving away from a traditional party membership base of inherited loyalty founded on Civil War politics – which side your family had taken on the Treaty. Since 1921, Éamon de Valera and Michael Collins had divided the nation for at least two or three generations, depending on how diehard your parents and grandparents were. Garret FitzGerald wanted none of that old tribal stuff. He called on young people and women, who had no political pedigree in their family, to join Fine Gael. I was up for that.

His policy platform of common sense, sound economics and fiscal responsibility in budgetary policy was enhanced for me by two other dimensions. He advocated a new liberalism: the state did not belong in the bedrooms of Ireland; the Catholic Church's teaching should be segregated from the state's laws on social issues. On Northern Ireland, he pioneered, with Paddy Harte as spokesperson, the principle of Unionist consent in any solution. The Sunningdale power-sharing agreement of 1973 had collapsed in disarray, but Garret strongly promulgated the need for an internal political settlement as a forerunner to any long-term constitutional change. Fine Gael, as a result, was infused with an almost palpable energy, a tangible sense of urgency, and I wanted to be part of the move towards a secular modern society.

My first dilemma was how to join the party. I knew nobody who was locally involved in politics. I had no one to contact about joining Fine Gael. I picked up the *Golden Pages*, found an address for Fine Gael in Wexford and wrote them a letter:

> *Dear Sir or Madam,*
>
> *I am a young farmer living at the above address and would like to join the party, but do not know how to do so, please advise ...*

After some weeks, I received a letter from Cliodhna Ó Tuama, the Enniscorthy town branch secretary. She advised me that my correspondence had been referred to her by the local Fine Gael Waterford TD, Eddie Collins, and she would send me notices to attend future monthly meetings.

I was apprehensive before my first meeting in Murphy Floods Hotel in Enniscorthy's Market Square. I hadn't a clue who would be there, what would be discussed or what they might make of me. As it turned out, they made the best of me. I was warmly welcomed, partly because it was a novelty to have a raw recruit, especially after the rout and rejection at the previous year's general election. They all knew and respected my father, and assumed I was following a family allegiance to Fine Gael. They couldn't have been more wrong. Throughout the period of the Fine Gael/Labour coalition government (1973–7), my father had grown increasingly opposed to that administration's taxation policies. He sneered at 'Red Richie' or 'Richie Ruin' as the then Minister for Finance, Richie Ryan, was known: businessmen and farmers alike detested the wealth and other capital taxes he introduced. My parents would have voted for and supported Seán Browne, the local Fianna Fáil TD, for many years.

I sat quietly through my first few meetings, absorbing all the procedures and discussions. The chairman of the town branch was a farmer and former senator, Pat Codd. He would open the meeting by calling on the secretary to read the minutes of the previous meeting, followed by matters arising. There would then be a report from the treasurer on the branch's finances and another from branch delegates who had attended recent district and constituency executive meetings.

The local councillors on Enniscorthy Urban District Council and Wexford County Council would outline their activities. Occasionally, the newly elected deputy Michael D'Arcy would attend. Ritual condemnation of Fianna Fáil in government happened all the time. Everybody blamed them for unemployment and every other problem, national and local. The meeting would invariably end with what I thought was an odd minute's silence, when we bowed our heads, for supporters who had recently passed away.

Fine Gael meetings may not sound like social events, but for me they were precisely that. They freed me to do things, like smoking, which I preferred not to do in front of my parents. The meetings involved lively arguments and led to a few pints at the end of the night. After my day on the farm, it was as exciting as a visit to a nightclub. Then there were church gate collections, visits to the constituency by members of the front bench or the party leader, attendance at the Ard Fheis in the Royal Dublin Society (RDS) and preparation for forthcoming elections.

Of course, if you attend meetings and contribute to them regularly, someone will decide, inevitably, that you would make a good district organiser. I was chosen to be chairman of the fledgling Enniscorthy unit of Young Fine Gael. Numbers were small: mostly sons and daughters of party members, attending out of a sense of duty and loyalty to their parents or grandparents. Any willing volunteer got lots of invitations.

'Would you like to be district organiser?'

'Would you kind of like to be sort of branch secretary?'

'Ever think about being chairman of Young Fine Gael?'

If I'd been naïve, I would have found it flattering. But even that far back, naïve I wasn't. Local politics is voluntary. The problem is that in a voluntary organisation, very few people actually volunteer for jobs. As a result, any eager beaver can make progress, and I was the quintessential eager beaver. I was always on time. If I'd said I would do something, I did it. In my teens, I was up for it all because I could see Young Fine Gael had a hell of a social element. Opportunities beyond politics presented themselves in the form of attractive girls. I eagerly attended a regional conference in Waterford, where the local TD, Austin Deasy, admonished the youthful attendance to deploy 'streetwise cunning' in their political endeavours, to realise that politics was a rough trade and not to be artlessly idealistic about it. At that same event, I got to hear my hero, Garret FitzGerald, for the first time. He addressed the audience without flourishes or rhetoric. Indeed, he spoke so fast, with such a wealth of technical detail and statistics, that no one actually understood what he was saying. We liked his tune, though, and decided we could leave the detail to him since he was so obviously an economic genius. From that first sight of him, I was a fully paid-up storm trooper on his behalf.

After my father died in February 1979, I was mostly answerable to myself and my mother, who was always supportive of whatever I wanted to do – no matter how hare-brained. When the two sitting urban councillors in Enniscorthy, Tommy Hayes and Jim Kavanagh, revealed they would not be seeking re-election in the forthcoming June local elections, Fine Gael headquarters wanted to run four candidates and stipulated a preference, almost an edict, that a place on the ticket be reserved for a Young Fine Gael nominee. No one else among the junior party membership was interested in standing. I went forward.

It was crazy because I was eighteen, lacking any experience and knowing hardly anybody in Enniscorthy. The only thing I had going for me, in the aftermath of my father's death, was time. I had little prospect of success, but even to run and lose would leave me well placed for a future election when I was older. I had no reputation to lose because I had no reputation. I was an unknown quantity – I didn't even know enough people to get elected. My initial objective was not to get a derisory result. I have always had something in common with Mr Magoo in the cartoons: the two of us just plough ahead and leave others to mop up the mess.

How was I to get myself known? I joined the local St Catherine's youth club, attended community and social organisations' meetings and socialised occasionally in the Castle ballroom nightclub on Saturdays. Not easy, particularly since none of my regular friends was remotely interested in accompanying me. Young Fine Gael organised a campaign to procure signatures on a nationwide basis to abolish the legal status of illegitimacy for children born outside marriage. Outdated legislation from the nineteenth century was still on the statute books. This allowed me to knock on doors in housing estates and introduce myself. I soon realised that to make a proper connection on the doorstep, you needed to have someone with you who knew – by their first name – the person opening the door. In ancient Rome, this was a treasured role for a slave, who was known as the *nomenclator*, the person who would whisper the name of an oncoming constituent to a politician. Wonderful, to be able to outsource such a central political task.

But, then, politics always generates people who selflessly gather around a prospective candidate to provide the support and expertise he doesn't know he needs and doesn't know he lacks. What I didn't know would have filled several volumes of the old *Encyclopaedia Britannica*. What I didn't know that I didn't know would have filled a volume all its own. There was nothing I could have done wrong that I didn't do wrong. I looked too young. I was brash. I argued with people on the doorstep who got stroppy with me. If they gave out to me, I'd think, What the feck do *you* know about it? Half the time I would say those words straight out. I hadn't learned any of the patter of politics: 'How's your mother doing since the surgery?' and 'Jaysus, you're getting younger every time I see you.'

But I had Nancy Connolly, a single lady in her fifties, who lived alone in a large housing estate in Bellfield Road, worked as an assistant in Garahy's pharmacy and, like me, enjoyed a night at the dog track. At every opportunity, she told people what a wonderful, brilliant prospect I was. I had Willie 'Hoppy' Davis and Willie Roche, who took me canvassing in different parts of Enniscorthy – the parts each of them knew best. They would introduce me and I would buy them a few pints at the end of the night.

One of the few advantages to my candidature was that I was John F. Yates's son. 'If you're half as good as your father, you'll be all right,' I was told constantly.

I had novelty on my side, too. It was unusual to have a Church of Ireland candidate standing for election, and I hoped the fifty or so Church of Ireland voters within the urban electoral boundary would come out for me, particularly since I couldn't vote for myself because I lived on the edge of town. I urged diehard Fine Gael supporters who wanted to get three seats to vote for me – tactically – as the weakest runner. Somehow I managed to get 154 first-preference votes out of an electorate of 2,581.

The quota for election was 254. I was well short. My running mates were Charlie Kavanagh, a son of the outgoing councillor and a prominent, popular, well-established local publican. He was certain of election and duly won. Dan O'Leary was a dashing secondary-school teacher at the Mercy Convent girls' school. He ran a storming campaign, with help from his pupils' parents, and promised a public swimming pool. Although a 'blow in' from west Cork, he sailed to victory for the first Fine Gael seat.

The fourth Fine Gael candidate was Mrs Kay Dwyer, who

worked as a staff nurse in a local hospital. She got 106 votes. Her elimination could push me towards success. I was so stressed out, I went on the piss on polling night after the booths closed. The following morning my hangover, combined with the tension of the count, kept me at home for the early counts. I eventually appeared in the late afternoon. On the twelfth and final count, I made it without reaching the quota, with a mere thirteen votes to spare. After a nerve-racking recount, I was deemed elected to the second last seat, the youngest councillor in the country. It was only afterwards that I realised – and, indeed, was told – just how bad a campaign I had run. I also got a telling-off from veterans over a deal with which I'd had nothing to do. This was when Fine Gael, Fianna Fáil and Labour combined to vote through on a 6–3 basis control of all positions. Charlie Kavanagh was elected chairman and the main parties were to retain the chair and vice-chair, to the exclusion of Independents, for the five years. It was branded 'an unholy alliance' and hated by diehard supporters of both Fine Gael and Fianna Fáil. Previously the chairmanship had rotated on an annual basis between each political group. The alliance was seen as sharp practice by Independent councillors and led to constant rows. The controversy enlightened me about brokering back-room political deals and particularly the fundamental fault line between Fianna Fáil and Fine Gael.

Once I'd attended my first council meeting, I realised that a priority was to grab headlines in the local weekly newspapers. Showtime for opportunists. I loved it.

I had a problem, though: the silver spoon. I had, of course, been reared with every comfort and privilege. My father might have been tight with money and averse to display, and have passed on both characteristics to me, but to an outsider I was a classic posh boy, protected from real life with a padding of cotton wool. Natural shyness – I was only a teenager, though it may be hard to believe now that I was ever shy – added to this cosseted image, until I met Paddy Walsh from Enniscorthy. A maintenance man in Davis's flour mill and a recovering alcoholic, Paddy had been in the British Army and lived in London in hard times. Now he was a settled, devoted, family man with a passion for politics and particularly for Fine Gael. As an Irish Transport and General Workers' Union official, he was untypical of your average Fine Gael member. He was blue-collar, working class and proud of it.

One evening when we completed canvassing, Paddy said he wanted a word. This was always an ominous sign. I was due a dressing-down, I figured. Another dressing-down.

'Yes, Paddy?' I said, bracing myself.

'Remember that woman who walked by you on the street? She nodded at you. You ignored her or didn't notice her. What sort of arrogant, stuck-up snob are you?'

'Well, Paddy, I didn't know who she was. I didn't want to be too forward.' Even as I said it, I knew it was a feeble excuse.

He waved it aside as if it was a wasp. 'In future, always remember that you may not know *them*, but they sure as hell know who *you* are. By word of mouth they'll tell others how snooty, offhand and distant you are. You don't seem to realise that class politics applies around here. They think you look down on them. If you think they'll vote for you, forget it. Cop yourself on quick.'

From then on, everyone I met, I said hello, nodded, winked at them or smiled, although I might not have known them from Adam. In his sitting room, late into the night, Paddy instructed me about human nature: the selfish perspectives of voters and how to pander to them; the jobbery and corruption of politics; the realities of nepotism; the importance of working on families as a group to change their political allegiance; the deep-rooted disconnection of Fine Gael from working people in urban areas. He was a political godfather to me, teaching me the essentials of dealing with people and hammering home that, first, last and always, politics is a people business. I often resented his strictures, bluntness and discipline, but benefited enormously from them. I followed instructions, never leaving home without a notebook and pen in my pocket so I could welcome a casual query and not lose its details.

The most significant training I gained on the urban district council was how to deal with public servants. If you wanted a tenant's roof fixed, a family rehoused, a pothole or streetlight repaired, or any other favour done to garner a vote, you were dependent on the town clerk, engineer, planner or health inspector to see that it was carried out. The working relationship between public representatives and public officials is one of interdependence, which has to be based on mutual respect and appreciation. From my mistakes, when I rubbed up officials the wrong way, I learned that cajoling, charming and persuading them was a hell of a lot more productive than slagging them off in public.

The council chamber was a theatre, full of actors on stage. The veteran councillors knew how to use colourful language to grab headlines in the local weekly papers. At the end of each meeting, under Any Other Business, councillors could raise every parish pump problem that had been relayed to them.

Developing a thick skin is an imperative in public life. In the beginning, I was often privately upset and torn asunder by personal criticism or derision. Abuse at the doorstep or on the street, disappointment at failure to deliver, bitter partisan remarks – they're all part and parcel of a public representative's daily routine. Sometimes such castigation is malicious or politically motivated, but that's not the whole story. Often people with problems are deeply stressed or unwell. As a public representative, you have to avoid attributing motivation and becoming paranoid. You have to swallow your pride, bite your lip and defuse the heat.

By the autumn of 1980, I was Fine Gael's district organiser, setting out to recruit younger members to the rural branches in my part of County Wexford.

All eyes nationally and locally were now focused on the general election, which was expected to be held in 1981. Charles Haughey had ousted Jack Lynch after two by-election defeats in late 1979. Fine Gael was making progress in the polls. The local elections had created a launching pad for new councillors who would stand for the Dáil.

One November night, as was customary after the branch AGM, we went for a few drinks in the local pub with Seán Kavanagh, district executive chairman for many years and a farmer from Screen, a rural parish near the seaside. He was an only son and now a fifty-year-old farmer, married to Eileen, with four children. Apparently, he had not wanted to be a farmer, but had taken up the role on the insistence of his father. Politics and Fine Gael provided an outlet for his organisational talent. He was driven, impatient, with a fiery temper. Seán didn't suffer fools gladly, didn't take no for an answer and could be moody. He had lost the sight of one eye in an accident many years before. The man was determined Fine Gael would win a second seat in the Wexford constituency.

'Well, my young man,' he began, 'I was talking to some of the lads in the organisation around the rural parts of the district, and we were wondering if you might be interested in going for the nomination to stand for the Dáil.'

'*Me?* For the Dáil? How do you mean?'

'I know it may sound crazy. You're only twenty-one, completely wet behind the ears and you're totally unknown. But I was thinking that we could try to sell you to the delegates as a young guy with great potential and probably the best chance of getting elected.'

'But, Seán, we all know Pat Codd will get the nomination,' I said. 'He's a former senator. He has all the key contacts among the delegates. Even if I was capable of standing, I couldn't win. Either way, I'm trying to manage the farm at home with my mother, find my feet on the urban council and enjoy politics at an organisational level. I can't envisage having the nerve to take this leap in the dark.'

'Pat Codd won't get the nomination if I've anything to do with it. He's a three-time loser and only got 845 first-preference votes in the local elections. With him, we're beaten before we start. I don't think there's anyone else who could or would go for it in the district. The second seat has to come from the Enniscorthy district. It's where the votes are. You'll be ideally placed geographically, bang in the centre of the constituency. You have a bit of a base in the town and the solid loyal party vote will come out for you in the country areas.'

'Jesus, I've never even thought about this.'

'Think about it now.'

Over the coming weeks, I walked around the farm, fretting and in a daze. This was an incredible, if audacious, opportunity. At times I thought the notion was absurd. Then again, if I turned it down for lack of bottle, the party might find someone else.

Another reality was knocking inside my head. This farming game was no career. There was no money in it. You'd do the accounts and find you'd made ten grand at the end of the year. Even back then ten grand wasn't much money. It would be less than the industrial average wage and it was a lot of hard work. I didn't mind that, but I knew I wasn't looking forward to twenty, thirty or forty years of the same thing. If, on the other hand, I put my name forward, it could only enhance my prospects for the next county council election. I thought I'd give it a go.

Because it is decided on the basis of one person, one vote, there would, I knew, be three delegates down in Wellington Bridge or up in Cranford who could make the difference for me, if I could talk to them personally and convince them I should be on the ticket. I took off in my granny's car to meet them.

'I'm going for this nomination,' I would tell them. 'Look, I'm doing my best, but I'm the young candidate, the newcomer. Maybe that's what's needed. I'm on the urban district council, I'm working hard, I've got a foothold, I'm geographically well placed but, really, I'm interested in you. You tell me what to do. You be my mentor, my adviser.'

To this day, people remember when I called around to them. They spotted that I wouldn't just run in and run out. I'd spend an hour talking with them.

Some of my most mortifying moments come from that time. I remember going to this farmer in Oylgate, halfway between Wexford and Enniscorthy, and I'd had so many cups of tea I was bursting to go to the loo.

'Do you mind me asking where the toilet is?' I asked the farmer, who has long since died.

'Just go out that door and turn left,' he told me.

So I went out the door and turned left, and couldn't find any toilet. Like an idiot, I came back in and said, 'I'm sorry, I couldn't find the toilet and I'm bursting to go.'

The minute I'd spoken, I knew there was no toilet. Embarrassing for him, humiliating for me. I was just so dim. That's what I call a real education: learning to cop on to what's said and not said, learning not to demean people by noticing what they don't have.

Travelling around in the Escort, I got to know about politics and people in conversations, not in high-flown theory. Each farmer would talk to me about his own political past. They would reminisce about what they had done in this or that election. They would describe being out canvassing for the Esmondes. From 1953 the Fine Gael County Wexford standard-bearer was Sir Anthony Esmonde. He was succeeded by his son, John Esmonde, who served as the Fine Gael TD from 1973 to 1977. In a hard-fought battle, where there was only one Fine Gael seat to be won, Michael D'Arcy ousted him. Remarkably, both candidates had their base close to each other in the Gorey–North Wexford area. John was subsequently appointed a judge, departing politics and Wexford.

The farmers I met had a long memory for who had been well or badly treated by those who were elected. They did instant performance reviews, telling me that this councillor did no work, while that other man or woman did a lot but was totally disorganised. Never mind Donogh O'Malley: this was free education at its best. I was learning the facts, but – even more importantly – I was getting a feel for the way things were.

As Paddy had told me, while Fine Gael traditionally got a great rural vote, and in the towns a great middle-class vote, the party performs poorly in urban working-class Ireland and always has. That was true even in Garret FitzGerald's heyday when the party got 39 per cent of the vote. I had to find a way of connecting with these people, not on the basis of Fine Gael but on the basis of Ivan Yates. I concentrated on making contact, on establishing my brand, not that I would have used those terms back then. Even early on, when Young Fine Gael ran a campaign to abolish illegitimacy, I got the old clipboard out, knocked on every door and explained what the campaign was about. Some girls from Young Fine Gael and I would go painstakingly from door to door and ask each householder their view. It was as simple and tedious as that, the building of a political candidate's profile within a constituency.

As the big night of the convention to select the candidate approached, I meticulously prepared my speech, had it typed up for the local newspapers whose reporters would attend, and rehearsed every word until I had it off by heart. I loved making speeches. I practised in front of the mirror for hours. The content included the usual anti-government rhetoric, but my emphasis was on asking the delegates to trust me with the nomination and in return I would pledge my adult life to working flat out for the party and the constituency. My commitment was 100 per cent. I concluded, 'When the going gets tough, the tough get going.' It's a cliché now, but was fresh enough back then.

The tension in the packed downstairs ballroom of Murphy Floods Hotel was electric. This was the blood sport that party activists loved. This was decision time, when they alone made the decision. The speech worked a treat. My timing and delivery were exactly as I wanted. The audience responded with applause and cheers. Many years later, people would reminisce about that speech, saying they voted for me as a result of it, not having intended to do so.

When the votes were counted, the result was announced: Michael D'Arcy 129, Ivan Yates 101. That surpassed my wildest hopes and the most optimistic tallies of my generals. The third candidate chosen was urban district councillor Mrs Louise Hennessy, a teacher from New Ross, a Fianna Fáil bastion. Oh, my God, I thought, what have I done? Will their faith in me be rewarded?

My supporters were ecstatic. The vanquished were less so. A few weeks later, Taoiseach Charlie Haughey dissolved the Dáil on 21 May. It was widely speculated that he had intended to call the election on 14 February from the stage at the Fianna Fáil Ard Fheis until news broke of the Stardust fire tragedy. The postponement facilitated my nomination. Now, my every waking moment went into campaigning.

It helped that I was on the council because, in the months coming up to the general election, if someone's gutter was leaking or they had a problem with their winter fuel voucher, I was on it in a flash. I set myself the target not of meeting but of *learning* fifty new people every week. I was hopeless on names. To this day I'm no better at it. But I would start a conversation, then think of a first name or a surname or I'd remember a detail about the person I was talking to and then I would be flying.

The dangerous times for me, during that and later campaigns, were when, through tiredness, I was on auto-pilot. That got me into awful trouble. I'd be on a roll canvassing house after house. 'Jesus, Andy's getting big there,' I'd be saying at one door. 'You have a beautiful garden,' I'd tell another constituent. 'I love those roses – you must put a lot of effort into them.' We might end up talking about Jack and Vera in *Coronation Street* or just about anything. But now and then, a mistake would happen.

'Be sure and tell the boss I called,' I told one woman.

'The boss died last week,' she replied.

It almost brings you to your knees when you do something like that. Or when you ask after the partner, only to find that the couple have separated. I made a point of having someone with me to help me avoid making hurtful mistakes.

Midway through any campaign, the pace, the rivalry within your own party, badmouthing, panic, the fear of losing and stress are frenetic. You live on adrenalin, shaking so many hands and asking for so many votes that you have to operate on auto-pilot. I had no experience of this crazy build-up towards polling day. My seriously bad asthma was a major drawback, complicated by hay fever and heavy smoking: it put me in hospital right in the middle of the campaign – I had to have steroid injections and stay in bed for a few days. But nothing dented the enthusiasm of my supporters. Nothing *could* dent their enthusiasm or their confidence: the entire party organisation now knew that, because we didn't have a strong candidate in New Ross and if Fine Gael were to get a seat, it could only be young Yates who stood a chance. Seán Kavanagh virtually moved into my bedroom. The campaign harnessed for the first time my dedicated crew of around twenty regular daily canvassers and a network of more than two hundred individuals throughout the county. The scale of the operation was immense. Seán's two nieces, Bernie and Breda Redmond, became the most formidable, effective and loyal component of my election machine for the next twenty years.

'Folks, it's up to ye,' I kept saying. 'You got me into this mess. You'd better get me out of it.'

They all – my team mustered about sixty people – worked their socks off. The Fine Gael manifesto was famed for a promised payment of £9.60 per week to stay-at-home housewives as a tax rebate. The party targeted women's votes and ran a large number of prominent female candidates, such as Gemma Hussey, Nuala Fennell, Nora Owen and Mary Flaherty. Fianna Fáil was a divided party after the ousting of Jack Lynch as leader and the consequent bitter rivalry between Haughey and George Colley. It had as a core principle the outright rejection of coalition. The party required 50 per cent of the vote to secure single-party government. Opinion polls predicted significant gains for Fine Gael. A neck-and-neck contest ensued. The outcome was uncertain. Predictions of a hung Dáil abounded.

My team realised from the convention campaign that my candidacy was tapping into a ready-made group of Fine Gael supporters: the Esmonde group, who retained their resentment against Michael D'Arcy. I was to satisfy their requirement for a Fine Gael TD other than Michael D'Arcy. I gave them a political home. We cultivated these contacts. Michael had a safe seat, having had four years to build up his base as the sole Fine Gael TD, front-bench spokesperson on agriculture, with reasonable prospects of being appointed a minister. This would be enhanced if he delivered a second seat.

My routine was hectic, exhilarating and exhausting. Each day I would team up with a group of local supporters and canvass the assigned areas. My mother became my greatest ambassador on the road, knocking on doors, smiling pleasantly and asking for votes for her son. My entire family was deployed around the county on my behalf.

Seán Kavanagh's home became a military headquarters, making dozens of daily phone calls to line up the teams of canvassers travelling from Enniscorthy so they met up with our local contacts without any hanging around. Large charts were assembled with a matrix of each polling booth, electoral register, our local contact and how long it would take to complete the canvass.

The constituency director of elections, Martin Breen, reported directly to Peter Prendergast, who became party general secretary in 1977. Although Martin was a close friend and supporter of Michael D'Arcy, he ensured that the rules of canvassing engagement in each other's home districts allowed me enough days to access and secure votes in D'Arcy's back door of the Gorey district. This was where most Fine Gael, one-time Esmonde supporters and Protestant voters resided.

I freely confess, in retrospect, that I was bossy, belligerent and unreasonable to all my unpaid volunteers. Many had taken annual leave from their job to assist me and the party. I would vent my anxiety on those closest to me, while on the doorsteps I was the epitome of charm.

I borrowed money from my mother to pay for the campaign. To deal with the media, I hired a public-relations guy from Arklow I had met at a conference. Vincent McElheron filled me with self-confidence and was always adamant that I was certain to get elected. Seán and he fought like dogs. One day when I turned up at the election office Seán and Vincent were there. Vincent wanted to go off and chat with me. He asked Seán to keep an eye on his briefcase, to which Seán replied, 'I've only one eye and, by God, that's staying fixed on you.'

Garret FitzGerald's visit to the constituency, culminating in a tremendous evening rally in the Market Square of Enniscorthy, was a memorable high point. There was a really loud PA system and a great crowd. It was unheard of for Fine Gael to be so visible in a Fianna Fáil heartland. This was the political base of Seán Browne, the regular poll-topping Fianna Fáil deputy for decades and the incumbent Leas-Cheann Comhairle. We were taking on long-standing political icons such as him and former Tánaiste Brendan Corish in Wexford town. Could an unknown youngster, who barely qualified on age grounds at twenty-one, cause a shock election result? At this stage I was so driven I didn't contemplate defeat, but I hadn't a clue what to expect.

As polling day, 11 June, arrived, the tension worsened as there was less and less we could do because we had already canvassed everyone.

Michael D'Arcy topped the poll with 10,290, comfortably exceeding the quota of 8,304. He was elected on the first count. I obtained 5,522 first preferences, plus 914 from Michael's surplus. On the sixth count, after the elimination of Louise Hennessy, I got a further 2,217 transfers to secure the second seat with 8,850. I delayed attending the count centre, but Seán had told me about early tally predictions of possible success. I was exhausted, but felt great elation and gratitude.

The ecstasy of my jubilant team was like a Cup Final win and lasted for weeks. Their faith in me was vindicated. They were on the high that is the main reason supporters work for the party at every election, surviving cruel outcomes as well as celebrating triumphs. Fine Gael had had a really good day, capturing 36 per cent of the vote nationally. The party gained twenty-two seats, with a final tally of sixty-five. FitzGerald could now become Taoiseach. It was a life-changing moment for me. The seemingly impossible had been achieved: three years earlier, I had not even been a member of a party, still at college, no achievements outside politics, no political lineage. Now? A Dáil deputy at twenty-one. One of the youngest ever. Hello, Leinster House, goodbye to the daily farming routine.

5: Two Commandments

The Dáil usher tapped me on the shoulder. 'Are you Deputy Ivan Yates?'

'I am.'

'Deputy Peter Barry would like to see you in his office. I'll show you where to go.'

Jesus, what have I done now? I thought, as I obediently followed his black serge uniform down the corridor. I can't be in trouble already, can I?

Peter Barry was the deputy leader of Fine Gael. He was quietly dignified, almost ambassadorial in his manner, despite his years of serving behind the counter of his Cork family grocery shop in a brown coat. I knew him with the spurious familiarity television gives, but had never met him. The usher stopped, gestured to a door and left. I knocked and, hearing what I assumed might be an invitation to enter, turned the polished brass handle and put my head around the door. 'My name is Ivan Yates. I understand you're looking for me?'

He immediately gestured me into the room and rose to give me a warm handshake.

'We want the oldest member of the new Fine Gael parliamentary party, Oliver J. Flanagan, to propose the nomination of Dr Garret FitzGerald for Taoiseach, and you, as the youngest TD, to second the motion. Would that be all right?'

Would it be *all right*?

'I would, of course, be honoured to second the motion.'

'I think it will be the first of many honours you may have in the years ahead in this House.'

Red in the face from the flattery, I went back down to the Dáil chamber, where you could almost touch the tension. Fianna Fáil had 78 seats and couldn't obtain the magical majority figure of 83 (half of the total 166). Fine Gael plus Labour amounted to 80 TDs (65 and 15 respectively). So it was a hung Dáil. Dr John O'Connell, formerly Labour but now an Independent, was elected Ceann Comhairle. After Charles Haughey's nomination was defeated by 83 votes to 79, Garret FitzGerald was elected by 81 to 78, with the help of Independent Jim Kemmy.

That day, all 22 new Fine Gael deputies were photographed as a group with FitzGerald. Many, such as Michael Noonan, Seán Barrett, Hugh Coveney, Gay Mitchell, Alan Shatter, Nora Owen, Mary Flaherty, George Birmingham, Alice Glenn and Bernard Allen, were old hands to a greater or lesser extent. Newcomers who had not been councillors included Alan Dukes and Nuala Fennell. None was remotely as youthful or lacking in life experience as me. I was the rawest recruit in the house, facing a learning curve that could not have been much steeper.

While I was trying to come to terms with it all, I must have looked anxious, because one day, veteran constituency colleague and former Tánaiste Brendan Corish called me aside.

'You'll get on fine here,' he told me. 'Keep your head down, stay out of trouble, do your constituency work, speak once a week in the Dáil chamber, table constituency-related questions – that's the best way to get noticed.'

Brendan Corish was not the only one who was kind to me, but most senior figures hardly noticed me. The only time I recall Charles Haughey ever speaking to me at that time was when, less than sober, he bumped into me in a corridor one night and called me a 'mush Baptist'. I had the impression that it was cordially meant, but I wasn't going to draw him on me, one way or the other, by demanding that he define his terms. (I suspect he meant to say 'bush Baptist', a term long fallen out of use to describe someone with no official religious affiliation.)

Because the proceedings of the Dáil were not broadcast on TV at that time, people at home did not get so exercised about the chamber being empty. Sometimes the empty chairs shown in the TV pictures give the false impression that deputies are skiving off outside the chamber. This misses the point that the primary purpose of a TD's life is to get re-elected. No votes are to be won sitting on your arse listening to others. Your survival depends on your ability to get things done for your constituents and constituency.

Each Wednesday morning after the order of business, the weekly meeting of the parliamentary party would happen. FitzGerald and most ministers would attend and the important political issues of the day would be discussed. I never missed a meeting and always sat at the front, figuring that well-informed contributions were the best way to make an impression on the senior hierarchy. A quiet curate never got a parish.

Along with most rural deputies, I either stayed in Powers, Buswells or Jurys hotels, as they gave a discount to politicians. We lived out of suitcases, not committing to an apartment in Dublin, fearing that the job might not last. It was a volatile time and you never knew when, having jettisoned a previous career in order to get into politics, the electorate might in turn jettison you.

Christianity, according to Christ, has only two essential Commandments (see Matthew 22:37–40). Chris Glennon, a seasoned political editor with the *Irish Independent*, maintained that the same was true of politics, the two essential Commandments being get thyself elected and hold thy seat.

No matter what you say or do, without votes you go into liquidation in this business. Your *raison d'être* is votes, votes and votes, and votes come from personal service to individual constituents.

'Tut, tut, my dear Mrs Murphy, do you not realise I am a national parliamentarian, not a messenger boy?' you may ask such a constituent, conscious of your elevated status as a legislator. The answer will come from her at the next election, and it will be a P45. It doesn't pay, when you're a politician, to take yourself too seriously, or to miss the point that – to a constituent – what might seem to you the most trivial of requests is crucially important to the person making it and should be taken seriously.

I found that if I wasn't immediately helpful, I would be smartly told, 'Don't worry, I'll call on Deputy Browne or D'Arcy about my problem,' with the latent threat that the speaker would not vote for me the next time around.

Of course, not all 'problems' were really problems. Enda Kenny, when I shared an office with him, would gleefully brandish a letter from a constituent in the remote hills of Mayo, requesting him to have a word with the bosses in the *Sunday Press* about their weekly X the Ball competition. The correspondent felt sure that Enda would have the inside track, and be able to get the X placed in the spot the constituent had chosen, allowing them a cash windfall.

I operated the system more competitively than most. Every weekend I would hold, on average, four clinics to meet constituents. I would spend about forty pounds a week advertising them in the local papers, so that even those who didn't take advantage of my services could see how diligent I was. Any time I persuaded an official to reverse a decision, I was thrilled with myself. Even when I failed, most constituents understood that I had done my best for them and appreciated the effort.

Every Saturday morning I held my main clinic in Enniscorthy. On Saturday evenings I would alternate between the other main towns of Gorey, Wexford and New Ross. On Friday or Monday evenings I would hold two clinics in rural villages, maybe fifteen miles apart, where I would have a local party activist present to update me on local issues. I was a glorified social and community worker on wheels, criss-crossing the county to eighteen different venues, from Fethard in the south to Coolgreany in the north, and from the Blackstairs mountains to the eastern coastline. I preferred not to have people calling to my house, remembering the story of a former rural Fine Gael deputy who was at home carving the turkey on Christmas Day when the family meal was interrupted by a caller seeking his assistance to complete a medical-card application form. The TD stoically and dutifully did so. On completion, he explained to the person that he would have to get his doctor's signature on the form before submitting it. 'Ah, sure, I wouldn't like to disturb the doctor on Christmas Day' was the shocked answer.

Such was the electoral significance of correspondence, phone calls and clinics that TDs undertook – and continue to undertake. In addition, deputies must do constant door-to-door house calls seeking extra business. This, despite the frequent criticism on the doorstep at elections that 'We only see you when you're looking for votes.' If you want to get several thousand first-preference votes, there is no substitute for the endless slog of constituency work. A success rate of one in three will engender word-of-mouth praise among neighbours and relatives in appreciation for favours done or perceived to have been done. The most valuable asset of any TD is a reputation as a reliable worker. There's no point in bitching about it: those are the terms and conditions under our present electoral system. Nowhere else in Europe is the same proportion of parliamentarians' time dedicated to constituency work. The way to survive in politics when the tide goes out on your party support nationally is to have a sufficient personal vote to see you through.

How do you gain votes from people who do not have problems? The first priority is to be seen around. The second priority is to be known to be seen around. This involves turning up at every official or public event in each parish or town. Your yearly diary includes summer festivals, St Patrick's Day parades, exhibitions, pantomimes/dramas, school openings, county hurling and football finals, state agency announcements, tidy-towns competitions, annual conferences, religious events, dinner dances – simply any bun fight with photographers or voters present.

More important than any clinic, party or public event is to be present at funerals. It is impossible to overstate the importance of this. The funeral is the most significant event in many people's lives, registering the loss of a close relative. It may be cynical, but the reality is that the deepest appreciation of people and conversely resentment relates to the presence or absence of their TD from a family funeral. If I was unavoidably absent, I would try to call to the house of the bereaved within a few days to convey my condolences. The daily newspaper and subsequently local radio obituaries were vital sources of information. Letters of sympathy are dispatched systematically from TDs' offices, regardless of whether or not they knew the deceased. It is safer to err on the side of over-sympathising than the reverse.

Most weeks I attended several funerals, as many as three a day. Mates working for undertakers would tip me off in good time about the arrangements. Attending wasn't enough. I had to shake hands with as many family members as possible. 'I'm sorry for your troubles' is the standard phrase. Some politicians become professional sympathisers, knowing the most appropriate small-talk, the double handshake and fake sincerity/grief for people they did not know. They can loiter with intent and be seen, while timing their arrival and departure to coincide with the most opportune moments of visibility and minimise time wasted sitting through mass. Some enormous funerals involving multiple tragic deaths (drowning or road fatalities) are community-wide bereavements, at which TDs *must* be seen.

I realised early that a crucial category of professionals who require the most careful and sensitive glad-handing are the local media. In the 1980s there was no local radio, so the weekly provincial press provided the best medium to make a public impression throughout the Model County. I was attentive to the needs of local hacks working for the *Echo* and *People* group of papers, bringing them printed copies of speeches and always being available to chat and confide on and off the record on local stories and scoops. I treated the journalists as pals and enjoyed their company.

Learning all this in the 22nd Dáil was like learning to ice-skate in a thaw. The circumstances could not have been more precarious. The new Fine Gael /Labour government found the public finances in a much worse state than they had been led to believe. The exchequer borrowing requirement exceeded 20 per cent of GNP. The current budget deficit was spiralling out of control. A savage hair-shirt budget was being planned for early January 1982. A Dáil majority to pass these measures was in doubt because Haughey's Fianna Fáil would oppose everything.

Nineteen eighty-two was an unprecedented year in the history of the state because of its political instability. On budget night TDs marched up the steps of the chamber to walk through the Tá or Níl lobby gates to enact the VAT resolutions. The large figure of the bespectacled Jim Kemmy sat ashen-faced, then voted against the measure to impose 18 per cent VAT on children's clothing and footwear. The government was defeated, and a general election an automatic consequence. Unconcealed panic broke out among government TDs.

The abrasive but able minister for education, John Boland, came into our small office. I admired him for his tenacity in standing up to the primary-teachers union, INTO, over previous weeks as the government raised the school entry age from four to five years. In one Dáil debate, he railed against a packed visitors' gallery of teachers. He had no lack of courage, but now he was crying after the government defeat, bewildered with shock. A general election was fixed for 18 February. A mid-winter election, without any of the excitement and expectations of the previous summer.

Could I be one of the shortest-serving members the Dáil had ever played host to? In theory, yes. But that was one possibility I was determined to prevent. One advantage I had was that this time I knew the ropes and my team knew how to campaign effectively. We convened an emergency meeting of all my main supporters for the following night. Names were enlisted and days selected for canvass teams to be available. A system of petrol vouchers was put in place in two local garages; we would also pay for canvassers' meals where they weren't provided by the local host canvasser. Posters were erected on all main roads, with particularly high visibility at junctions. Up-to-date registers were obtained for every parish, housing estate and urban area.

We drilled every canvasser. Bring a notebook and record the exact details of everyone's identity and problem. Before starting each day, they were asked to bring ample canvass cards with my name and photo in first position and to bring 'Sorry to have missed you, Ivan Yates' cards for when knocks on the door evoked no response. (I know it was a bit bold, but I would ask them to handwrite those cards in order to give recipients the impression that I had actually called to their door.)

Our pitch to voters was to be tilted towards my vulnerability, compared to Michael D'Arcy's invincibility. In order to hold the two Fine Gael seats, I needed the number-one vote where possible. 'Always ask for a minor-preference vote, if there's negative feedback,' we told canvassers. 'Pass only houses of known Fianna Fáil canvassers. Otherwise visit every home.'

We negotiated and secured satisfactory two-day access into all electoral districts of the constituency, especially D'Arcy's Gorey district, where I believed we could pick up at least two thousand votes.

I hired a personal driver for the three weeks of the campaign to improve the efficiency of my own door-to-door canvass. He would be turning the car while I did the talking. In housing estates, we would operate in teams of four to six, so I could run around and shake people's hands instantly and continuously, not stand waiting for them to come to the doorway.

We had learned the importance of smiling and eye contact. We were proper charmers. My line of *plámás* had improved.

'The hair looks well today,' I'd tell an elderly constituent.

'Gosh, the kid's gone that big now,' I would wonder aloud, as a youngster streaked past me into the hall.

'The garden's come on a treat – it's a credit to ya' was another sure-fire opener.

'Be sure to tell himself that I was asking for him,' I'd say when leaving. 'Do the best you can for me, I'd really appreciate it.'

If they mentioned another candidate, I would praise that candidate. We would badmouth nobody. My doorstep companions alerted me to the first name of the householder and any recent family incidents of note. Any delivery of work done in the area was emphasised. My network of clinics was mentioned and we encouraged voters to be sure to call on me in future if I could ever be of assistance.

As many relatives and friends as I could muster were harnessed into action. We understood not to make false promises. In this campaign, my canvassers made a virtue out of our horror story. Our austerity was the only honest approach to tackling the nation's problems. Any opponent promising soft options was being dishonest. Now and then we unwittingly called on a strong or bitter Fianna Fáiler or Sinn Féiner who gave us serious flak.

'Of course we knew you would be unlikely to vote for us, but we didn't like to pass the house. It might be considered rude,' I would say, with quiet politeness. That usually shut them up fairly quickly.

I learned that when people used the word 'Anyway' before or after saying whether they'd vote for me or not, it was going to be a negative. But when that happened, I wasn't crushed because I had become a lot more self-assured and confident that I was worthy of their vote and that they could depend on me to work on their behalf. Whatever else, no one would work harder than Ivan Yates.

We survived the vicissitudes of contrary dogs, made sure to shut the gate behind us and struggled through long days and darkness, canvassing from nine in the morning until nine at night. Then we would head to a local pub to buy drinks for the troops and afterwards back to the election office to co-ordinate all the problems picked up from the entire canvass and to review progress. Every few days I would bring sackfuls of notes to my local part-time secretary, Lily Quirke, to ensure prompt replies and follow-up responses. All the problems picked up on the canvass trail were processed and acknowledged by letter within days.

One of the high points of any election campaign is the visit of the party leader. This time it was to provide a truly tragic moment. Garret FitzGerald was on a whistle-stop tour of the county, briefly stopping off in Enniscorthy to meet and greet people on the high streets. A media entourage followed his every move. The legendary television cameraman Bill St Leger was running in front of them to get the best shots. Suddenly he stumbled and fell to the ground, dying right there on the footpath outside the post office from what we later learned was a stroke. I was numb with shock, feeling so sorry for him and his family.

Each party candidate is entitled to a free postal delivery to every voter on the electoral register. A major organisational feat for every campaign is to pack a single leaflet/letter on behalf of the party ticket into envelopes for delivery; it involves tens of thousands of pieces of literature. In the final days of the campaign, I would hit the main shopping streets and employment centres to maximise personal contact with constituents. I used to call to the local convents to meet the nuns the night before polling day. They treated me like royalty and I would charm them to bits, greatly enjoying the visits. There was nothing I wouldn't do for a vote, up to and including, on polling day itself, personally visiting as many booths as possible.

It all went swimmingly. My first-preference vote increased from 5,522 to 8,005. Michael D'Arcy again topped the poll with 8,787 votes. I obtained 385 from his surplus and surpassed the quota of 8,136 on the second count. This time I didn't need the transfers of Louise Hennessy for victory. Job done. After just six months, I had secured a comfortable re-election through a combination of the honeymoon factor, enhanced credibility and a well-oiled political machine. Nothing succeeds like success. My team perceived me as a winner and they loved winning.

Without Brendan Corish, Labour ran his brother Des and a second candidate from New Ross. They lost the seat to Fianna Fáil. Seán Browne came out of retirement and contributed to Fianna Fáil winning three seats. Wexford's Fine Gael vote actually increased to a new record level of 37.7 per cent, despite unpopular spending cuts and tax increases. It taught me that the public can and do reward courage in politics. A significant number can see through short-term unsustainable attempts to buy votes with the people's own money. That said, it has to be acknowledged that Ireland does not have the most sophisticated electorate in the world. Plenty of voters are gullible enough to believe false promises. The desire for a change of administration usually ensures that the incumbent crowd are cyclically turfed out.

The 23rd Dáil was also a hung parliament and equally short-lived. The minority Fianna Fáil government collapsed before the end of 1982, despite Charles Haughey buying the allegiance of Independent TD Tony Gregory and appointing a Fine Gael deputy, Richard Burke, to the EU Commission. We were plunged back into the morass of another campaign. Three general elections in eighteen months . . . It was the ultimate baptism of fire. Many Dáil deputies have got fifteen years' service out of three election wins. Polling day this time was 24 November.

Whenever a government collapses, the ruling party tends to lose seats in the ensuing election. I decided that whoever lost, it wasn't going to be me. Not if energy and effort counted for anything. For the next few weeks I moved around that constituency like a blue-arsed fly. Whatever happens, I'm going to hold my seat, I would think, when I saw the other Fine Gael candidates on the stump. If that means one of you loses out, so be it.

I was in a paradoxical situation. On the one hand, I was at extreme risk. On the other, Wexford nearly always delivered two seats out of five to Fine Gael. I just had to make sure I didn't start on the bottom rung of the ladder.

The critical difference this time was a change of candidates. Fine Gael's ambition was now elevated to obtaining a third seat. Step up, Avril Doyle. Avril was a bright, formidable, articulate woman. She had been successfully elected a member of Wexford County Council and Wexford Corporation since 1974 from her base outside Wexford town. She had married Freddie Doyle, a prosperous farmer and well-known cattle dealer, having been steeped in Fine Gael as a member of the Belton family in Dublin. She was the first-ever female lord mayor in Wexford town. She looked and sounded the part. Avril was in it to win it. This spelled real competition for the second seat.

If that wasn't bad enough, Fianna Fáil decided to run Seán Browne's nephew, John Browne, who had topped the poll in the local elections for the Enniscorthy district of the county council and urban council in 1979. He was thirty-four years of age and obviously much more vigorous and energetic than his veteran uncle. As well as having a solid party vote machine behind him, he was chairman of the dominant local Enniscorthy GAA club, which had a thriving social centre in the town. He knew everybody and was really well liked for his charm and genuine helpfulness. Not only was he a hard worker but he was teetotal. John Browne was well placed to secure 40 per cent of my back-door vote in perpetuity.

By this third election, I had realised that campaign finance was vital to oil the wheels of my election machine and I organised collections among the business community and other professionals in the town in August of each year. All the proceeds were receipted and placed in a separate deposit account fund in the name of the town branch. Any time anyone gave me a donation, I would issue a receipt and lodge the money in that account. It built up a slush fund to pay exclusively for the campaign. I didn't reveal this war chest to anyone other than my closest campaign confidants and even they never knew how much was in it.

The result of the November 1982 election was the best ever achieved in the history of the state by Fine Gael. The performance in Wexford has never been repeated. In 1973 and 1977 Fine Gael obtained respectively 11,448 and 11,364 first-preference votes. This time we got 41 per cent of the vote and an impressive 20,862 first-preference votes. Instead of me being a beneficiary of vote management, the emphasis was now on lifting Avril Doyle's tally and reducing those of Michael D'Arcy and myself. This worked as Michael got 7,943, I obtained 7,166 and Avril got 5,753. All three of us were duly elected, reversing the former allocation of seats. Labour ran one candidate, a young teacher named Brendan Howlin, based in Wexford town, whose elimination and preferences elected Avril for the second last seat on the sixth count.

The ecstasy and jubilation of the party organisation at this unprecedented breakthrough continued, with organised celebrations for months, well into the New Year. The long-standing older members, steeped in traditional Civil War rivalry, were in seventh heaven. They had never seen the likes of it. The good news was that Fine Gael and Labour now had an overall majority and could govern for a full Dáil term, providing us with some sort of job stability. The bad news for me was that this result was utterly unsustainable. Fine Gael could not retain, under any circumstances, 60 per cent of the seats in the constituency, even on 40 per cent of the vote. Brendan Howlin's tenure in the Senate meant he would most likely win back Brendan Corish's seat.

Three into two simply wouldn't go. Avril, Michael or I would lose our seat in the next general election. Now, with John Browne on my back, I was going to be under even more pressure as a government backbencher in my home area. The prospect was perilous. You didn't need to be a political scientist to know we were on a type of political Death Row. The whirlwind pressure of campaigning was to be replaced by a deep-rooted anxiety of medium-term unsustainability.

I had one big advantage. I was placed geographically in the centre of the county, whereas Avril Doyle was in the south and Michael D'Arcy was in the north. If I could stay off the bottom rung of the ladder, even in second place, the likelihood was that the elimination of either Michael or Avril would favour me in transfer preferences to be the top vote-getter of the three. My base was nearest to each of theirs.

Political pundits often mistakenly ignore this vital element of people voting for a local TD in their town or area, irrespective of party allegiance or individual popularity. The geographic factor can be crucial in determining the last seats in every constituency.

My determination to survive had no limits. Whatever it took, I was going to do it. If I had to hold more clinics, attend more funerals, be most active in every Fine Gael branch and get greater profile locally and nationally, it would be done. Over the next five years, I learned that native cunning is by far the most important ingredient in individual success, next to desire and determination. These characteristics outweigh ability. There is no substitute for hard work and I was a dedicated workaholic. I was in my twenties and had unlimited desire and determination. Whoever lost, it wasn't going to be me.

6: Serving Your Time

From 1983 to 1987 I was a government backbencher. It was a torrid time economically. A prolonged recession meant rocketing unemployment, peaking at 19.9 per cent in County Wexford. The most painful meetings were with groups of workers who had lost their jobs, many of whom were middle-aged and might never work again. The local TDs collectively would meet the receivers/liquidators on the workers' behalf to ensure they got the legal entitlements of redundancy and holiday pay. We had to ascertain what prospects there were for job retention through a new investor. Often the news was grim. The finger of blame was regularly pointed towards government bodies such as the Revenue Commissioners or lack of support from the state rescue agency, Fóir Teoranta.

The list of companies affected by insolvency or rationalisation was endless: Buttles Bacon, Top-Quality Products (compost and mushroom production), Barna Buildings, Ansil, Clover Meats, National Aluminium, Viners Cutlery, Ross Co. (boat builders), Janelle, Fox Engineering, Albatross Fertilisers, Irish Continental Line and B&I Ferries, Great Southern Hotels, Shepp Velours, Premium International, Davis Mosse – covering all types of manufacturing industry, particularly long-standing traditional large employers. Thousands of layoffs happened, and closure often left aggrieved, unpaid and unsecured creditors.

The downside of European Community (EC) membership was a flood of cheap imported products, against which Irish firms could not compete on price. Workers and their families would be bitter against the government politicians and I would be directly in their line of fire at the next election. New state-won projects seemed to materialise only for larger centres of employment, cities closer to universities and airports. I constantly castigated the Industrial Development Authority (IDA) boss, Padraic White, for his neglect of the south-east region. Lack of disposable income and emigration meant further knock-on unemployment in the service sectors.

The early 1980s were also characterised by one of the most vicious and insidious lobbying campaigns. PLAC (Pro-Life Amendment Campaign) and SPUC (Society for the Protection of the Unborn Child) took no prisoners. Their correspondence campaigns produced hundreds of abusive letters enclosing photographs of aborted foetuses. When deputations accosted you, they were explicit in their voting threats, accusing you of being a murderer. Some were nutters.

The national political leadership of all parties was hijacked into giving written commitments to support a referendum providing a constitutional ban on any form of abortion before the 1981 general election. This was overwhelmingly passed nationally and in the Wexford constituency by 28,843 to 10,752. Between Haughey's opportunism and the cowardice of other senior politicians, the Irish body politic allowed the views of the Roman Catholic Church to prevail. It was the only time in my political career that I felt uncomfortable as a Protestant TD. From clerics in the pulpit came arguments justifying Catholic laws for a Catholic state. For every Protestant vote I ever got, I obtained eight Catholic votes. Keep the head down, Ivan.

I was always a liberal, but respectful of all religions and their clergy. Two of my best friends were (still are) Father Walter Forde and Father Aidan Jones. We had dinner in each other's houses on many occasions. It was laughing-out-loud conversation. Through them, I got to know and like Bishop Brendan Comiskey, who was appointed to Ferns in April 1984. All three were deeply committed to ecumenism. Each January I would attend special ecumenical services. My clerical friends pioneered new protocols for mixed marriages. So much so that if there was a vacancy for a rector in a Church of Ireland parish, I would tell Father Aidan that he was being considered for the post.

I had direct encounters as a TD with Father Seán Fortune in both Poulfur and Ballymurn. He was a deeply manipulative bastard. I didn't cop onto him and his evil ways for a few years. Avril Doyle, who had in the past directly confronted Fortune on the matter, tipped me off that he used to manipulate huge community employment and training schemes for his own benefit. Loyal parish members became deeply divided for or against Fortune wherever he went. Much of the overall sexual-abuse culture seemed to emanate from St Peter's College seminary in Wexford town. Judge George Birmingham's eventual report beggared belief. The pain and emotional scars of the victims savagely damaged their lives. Great credit should be given to the courage of the victims and their relatives in many parishes and also to the local media, particularly Ger Walsh, the editor of the largest newspaper group in the county (People Papers). He and others knew the truth and relentlessly exposed it.

Garret FitzGerald's constitutional crusade and the 1985 Anglo-Irish Agreement were for me the highlights of that Fine Gael/Labour government. The divorce referendum was defeated in June 1986 and it took more than a decade thereafter for the Belfast and subsequent agreements to secure cross-community power-sharing and peace. However, Garret's leadership provided a battering ram to begin the process of changing public opinion about Articles 2 and 3 of the Constitution, away from an acceptance of historic republicanism, based on an all-island state. Journeys start with significant small steps.

It was fascinating attending plenary sessions of the New Ireland Forum with all parties and the SDLP members. I gained deep respect for John Hume and nominated him for the person of the year award, which he won. We used to attend preparatory Fine Gael meetings, reviewing lengthy working papers, in Garret's home on Palmerston Road in a tiny basement flat where every wall groaned with shelves and shelves of books. In the adjoining bedroom, his wife Joan was confined to bed. She would call, 'Garret, Garret ...' He would immediately drop everything and attend to her. He was a devoted husband and, subsequently, a lonely widower.

For a relatively brief period, I became involved in the affairs of the Church of Ireland. I had attended my local diocesan synod, got nominated to the national General Synod and from there to the standing committee of the Church. Monthly meetings were held in Rathmines. Unreconstructed hard-line northern Protestants, including MP William Ross, were bitterly opposed to the Anglo-Irish Agreement. I spoke at the General Synod in 1986, defending the Agreement, and got a round of applause when I said Unionists were entitled to be British and have full civil and religious liberties, but were not allowed to refuse the same rights to the minority community.

The goal behind Garret's leadership drive was to develop a modern Ireland in which the valid roles of church and state were separated. He envisaged reforms in relation to contraception, divorce and remarriage, health and education. Powerful vested interests, including the Roman Catholic Church hierarchy, its priests and lay organisation, energetically resisted ceding control and authority in Irish society. Garret's other great passion was Europe. Under his leadership Fine Gael joined the Christian Democratic Union/European People's Party. He was an unswerving Europhile. Leaving aside the gravy train and net transfers from Brussels over three decades of billions in cash (from the Common Agricultural Policy, the European Social Fund and others), European directives greatly contributed to reforming outdated Irish laws in relation to gender and other forms of equality.

I believe that FitzGerald's faith in future generations was amply rewarded. The downside of his tenure was clearly his administration's failure to rectify the public finances. While inflation was reduced from 16 per cent to 7 per cent, the unsustainable current budget deficit and national debt levels remained unresolved when he left power in 1987. He retained power by keeping Labour onside. The price of this was that Fianna Fáil ultimately got the medium-term credit for taking the tough decisions in the late 1980s. It is ironic that FitzGerald's original appeal was as an economist and statistician, yet his lasting successes were elsewhere: he laid the foundations for much social modernisation that followed, including the availability of contraception for all, legal divorce, the removal of Articles 2 and 3 of the constitutional claim on Northern Ireland and more. These came after his time as Taoiseach, but he dedicated his later life to seeing them to fruition. His micro-management of the cabinet was ineffective, though: cabinet meetings often resulted in procrastination and indecision.

Against this national backdrop of growing government unpopularity, my survival task was to replace lost party votes by persuading people to vote for me on an entirely personal basis. I hope you've got the picture by now that Tip O'Neill's hackneyed 'All politics is local' doesn't begin to describe how the Irish political system operates. The immediacy of contact between senior politicians and their people is without comparison. Top politicians' first and last waking thoughts relate to parish-pump concerns in their backyard.

Within this context the role of the local councillor is critical to the deputy – they are his or her eyes and ears on the ground. The time for local-government elections, for those councillors elected in 1979, was extended by a year. They were held in June 1985. I needed to put my imprint on the outcome in Wexford. This meant seeing that loyal councillors, who were committed to feeding me with the problems and information in their patch, were elected. The relationship between councillors and TDs can be tricky. Councillors in the local electoral area can covertly work against their local TD in passing on issues and generally establishing a separate identity. The trick is to do it without being so obvious as to provoke the sitting TD into taking action against them. I benefited from this situation because councillor and former senator Deirdre Bolger, along with her supporters, worked hard for me, despite being in Michael D'Arcy's territory. Former councillors also carry clout and are to be respected. We had a famous guy from Kiltealy, J. J. Bowe, who stood unsuccessfully for the Dáil for Fine Gael eight times, but was a long-standing councillor. Even after he lost his seat, his influence continued.

Councillors, God love them, are a special species – as wily a bunch of cute hoors as you will ever meet (that's a compliment). Their most coveted power is their entitlement to form the electorate for most of those seeking election to Seanad Éireann.

Those were the days of the dual mandate, when Dáil deputies were usually councillors as well. Being on the council meant you provided for your constituents a one-stop shop, dealing with every conceivable problem. You met with the important officials on a constant basis and were able to cajole favours from them behind closed doors. I therefore had to stand for the Wexford County Council as well as seeking re-election to the Enniscorthy Urban District Council.

My previous adversary, Pat Codd, whom I had defeated for the Dáil nomination, had resigned from the party and was due to stand as an Independent. We ran a local farmer from his parish, Jack Bolger, to retain the seat for the party. I was blamed for favouring a close pal and senior party officer, Tommy Neville, over outgoing councillor John Quirke. He went on to *Morning Ireland* to claim discrimination, that he had not been selected because he was blind.

In a successful vote-management exercise, I obtained 1,770 votes, just exceeding the quota of 1,716, with Jack Bolger winning a seat. The tide had started to turn against the party because our vote share was down to 28 per cent on that polling day. I was re-elected to the urban district council, but Fianna Fáil gained a seat at Fine Gael's expense. On these figures, I worried that we could lose two Dáil seats at the next general election.

Arising out of the councillor changes, I was in a stronger position throughout the four districts of Enniscorthy, Wexford, Gorey and New Ross by having public representatives sympathetic to me and I had built up a working relationship with them in the county-council chamber. It helped that I would give away my quota of conference travel to other councillors because I was too busy to attend. I never went to overseas conferences because I didn't like flying or being away from home, so the travel crumbs that fell from my table were often worth having.

There are four types of Dáil deputy. Some are glorified county councillors: they are so happy to be well-paid and to be big fish in a small pond in their locality that they have no aspirations to ministerial office. As long as they can secure and hold their seat, and perhaps pass it on to their son or daughter or other relation, they are perfectly content.

Also relaxed are TDs who have an interest or income outside politics. They either had a successful local business or a profession before becoming a TD. That other outlet occupies part of their time; they would not like the full-time commitment of a ministry because they would have to give up this external activity. Their political judgement is usually sound and they are unpretentious. They confine their Machiavellian tendencies to their home turf.

The next two categories are 100 per cent career politicians. They see membership of the Dáil as merely a means to an end – being a minister. They would regard their political career as a failure if they weren't at some stage an office-holder. Their singular focus is to be a full-time politician and climb the greasy pole as near to the summit as they can get. The first task is to get onto the party's front-bench, wait the party's turn in government and jockey successfully into position to be appointed a minister. Fulfilment for the first of these groups is to reach the cabinet table or have a decent tenure as a junior minister.

But the final cohort are inwardly manic. Their whole life is dedicated towards becoming party leader and Taoiseach. Their ruthlessness knows no limits. I think it is impossible to become party leader without these characteristics.

Frank Cluskey, Labour leader, 1977 to 1981, once said, 'If you wait around long enough in politics, you will eventually get the job you desire.' The stamina and durability required has to be matched with the tunnel vision of your entire adult life and a preparedness to sacrifice everything to achieve your goals. Your marriage and children are secondary to the pursuit of power. I don't decry ambition: it can be the dominant driving force of national politics. Even when these individuals are not working, they are thinking about politics. They see most topical agendas through the prism of how it affects their hold on government offices and power.

After the November 1982 election, and with the prospect of an uninterrupted handful of years in the Dáil to establish myself, I wanted to ascend gradually and incrementally to the top jobs. I was a quick and hungry learner. I was twenty-three, so time was on my side. I had learned how the game worked inside the Dáil, survived three gruelling general elections, understood and operated the party's local structures and hierarchy. I had earned credibility on the stump in the Wexford constituency.

My attitude to ministerial promotion was quite easy-going up to 1987. This meant that when Garret FitzGerald conducted a reshuffle in February 1986 I had no expectation of promotion to the position of junior minister. I was always being told that I was too young. But the dynamic of his changes had an impact on my constituency. Michael D'Arcy was shafted as minister for state for agriculture. When he refused to resign as part of a ministerial reshuffle, he was fired: public humiliation. This was compounded by the promotion of Avril Doyle to minister of state at the departments of finance and environment. This provoked deep animosity between their rival supporters. No interpretation could be put on the moves other than that the party leadership felt that D'Arcy was expendable and Doyle's seat should be saved. I blissfully evaded the flak and bitterness, consolidating my case for preferences from both candidates.

For the brief period of 1982 in opposition, Garret had appointed me a junior spokesperson on employment creation. I had no illusions about the significance of this. The practice was to appoint nearly every Fine Gael TD to something in a kind of 'one for everyone in the audience' syndrome. My plan for the 1983 to 1987 period was to prioritise my seat retention, work locally and cultivate a national image that provided a little clear blue water between me and an increasingly unappealing government. At parliamentary party meetings I was openly critical of government decisions and individual ministers. The ideal platform to launch a credible case for my future promotion came when I was appointed chairman of the brand-new Joint Oireachtas Committee for Small Businesses.

To progress in politics, you have to seize molehills and turn them into mountains. I was determined to make this only marginally relevant Dáil and Seanad committee the best thing ever. An earnest and industrious guy, Shane McCauley, was seconded from the IDA to be clerk of the committee. No research budget for consultancy services was provided, so I recruited individuals with expertise to serve on a private subcommittee, which I ran, to produce draft reports on small business for the committee's approval. Foremost among these contacts was John Lynch, who had worked as a policy strategist with the CII and would go on to become the first executive chairman of FÁS and later the CIÉ group. Ever since, he has been a close mentor and friend of mine.

We decided to produce four reports, covering manufacturing, retail, catering/leisure/tourism and construction. We defined small businesses as every economic enterprise with a hundred or fewer employees. My personal goal was to become a champion of the self-employed and indigenous business. We advertised to invite every conceivable trade organisation and association to make written submissions.

I had a dynamic and forceful attitude to the committee's output. Each report contained at least seventy recommendations of practical proposals to deal with the A–Z of business issues: taxation; the black economy; employment law; loan finance; personal guarantees; the effectiveness of supporting state agencies; company law; job creation incentives; industrial policy; and reducing the myriads of red tape being encountered by employers. I could leak each report to friendly journalists. We organised a full-blown press conference, with the members of the committee present. Out of a nondescript backwater opportunity, we created a credible platform for the steady flow of new ideas.

I followed up the retail report with a private member's bill to ban below-cost selling. Five thousand independent retailers had closed over the previous decade. The increased concentration of purchasing power by the large multiple stores meant that they were screwing Irish indigenous manufacturers into providing unsustainable discounts on selected items as loss leaders, as well as extorting promotional payments such as 'hello money'. Michael Campbell of the Retail Grocery Dairy & Allied Trades Association

(RGDATA), the representative organisation for independent family grocers in Ireland, assisted me with the parliamentary draughtsman's legal expertise on the text. The Retail Sales Below Cost (Groceries) Bill 1986 eventually became law when Albert Reynolds, as minister for industry and commerce, implemented the ban in 1988.

Initially I had a stand-up row with John Bruton, the relevant minister, who had an ideological antipathy to any market interference. I said bluntly that I was going to bring the bill before the parliamentary party for approval to publish it. He was furious and warned me that such action would not be in my own best interests. I proceeded regardless.

Fortunately for me, the cabinet reshuffle meant that Michael Noonan became the line minister with responsibility. He was pragmatic and supportive. He set up an inquiry into the topic by the Restrictive Practices Commission, the forerunner for legislation. They duly recommended new controls on the capacity of large multiples to manipulate the market. Their profits continued to increase. I believe it helped secure seventy thousand jobs between retail and food-processing, until it was scrapped a decade later.

My next big breakthrough was a public assault on the five large building societies. I had help in researching this from Hilary Haugh. Over a dozen years, these originally mutual societies had grown to be mega-financial institutions. They accounted for 75 per cent of all mortgages and 20 per cent of all savings accounts in the country. Instead of being truly democratic, they were operated almost as private fiefdoms by the likes of Edmund Farrell and Michael Fingleton, through the use of proxy votes at AGMs. Their operating expenses mushroomed out of all control. I railed against the differential between lending and deposit rates, leading to excessive profits.

I challenged the building societies to justify why they should appoint their own solicitor and house insurer on mortgage transactions. Redemption and other fees were penal. This was a really populist issue and exposed a lack of accountability and transparency. I accused the registrar of friendly societies of being a 'toothless lion' and inept. I called for building societies to be taken under the auspices of the central bank. I challenged their umbrella body, the Irish Building Societies Association (IBSA), to debate these issues. It initially agreed to do so, on RTÉ radio's *This Week*, then chickened out. The media loved proper full-frontal rows. Then the minister for the environment, John Boland, announced a government inquiry into the matters I had raised. This ultimately led to a new Building Societies Act incorporating many of the points I had campaigned on. It was a direct hit, proper David and Goliath stuff.

Encouraged, I took up other causes, such as the restrictive practices operated by opticians in having a monopoly over dispensing all forms of glasses. I could not understand why you could buy basic reading glasses from a variety of outlets for fifteen pounds in Newry, but had to get a prescription in the Republic and pay up to a hundred pounds through an optician. I accused the Opticians Board, made up almost entirely of eye doctors, of representing the profession rather than the consumer. I called for it to be disbanded and replaced.

As time went on, national media realised I could be useful to them. Whenever a story surfaced about, for example, extra charges put on mortgage holders, reporters would always ring me, wanting my take on the move. I'd give it the full lash there and then. No point saying, 'Come back tomorrow when I've researched this.' It had to be instant and quotable, as well as accurate and angled. All that suited me. I was never afraid to have a go, even if it dropped me neck-deep in controversy.

I could also do the maths. Clearly, there were more punters needing glasses than there were opticians. On each issue, I assiduously gathered the back-up statistical and legal information to engender these battles. This meant that, at a moment's notice, I could contribute to broadcast programmes. I had only to grab my files. Spontaneous availability was the key to airtime. I was always ready to let rip immediately with catchy phrases aimed at generating maximum conflict.

The small business committee went on to do reports into topics such as crazy insurance costs, co-operatives and research-and-development (R&D) initiatives. I railed against excessive legal fees and practices. I challenged the ESB to justify its high prices, accusing them of excess capacity, over-manning and gross inefficiency. I believed that, because of strike threats by unions and fear of a national power blackout, management had been weak and ineffective. I called for the appointment of an independent regulator/watchdog since parent departments of state were often the 'downtown office' – the close, cosy relationships that can develop between trade organisations, corporates, lobby groups and their official departmental regulators. The state-sponsored bodies fought back trenchantly – just what I needed to keep the story running.

In 1985 I conducted a detailed analysis of the prospects for selling shares in state companies, such as Bord Gáis, Irish Life, Irish Steel, Aer Rianta, ACC and Bord Telecom. I estimated that their sale could raise over £1 billion for the exchequer. Up to then there had been very little advocacy for privatisation. The *Sunday Press* did a full-page spread on my proposals and similar developments internationally by other (even socialist) governments in Europe. It was a couple of decades before this became accepted public policy.

I was learning how to build relationships and make an impact. It also helped that journalists started to review the work rate of all TDs. League tables were published of the number of parliamentary questions (PQs) and words spoken in the Dáil chamber for specific sessions. Lo and behold, I came out on top. This encouraged me to be even more prolific in Dáil contributions and tabling PQs. I was branded the busiest TD in the Dáil. I cultivated media contacts, such as John Foley of the *Irish Independent* (a native of Enniscorthy), Seán O'Rourke, political correspondent of the *Irish Press*, Martin Fitzpatrick of the *Sunday Independent*, Brendan Keenan of the *Financial Times*, and many of the Dáil press gallery. I copped on that if you produced research-based arguments, you obtained column inches and air time while gaining credibility. You had to be prepared to stand your ground and disregard critical abuse if you were to get noticed and make an impression. Profile pieces in the Sunday papers and regular contributions on RTÉ radio panel discussions followed.

Each instalment of media mileage widened public awareness of my existence. My communication techniques, such as simplifying complex issues and reducing arguments to sound-bites, improved. The cumulative effect of all these endeavours was the gradual creation of a media profile that indicated I was tough, able, articulate and hard-working. There is a term in rugby, the 'hard yards', that describes the dogged physical drive the forwards carry out to gain ground before the game opens up for the backs. I describe this period of trying to make an impression as the 'hard political yards'. Any office-holder or minister with the back-up of a big department and their state agencies for research and public relations can raise their profile by just doing their job and dealing with the conveyor belt of daily issues. It's much harder to get noticed when you have to create the space, on your own, out of nothing. I did have the able assistance of the Fine Gael press officer, Peter White, a close friend, who wasn't part of the government PR machine and therefore was quite happy to make independent backbench mischief with me.

Such was my relatively right-wing image (pro-business, anti-public-sector waste, favouring self-reliance and lower taxation) that in 1986, after Desmond O'Malley had formed the Progressive Democrats, senior figures in that fledgling party made informal approaches to me to join them. I admired the Progressive Democrats' principled policy positions. I agreed with their unambiguous stances on a modernised secular state and Northern Ireland. I viewed Des O'Malley as a courageous, formidable operator, who stood up to Charles Haughey's self-serving arrogance and later proven corruption.

Nevertheless, I stayed with Fine Gael, despite many of my farming supporters turning against the party on issues such as the land tax and resource taxes that were to replace agricultural rates. I did so because loyalty is a characteristic that I rate extremely highly. In the long term I believe you gain more by being seen to be reliable and steadfast in your commitments rather than seeking immediate advantage. Furthermore, the record of new parties lasting longer than a decade against the Civil War traditional parties was self-evidentially disastrous – remember the Workers' Party or Clann na Talmhan? Instead, within the Fine Gael parliamentary party I sought to advocate similar policies to those of the PDs.

The best arena for backbenchers to influence government decision-making directly is the weekly parliamentary party meeting, which offers face time with the party hierarchy and cabinet members. All political business was up for discussion: budgetary matters, current legislation, internal party affairs, election post-mortems, front-bench or leader's performance, lobbying campaigns, opinion polls, forward planning, party strategy, or any current controversy you wanted to raise.

There is a sense of collegiality at such meetings. We are all on the one team. This provides a context of openness and directness that cannot happen in any more public forum. There is equality between all TDs. No non-public representatives are allowed to attend, so you can freely speak your mind. The proceedings are supposed to be in camera, but are often leaked to suit hidden agendas or to curry favour with political correspondents.

The chairman usually gives latitude to backbenchers to state their views at these meetings because, of course, they do not attend front-bench meetings when in opposition or cabinet meetings when the party is in government. Throughout the 1980s, these encounters became increasingly fraught with dissension on a 'them and us' basis. Many backbenchers regarded some cabinet ministers and ministers of state as intellectually over-endowed but lacking in political savvy. Some members of the cabinet could barely tolerate those they clearly regarded as country yahoos with throwback ideas. Garret FitzGerald would sit through long hours of thinly veiled criticism and abuse, sighing heavily, rubbing his eyes. His body language conveyed he would rather be anywhere than where he was.

In theory the parliamentary party is the ultimate democratic decision-making process. In reality it is used as a rubber stamp by the leader to get retrospective approval for the cabinet's decisions, but it can spark a U-turn.

The most bruising episodes occurred when Peter Sutherland, as attorney general, sought to change the wording of the Pro-Life constitutional amendment. Backbencher Alice Glenn, former minister Tom O'Donnell and Oliver J. Flanagan, who was a papal knight, lacerated the leadership for its U-turn. They made it plain that they were prepared to vote against the party whip and sought a free vote in the Dáil chamber.

The veteran Oliver J. was a wily and formidable character. In one long-winded speech he put out a hand and slapped it with the back of the other for emphasis as he said, 'The party has turned into a crowd of adulterers, abortionists and homos.' Some deputies laughed. He wasn't joking. Strong liberals, like Monica Barnes, were apoplectic with rage. I liked Oliver J., although I disagreed with his views.

John Kelly, a professor of constitutional law, and former minister and attorney general, was the most theatrical orator. 'Why do Fine Gael, in their present incarnation, have to go up to a sleeping dog and kick it in the balls?' he once asked. Another character was the infamous Dr Hugh Byrne, who was indifferent to authority and political correctness.

In my early contributions, I tried to be constructive with new ideas. I suggested that Tom Fitzpatrick, a vastly experienced TD from Cavan/Monaghan, would make an ideal Ceann Comhairle and gain a seat for the party at the next election. He was duly successful and often thanked me afterwards for being the first to put his name forward, without being asked to do so.

I could sometimes be scathing in my criticism. In the post-mortem debate on the collapsed budget in early 1982, I accused Garret of having less political cop-on 'than Chrissie in the restaurant'; she was the most fearsome sharp-tongued waitress on the Fine Gael tables in the Dáil restaurant. This drew guffaws and became quite a celebrated quip. I was among a group of backbenchers who openly castigated government indecision and ineffectiveness on the economy. Often ministers would respond in defence. One of the most memorable quotes I recall came from transport minister Jim Mitchell, when he said, 'It is wrong to give hope where there is no hope.' I thought it summed up the reality that the government had no hope of re-election.

Garret clung to power for too long. It was a doomed exercise. When the political tide goes out, things that were once seen as innovative and clever, like his use of national handlers (smart strategists such as Bill O'Herlihy, Enda Marren, Shane Molloy and Frank Flannery), come to be viewed as cronyism. The general election should have been held in 1986 as cabinet credibility eroded with each passing calamity, backbench revolt and u-turn. Ever-increasing taxation measures, such as higher VAT, the introduction of 35 per cent DIRT (Deposit Interest Retention Tax) and a top marginal income tax rate of 65 per cent were stultifying any growth. The election took place on 17 February 1987 after the Labour ministers walked out on 23 January. The anticipated disaster became a reality when Fine Gael lost nineteen seats and suffered its worst electoral result in thirty years.

I cannot emphasise adequately my dependence on my loyal party workers. Still under the baton of Seán Kavanagh, Bernie and Breda meticulously organised around fifty men and women to call from house to house across the constituency exclusively on my behalf. Instead of the tailwind that had been behind us in the early 1980s, they now faced a stiff headwind of resistance to Fine Gael canvassers. But they kept going. I will always be indebted to them. Their commitment to me personally often exceeded their faith in the party. They constantly endured foul conditions and abuse. For me, they made the difference between success and failure.

All my running around on the ground in Wexford for four long years did pay off. The party vote slumped to 31.6 per cent. I secured 6,018 first preferences, ahead of Avril Doyle's 5,518 and Michael D'Arcy's 5,247. D'Arcy lost his seat. Senator Brendan Howlin won back the Dáil seat for the Labour Party to restore the county balance to two Fianna Fáil seats, two Fine Gael seats and one Labour seat. It was inevitable that there would be a change of government and Haughey would be back as Taoiseach. I relished the prospect of the party going into opposition, where I would no longer have to defend the indefensible.

I had waited patiently for this opportunity. In the aftermath of elections, particularly where there is a change of power, the greatest personnel changes occur – retirements, exits from defeat, new vacancies and, most of all, a potential change of leader. I had made up my mind that FitzGerald was a goner. He had always said that he would lead the party for ten years. That time was now up.

For the previous eighteen months, I had studiously if covertly planned for what I felt would be the inevitable succession race to replace him. Before the election, I told Seán O'Rourke, 'You wait and see. There's going to be a leadership change in Fine Gael and, come what may, I'm going to lead the victorious horse by the halter into the winner's enclosure. Watch this space.'

I had served my time. I wanted to get onto the front bench at all costs. I knew the best way to secure that was through closeness, loyalty and indispensability to the new leader. Meritocracy, my arse. I'd had my fill of playing second fiddle on the back benches. Before the election, I decided whom I was going to support. The necessity was now to make sure he stood and to get him elected as party leader.

7: Snakes and Ladders

'Alan, here's the thing. Yeah, you're up to your eyes with all that shite in Justice. I know, I know. But I still want to have a serious political chat. Polling can't be far away now that Dick Spring and his boys have walked. This will end in tears. The party is going to be decimated, if the polls are even half right. It's time to start planning. My guess is Garret won't stay on in opposition. He's totally drained and he's done the ten years he said he'd do as leader.'

Alan Dukes sat impassively behind the small table in his ministerial office in Leinster House. On that Wednesday evening in February 1987, we were alone. He sucked hard on another cigarette and said nothing. He did nod, though.

'I've been thinking about the succession stakes. I'm going to back you to be the next leader. Doesn't matter to me if you haven't decided to run. You can win. You *will* win, with the right campaign.'

Still no response. I went through the party's prospects under all the other possible contenders: Peter Barry, John Bruton and Michael Noonan. I suggested the names of some critical TDs who would be needed for support, with a regional spread across the country, and indicated those likely to oppose him. 'You'll have to position your candidacy strategically,' I told him. 'You'll need to be seen as continuing Garret's legacy, not revert to old-style conservatism. You must stress your ability to work a coalition with Labour, unlike John Bruton. It'll need to be subtle, but you'll also require to be seen as the one who can open up a new generation of Fine Gael, a fresh start, unlike Peter Barry, who's heading for sixty.'

Long silence. Prolonged sucking at the cigarette. I made some more comments. The long ash fell off the end of his fag, but he didn't seem to notice.

'We'll talk about this again,' he said, unfolding to his full height. 'I suggest you keep this conversation between us.'

I went away without a clue as to where he stood. I knew where *I* stood, though. As far as I was concerned, it was time for me to move to the front bench. Nobody was going to put me there by measuring my talent, profile or popularity. My career prospects would be decided at the whim of the party leader, so it was time to get close to the one who would succeed Garret FitzGerald.

Dukes had experience as an economist and technocrat with the Irish Farmers' Association (IFA) and the European Commissioner's office. He had worked in the senior ministries of finance and justice, as well as agriculture. At forty-two, he could be a leader for the long term, rather than a caretaker. He was urbane, cerebral and from the commuter belt constituency of Kildare.

The 25th Dáil reconvened on 10 March and elected Charles Haughey Taoiseach of a minority Fianna Fáil government. That night, Garret FitzGerald asked party chairman Kieran Crotty to convene a meeting of the parliamentary party the next day, Wednesday. I was slightly late for the meeting and walked in while members were paying full-hearted tributes. I thought someone had died until I realised they were talking about Garret, who had announced his resignation as party leader. After all the accolades, it was agreed that the election of a new leader would take place eleven days later on Saturday, 21 March.

I was ready for battle. Dukes readily agreed to stand. Names of definite supporters were drawn up: backbenchers Gay Mitchell, Alan Shatter, Dinny McGinley, Jim Higgins, Madeleine Taylor

Quinn, Brendan McGahon, Bernard Allen and Nora Owen (all elected for the first time in June 1981). Most deputies and senators did not want to be publicly associated with any particular candidate: it might damage their future career if the one they backed didn't make it. I had no such fears and broadcast my support for Dukes anywhere and everywhere.

Wavering voters always want to know who the winner will be. Once they are pretty sure, they then back that winner. Therefore my priority was to brief the media and anyone else who would listen that this contest was over before it started. 'Alan Dukes will win decisively,' I said. 'He has a clear lead and is the front-runner by far.'

Even if it wasn't true, I would have said it. In this case, though, it *was* true. From the first day, Gay Mitchell, Alan Shatter and I became a triad, running the most intense campaign of my experience. Each of us had to speak to an allocated TD and senator, persuading them that Dukes was their best option. Then we would meet to compare notes. It was the steepest learning curve of all time.

It quickly became clear that Michael Noonan's candidacy, despite strong support from George Birmingham, was not going to get off the ground. Peter Barry had been a distinguished deputy leader and a great foil for Garret, with a track record as minister for foreign affairs, but because his was the last campaign to go live, we had a head start, despite members of the former cabinet – with the exception of Gemma Hussey – circling the wagons around him. Garret went to America, detaching himself from the process, although he promised to return and act as one of the tellers to count the votes.

John Bruton and his constituency colleague John Farrelly drove around the entire country, calling to the houses of the eighty-two voters, including MEPs. He had strong supporters in Austin Deasy, Enda Kenny, his brother Richard and John Donnellan in Galway

West, but he had nothing approaching a campaign team (surprising for someone who clearly had long-term leadership ambitions). Bruton was regarded as being too conservative and ideological.

As the days went by, the party hierarchy seemed to articulate effectively, inside the party, the need not to jump a generation. They argued that, since the new government was a minority administration and a snap general election was possible, it was time for an interim 'steady hand on the wheel' in the shape of Peter Barry. This would also, of course, buttress the status quo and the position of big hitters in the party.

'We can't afford to mark time,' I said, every time this argument was put to me. 'We've got to chart a new, modern identity for the party. Make it appeal to younger voters.'

The top brass at the time, such as Michael Noonan, Seán Barrett, John Boland, Paddy Cooney and Fergus O'Brien, had a clear interest in keeping out Dukes *and* Bruton. We undercut that by going directly to the grassroots in the constituencies. Party meeting after party meeting endorsed Alan Dukes, who had obviously worked the rubber-chicken circuit relentlessly as a minister, and was now reaping the dividends. Even in Munster, Dukes was preferred to Peter Barry.

As each of the eleven days fell away, we grew more confident – and had more fun. It was intense and demanded constant contact, which, in the days before mobile phones and the Internet, was not easy. But we did it, coasting on the adrenalin that comes with conspiracy.

Mitchell, Shatter and I had a final meeting in Mitchell's house in Rathmines. We allocated different people who were supporting Dukes to approach their friendliest colleagues. We checked final tallies of different assessments: 'definites', 'possibles' and those not supporting Dukes. Dukes's own tally had lots more people in the first category than was credible. Floating voters promise everybody their vote when asked face to face.

Unusually, this election was conducted without acrimony. The magic figure was forty-two votes to attain a majority. If we had more than thirty on the first count, we would be okay to win on transfers.

On the morning of the vote I was quietly confident. 'Write your stories,' I told my political hack friends Stephen Collins, Seán O'Rourke, John Foley and the late Gerald Barry. 'Dukes is home and hosed. Winner, all right.'

The only unexpected drama at the meeting related to my constituency colleague Avril Doyle. She was supposed to second her old boyfriend John Bruton's nomination at the meeting but arrived too late, although whether this happened through naïveté or subtle cunning was never established.

Constituency supporters and family members of the candidates assembled outside the Dáil gates and Buswells Hotel, nervously awaiting news of each hopeful.

It was over in an hour and a half, and Alan Dukes won. We beat the entire outgoing cabinet. The two tellers, Kieran Crotty and Garret FitzGerald, never revealed the count figures. I was on an emotional high. It had been all chips in as far as I was concerned. Everyone knew I was Dukes's right-hand man. For a man who doesn't do emotion, he had a broad smile. We shook hands. I congratulated him and wished him good luck.

The tension of the week was starting to catch up on me. I wanted to escape the whole scene and, although Dukes invited me to the victory celebrations in Newbridge, I went instead to Lansdowne Road with Deirdre to watch the Ireland v. France rugby match. Despite tries by Trevor Ringland and Michael Bradley, we lost by six points. Still, one victory was enough on that momentous day. I couldn't focus on the match, anyway, such was my relief and elation. This was the beginning of regime change at the summit of Fine Gael. Bring on the new front-bench appointments.

The following Tuesday I visited Dukes, at his invitation, in the leader of the opposition's plush office. We laughed together over anecdotes of the drama, tension and elation of the previous week's events. 'A good plan well executed,' he said, expressing his deep appreciation and gratitude.

'You don't owe me anything,' I told him. 'It was a pleasure.'

I didn't mean that he didn't owe me anything, of course, but two days later, he picked his front bench. Neither Alan Shatter, Gay Mitchell nor I was on it. Instead, he had reappointed the former ministers, nearly all of whom had opposed him. I was almost concussed with shock and disbelief.

'Does this guy *know* how we worked for him, what we achieved for him?' I kept asking. Because, polite self-deprecation aside, he *did* owe me and his campaign team. He *so* owed us, the 'class of '81'. Had he not understood what our whole campaign had been about? Could he be that naïve? Did he not realise the barely concealed contempt some of these front-bench members had for him? Did he not see the need to develop a close-knit coterie of diehard supporters to cover his back? Was he a loner with a brilliant mind and a complete absence of emotional intelligence?

The answer to most of those questions turned out, over time, to be a resounding yes. At the time, I was neatly caught. If I expressed any of the rage and betrayal I felt for myself, Alan Shatter and Gay Mitchell, indeed for all our troops, I would look like a fool whose poor judgement was equalled only by his personal opportunism. So I smiled, laughed and expressed constant support for the new leader.

I was in despair when I went home to Deirdre the following Thursday evening. On the doorstep we embraced and cried. It was the worst setback of my life up to that point. I was gutted. The media had speculated since Dukes's victory that there would be a wholesale reshuffle of the top rank in Fine Gael, with my name foremost in speculations about those who would benefit from the change in leadership. Instead, Avril Doyle was subsequently appointed front-bench spokesperson on agriculture. I had no choice but to face into the open humiliation of colleagues' jeers.

'After all you did for him, he still didn't appoint you,' Austin Deasy commented. 'What a fool.'

It was up to me to decide whether it was Dukes or me who was the fool. Austin Deasy regularly ridiculed Dukes, but he was nonetheless reappointed. But, then, Dukes appointed all the people Peter Barry would have appointed. I realised then that he knew little about *realpolitik*. He had no sense of what Anthony Jay called 'The 10 Group', the inner circle of your own people. He thought it was about picking the longest-established good boys at the top of the Fine Gael class – the prefects. He regarded the leadership as a full stop, rather than an indicator of progress. He never seemed to take on board that as soon as a leader wins, the seeds are set for the next leadership contest, and that the ones he positioned and where he positioned them would establish whether those seeds were deep in the soil or near the surface. In his case, they were dangerously near the surface.

Alan Dukes is a clever man, but politically naive. He never appreciated that appointing leadership rivals to your front bench not only fails to extinguish their ambition but positions them perfectly for a run at the top job the moment an opportunity presents itself.

Not that my thinking was so discriminating at the time. I was just hurt and rattled by the smart-aleck comments of those on the new front bench who had openly opposed him: 'Ah, Jaysus, did you not even get to be the junior spokesman for burned sausages?'

The experience taught me a tough political lesson: always nail down an advance deal. Define the *quid pro quo*. Don't presume anything. I let the dust settle, and got on with my constituency work as normal. Some weeks later, in May, Dukes rang and asked me to meet him in his office.

'Look, I want to transform the role of the chairman of the parliamentary party,' he said. 'I want to make it a substantial role, as it is in Britain. Substantial and dynamic, and I believe it would give you a great opportunity.'

'I'm really not up for that,' I said.

He told me he could understand me not wanting the role as it had been configured up to that point, but added that in Britain the Labour and Conservative parties treated the party chairman role as a high-profile front-bench position without portfolio. He envisaged a similar function for me and eventually he talked me into it. Like an idiot, I let my name go forward, only to find Kieran Crotty, who had been in the chair for a decade, standing down and proposing Donal Creed, a long-standing TD from north-west Cork who attracted sympathy because FitzGerald had dropped him in the last reshuffle. Creed was popular and understated. Unlike me, he had no enemies.

Avril Doyle proposed me for the post and Senator Maurice Manning, who for many years was a most likeable Fine Gael leader in the Senate, seconded me. John Kelly, who had opposed Dukes and declined a post, made a strong speech stating that the chairmanship should be completely separate from the leadership, independent of the front bench and representative of backbenchers. Now it was payback time for those who resented Dukes's victory. I was defeated, this time for a position I did not even want. I was furious with Dukes for the double dose of grief. There was open glee among some that his authority had been so undermined.

Enough was enough. I refocused my life, and not only on my constituency work. Deirdre and I were contemplating starting a family. That summer I took the first steps to pursue a career in business outside politics and researched the potential of a high-street business, such as a fast-food outlet or a betting shop. I wasn't going to waste the best years of my life as a backbencher.

At 6.15 p.m. on 8 August 1987, I took the second-best decision of my life (after marrying Deirdre) and quit smoking. I had constant severe bouts of asthma and bronchitis and often needed inhalers and injections to be able to breathe. On holiday in the west when I became ill, the young locum doctor refused to give me a cortisone injection. He said it was ridiculous to be on such heavy medication when I was still so young. I should cop on and give up smoking. I haven't smoked since – and I had been smoking forty a day. I couldn't have done so without a health scare and Nicorette chewing gum, which, in turn, I found difficult to stop using.

Alan Dukes continued to smoke but, then, he couldn't even have considered giving up in the middle of an increasingly tricky situation in the Dáil. Having advocated in government and throughout the general election campaign the absolute necessity of fiscal rectitude, when Charles Haughey and Ray MacSharry wielded the axe, making savage cuts on public expenditure, Fine Gael would have been hypocritical to vote against them. Every lobby and local group on the receiving end of this hardship wanted the opposition to reverse the measures by voting against the government, which had no Dáil majority. Dukes was faced with a choice every Wednesday night on a private member's motion of whether to bring down the government or not.

He did not want an immediate election, especially if precipitating one made him look like a short-term political opportunist without care for the long-term national economic interest. Dukes and Fine Gael were damned whatever he did. Then, on 2 September, he made what was to be a defining speech to the Tallaght Chamber of Commerce: 'When the government is moving in the right direction, I will not oppose the central thrust of its policy,' he announced. 'If it is going in the right direction, I do not believe that it should be deviated from its course, or tripped up on macro-economic issues.'

This became known as the Tallaght strategy. Dukes launched a major political co-operation initiative without prior consultation with his front bench, a schoolboy error that totally undermined their trust in him. Open disrespect was soon apparent in the mutterings along the Dáil corridors. That disrespect grew, as did discontent with Dukes from all elements of the party. Fine Gael was slumping in the opinion polls. And I was bored. On 3 March I got bored and angry, a dangerous combination, and prepared a speech for a mythical local branch meeting in Enniscorthy. In it I called for a pre-election voting pact between Fine Gael and the Progressive Democrats. I argued the case for an alternative government of like-minded people to replace Fianna Fáil and said that the Tallaght strategy should be only one aspect of the party's tactics. I circulated it personally to the media, deliberately avoiding the Fine Gael press office, which would have spiked it. Then I left the Dáil and went on the piss at Wexford races for the day.

I didn't know if it would get any coverage. But it was a broadside shot at Dukes, contradicting his line of contempt for the PDs and openly rejecting his authority. His position was that Fine Gael could obtain an overall majority at the next election and would go it alone, which was too silly for words. In calling for closer co-operation with the PDs in opposition, I was, by implication, accusing Dukes of failing to provide a clear, positive direction on our electoral strategy beyond the temporary pragmatic necessity of propping up Fianna Fáil in office, which was deeply hated by party diehards. I knew he would resent my outburst, but couldn't have cared less. It was a brazen attempt to let him know that I 'haven't gone away, you know'.

Unknown to me, that same day Austin Deasy resigned as front-bench transport spokesperson. *RTÉ News: Nine O'Clock* ran both stories together. Next day's front-page story in the *Irish Independent*, *Irish Times* and *Irish Press* related how Dukes's leadership had been undermined and threatened by this 'double blow'. Editorials relayed how I had been one of Dukes's staunchest supporters and was now precipitating a crisis for him. I said nothing further, did no interviews, just let the fallout happen.

Dukes went ballistic. Peter White, now his spokesman, described me as 'a very foolish young man'. It was hinted that I would not get the front-bench vacancy created by Deasy's departure. The PDs welcomed my initiative and political media pundits saw sound logic behind my argument on the need for a credible alternative government to Fianna Fáil at the next election. Over the next few days Dukes's line on the PDs softened to a position of my having been *tactically* wrong, rather than wrong in principle. The following Tuesday Dukes summoned me to his office. He was in a rage, smoking the latest in what, to judge by the ashtray, had been a dozen cigarettes.

'I don't have long, Alan,' I cheerily told him as I walked in. 'Busy day, you know.'

'What the fuck are you at?'

'How d'you mean?'

'You know what I fucking mean. This speech about the PDs.'

'I issued that in an entirely personal capacity, not using the press office. I didn't want to compromise your position, because of our past association. I believe in what I said and stand over it. Okay, the timing was unfortunate with the Deasy resignation, but I was unaware of that. Anyway, I'm only a backbencher. What I have to say doesn't matter a whole lot.'

'You know bloody well that a major initiative such as a strategic alliance with the PDs is the prerogative of the party leadership. You know you're not entitled to go off at half-cock unilaterally with this bullshit. You made a big mistake. I will be raising these matters at tomorrow's party meeting.'

The next day I was duly rebuked in front of my colleagues for the content and timing of my statement. Neither the meeting nor the subsequent media reports took a feather out of me. I had got huge media coverage, let Dukes know he couldn't take my support for granted, and a lot of grassroots members agreed with me. Whether as a peace offering or to distract me, Dukes nominated me to be the Fine Gael representative on a two-week parliamentary trip to Japan. It was my first and last political junket. I went with Ceann Comhairle Seán Treacy, Charlie McCreevy and Mary Harney. In advance of a meeting with an Irish Jesuit priest, Father Donal Doyle, who worked at Tokyo University, I asked Charlie McCreevy to explain to me the difference between the Jesuits and other orders.

'It's like this, Ivan. If you go to confession with a Jesuit priest and admit you murdered someone, he would reply, "Yes, and what else, my son?" In other words, they are extremely worldly.'

I have never consumed so much whiskey or laughed as much as I did during that trip. Charlie is an amazing character, outrageously bold in the context of political strokes, women, drink and gambling. He is fabulous company. His tales of battling Haughey's dark forces made Fine Gael's parliamentary party members seem like altar boys.

On 31 August Alan Dukes reshuffled his front bench, asking me to be spokesperson on health, because the incumbent spokesperson, Bernard Allen, was going to concentrate full-time on being Lord Mayor of Cork. In the same reshuffle, he shafted John Boland, Fergus O'Brien and Enda Kenny, while promoting Alan Shatter, Jim Higgins, Dinny McGinley and Madeleine Taylor-Quinn. Dukes had put his own stamp on the front bench.

At last, my seven-year apprenticeship on the back benches was over. Dukes was my best pal again, although I suspected that forces within the party were already planning the first heave against him.

Many of the mistakes Dukes made as leader can be attributed to his meteoric rise when he was first elected. The very first day he stepped into the Dáil, he was a minister. He hadn't come through the school of hard knocks or been kicked around the back benches. He was immediately and quite properly focused on the policy details of his portfolio and, because he was so clever, quickly enmeshed in the policy details of other ministers' portfolios, since Garret FitzGerald valued his contributions to cabinet decision-making. Which was all well and good but – added to his love of the abstruse – gave him an essentially skewed viewpoint, a long-distance perception of party politics.

However, he had hired me as health spokesperson and I believed health would be *the* issue of the next election, so my first priority was to immerse myself in the health sector. I set up in-depth lengthy meetings with anyone and everyone: senior officials in the Department of Health; chief executives of the eight health boards and the VHI; hospital administrators; trade-union representatives of nurses (INO), general practitioners (IMO/ICGP), hospital consultants (ICHA); officers of every conceivable health organisation covering asthma, HIV/AIDS, various disability groups, cancer, the elderly. I filleted the annual yearbook of the Institute of Public Administration for relevant contact details and sat down with them all to listen to their problems, perspectives and ideas.

I needed a credible, robust policy platform consistent with reduced public expenditure on health while directing resources to front-line patient needs. My mantra was 'greater efficiency and value for money'. Fianna Fáil had made itself a serious hostage to fortune by campaigning on the election slogan 'Health cuts hurt the old, the sick and the handicapped.' I wasn't about to let them forget it.

I advocated abolishing the health boards, replacing them with a single state agency – Bord Sláinte – to reduce administration.

I wanted to computerise labour-intensive processes, such as the keeping of medical records, obtain better procurement value, replace expensive branded medicines with generics, centralise purchasing for all hospitals, carry out more diagnostic tests in local doctors' surgeries instead of hospitals, shift income maintenance programmes to the Department of Social Welfare, pay per treatment, develop day hospitals and centralise resources into fewer centres of excellence. I produced detailed costings of savings to be made.

My next tactic was to wage all-out guerrilla warfare against the minister for health, Dr Rory O'Hanlon. Everything that moved in his sphere was subject to an instant critical response from me. I rigorously pursued topical issues, such as a financial crisis in the monopoly VHI, with mounting losses and consequently reduced benefits. I highlighted the rip-off factors of pathology consultants' fees and the impact of abolishing the drug refund scheme. I was the only TD to attend the launch of an AIDS documentary, and got to know individual patients dying from the virus. It was very moving, especially the plight of haemophiliacs who had been infected by contaminated products from the state's Blood Transfusion Service.

My clusters of contacts were invaluable. I could get briefed by them on an off-the-record basis. I might be their political boss one day; I needed to be a magnet for anyone with a grievance. The mismatch of resources between a minister and a shadow spokesperson is titanic, and I was very aware that I had to be informed to provide responses for journalists who needed a few paragraphs to round off their story.

I learned to admire and respect some of the clinicians in hospitals, such as Crumlin Children's Hospital and the HIV unit in St James's Hospital. Dr Finn Breathnach and Dr Fiona Mulcahy had a passion for their work that I found inspirational. I also took advice from cardiac surgeon Professor Maurice Neligan and former minister for health Dr John O'Connell, who owned the *Irish Medical Times*. Health issues were a matter of life and death, affecting every household.

The collective impact of health cuts was starting to bite. Some fifty thousand people were on waiting lists, with elderly pensioners queuing for three years for hip replacements and children for two years for heart operations. The public dental service was a shambles. I bluntly blamed the minister for all these problems. He in turn accused me of being a scaremonger.

'Either you do not know the extent of the problem,' I would respond, 'or you don't care about the impact of the cuts.'

It was a lose/lose scenario for O'Hanlon, particularly because he was a doctor himself. For me, it was a gift. I realised that the best way to get RTÉ television coverage was to put a human face on stories. I sussed that, within RTÉ, the regional correspondents were in competition with the business, political and courts correspondents to get their story up the news agenda, and I played to that.

Through a midlands Fine Gael TD, Paul McGrath, I came across the case of an elderly lady who would die if she didn't get cardiac surgery. I contacted Gerry Reynolds, a young go-getter trying to make his name in RTÉ. 'Gerry, I have a great story for you,' I said, and outlined the details. 'Now, the reality is that this woman is going to die – she's going to *die*, Gerry – if she doesn't get her heart operation immediately. No exaggeration. She'll tell you herself. Here's her phone number.'

He took a camera crew to her home just outside Mullingar. I went along with them. She had this lovely cat – a fat, easy-going, really furry cat with a long tail. She put the cat on her lap, and when the cameras started up, she began to talk, stroking the cat. She told her story brilliantly, even producing a doctor's letter as evidence. She was so short of breath, her need of urgent treatment was obvious. I did not have to make much in the way of a political point. Just being in the background of the shot, just having brought this case to public attention was enough. It moved the issue from being one of administrative detail about just another statistic to an account of a likeable sick woman facing death because the system had lost touch with its responsibilities. It was great television, and television had never been so important politically. What people saw on their screens changed the way they felt and radically altered how they viewed the issues. I exploited that for all it was worth. When, for example, people awaiting cataract surgery faced a delay, I was outside the hospital explaining the human consequences to Charlie Bird, then RTÉ's chief news correspondent, in the most blunt and vivid terms possible.

'What happens when you do not treat a cataract is that, sooner or later, the cataract may burst. And if the cataract bursts, then the eye can never [*pause*], never be fixed. We could be dealing with permanent blindness.'

I came across the case of a teacher, Ger O'Brien, who had no arms and only one leg but was able to drive his car, using his foot and mouth. Remarkably, the Revenue Commissioners had rejected his claim for a tax refund as a disabled driver, even though he had spent £7,500 modifying his vehicle. I held a press conference in the rear car park of Leinster House, with Ger showing how he operated the vehicle. I accused the government of heartless, inhuman laws. Because Ger had one good leg, he was denied eligibility. All the newspapers and broadcast media gave the story great coverage. This type of advocacy was politically priceless, with no downside to it. It resulted in tax concessions for disabled drivers.

As 1989 progressed, the minority Fianna Fáil administration gained in the opinion polls for its stringent fiscal policy. Economic recovery, growth, investment and business confidence were gathering pace. After my few failed attempts to win a Dáil vote on health motions, we hit the jackpot by eventually getting all opposition parties to combine against the decision not to give haemophiliacs £400,000. This was a critical confidence vote. The opposition won, 84 to 81. Haughey returned from a trip to Japan and called a snap election, combined with the already-scheduled European elections. This was perfect for me because health was to be the central issue of the campaign. Charlie Bird was assigned to cover health stories and I appeared on RTÉ's panel debates on programmes such as *Questions and Answers*, *Saturday View* and *Today Tonight*, the precursor to *Prime Time*. All of them featured health issues.

Polling day was 15 June. Fine Gael captured five extra seats, pushing the PDs back from fourteen deputies to six. My national profile helped me hold my seat in Wexford with 7,161 first preferences. This time Avril Doyle lost out to Michael D'Arcy. Her elimination gave me transfers to reach 10,734, electing me on the sixth count and establishing me as the party's big hitter in the constituency.

After the election, I continued in the health portfolio, getting a great buzz from being on the front bench. Each Tuesday morning we met, mirroring the cabinet format, before the week's parliamentary business. All aspects of political strategy, tactics, gossip, rumours were openly discussed. You were in the know. You could be openly crude, cynical and blunt: proper cut-throat politicking to undermine and oust Fianna Fáil. But internal trouble for Dukes was brewing throughout 1989 and 1990, which would undermine all efforts to advance the party's cause.

The 1989 election result – Fianna Fáil 77 seats, Fine Gael 55, Labour 15, Workers Party 7 and PDs 6 – meant that Fianna Fáil could not form a single-party government. Neither could the traditional alternative of Fine Gael plus Labour form a coalition government. This stalemate led to weeks of paralysis in which no Taoiseach could be elected. Eventually Haughey and O'Malley did a deal to form a Fianna Fáil/Progressive Democrat administration, with two PD seats at cabinet. This ended a historic Fianna Fáil 'core value' of principled opposition to participating in a coalition: a watershed in Irish politics. Fianna Fáil no longer had to get 50 per cent of the vote or seats to be in power. The party could pick its political dance partners from election to election and could stay in power for decades. Political parties survive on the oxygen of power. And under these circumstances Fine Gael could be starved of oxygen indefinitely.

From 1989 to 1994, many Fine Gael parliamentarians, members and supporters failed to grasp the significance of the impact on the party of this altered landscape. They also did not absorb the net impact of the Progressive Democrats. For every election when the PDs were on the pitch between 1987 and 2007, Fine Gael failed to exceed 30 per cent of the national first-preference vote. The bulk of PD voters were disaffected Fine Gael supporters.

The PDs presented Fine Gael with an identity dilemma. The PDs had clearly defined positions on lower taxes, reduced public spending and liberalising social laws. Fine Gael was essentially 'not Fianna Fáil'. Labour and the Workers Party had strong and strident identities. That left no hiding place for bland equivocation by Fine Gael, but Fianna Fáil could occupy the centre ground by being the party of power in government, delivering results.

The profound implications of these shifts following the 1989 election were blithely ignored, countered by a shallow analysis that concluded the reason for Fine Gael's poor showing in opinion polls in 1990 was Alan Dukes himself. What were the charges against him? His lack of charisma, his political inexperience, the naïveté of the Tallaght strategy and, most of all, his failure to procure a viable candidate in the presidential election of 1990.

Gay Mitchell and I went to Dukes in the autumn of 1990, explaining that we were likely to finish a bad third in the race to Áras an Uachtaráin, which seemed probable from private party polls. Dick Spring's nominee, Independent senator Mary Robinson, had covered considerable ground over the summer. She had established herself as the credible non-Fianna Fáil candidate. There were two options: swallow your pride and support her, instead of running any Fine Gael candidate, or run a great campaign. We offered to run that campaign. Dukes dismissed the dangers for himself and his leadership and appointed Jim Mitchell as director of elections for a campaign that turned into an expensive disaster. Many senior party figures secretly shrugged: losing this battle was fine if it meant dislodging Dukes. He had no inner circle, relying on his chief of staff, Joe Kenny, to make contact with the world outside his bunker.

The presidential battle became a two-horse race, as often happens in by-elections with tactical voting in the final stages, between Fianna Fáil's Tánaiste Brian Lenihan and Mary Robinson. Austin Currie, despite his best endeavours, finished with a woeful 16 per cent – the worst ever result for Fine Gael in a national election. Within hours of Mary Robinson being deemed elected at the count centre, a motion of no-confidence in Dukes was tabled by long-term disaffected foe John Donnellan, who had adapted Brendan Behan's maxim to 'If it was raining soup, Alan Dukes would be out in the street with a fork.' Now, the cutlery of choice was a knife and the objective was leader decapitation. Dukes had never prepared for this moment. He had not built relationships either with antagonists or with those who were prepared to back him. He was distant and remote to those who had propelled him into the top job.

John Bruton, as deputy leader, had most to gain if Dukes was deposed. I knew the score. He was going to take over the leadership, no matter what, and it would be payback time for all the senior figures who had ever disrespected him – and party time for hard-core Bruton loyalists.

I assured Dukes when we met that I would back him in the vote and strongly advised him not to be pressured into resigning. 'Make them eyeball you and vote you out. Let's see if they have the courage and numbers to do it. Don't be psyched out of it, under any circumstances. They may not have the numbers. A lot of these TDs never accepted you as leader. Their lack of support for you as team leader has been disloyal and unfair. I'm not so sure this meets with universal approval among the grassroots. Stand up to them. Fuck them. I warned you of this danger months ago.'

It came as no surprise to me when Dukes convened a front-bench meeting just prior to the parliamentary party meeting to announce his resignation in the best interests of party unity. He did not wish, he said, to drag everybody through a divisive and damaging process.

Yeah, you obviously believe those who are telling you the numbers are gone from under you, I thought, watching him, knowing he had been crying. Those tears were understandable. It is not unreasonable for a Fine Gael leader to presume they will become Taoiseach. It had been the case for most of Dukes's predecessors. That dream was now shattered for him and he was hurt and humiliated. I felt extremely sorry for him and his wife, Fionnuala, whom I greatly liked. I was angry that he took advice from those who had not striven to elect him. Their weak approach would never have got him elected in the first place, so it was inevitable that, at the crucial moment, they recommended that he capitulate. Alan Dukes never reciprocated the trust others placed in him and he took dubious advice from people who were already having an each-way bet. In currying favour with Bruton, they shored up retention of their own position by negotiating a bloodless transfer of power.

Now I was faced with a serious dilemma. I had been Dukes's strongest campaigner for the leadership. He had placed me on the front bench, so my career was clearly in jeopardy. There was no question about it: John Bruton was going to be leader. I hadn't supported him at any stage and had told him so. In a divided party I was now on the losing side and politically dispossessed.

My closest pal was a political soulmate and adjoining constituency neighbour. Phil Hogan had been a senator since 1987 and had successfully ousted Kieran Crotty in Kilkenny at the 1989 election. His late father had been a councillor and Big Phil had been reared to cut-throat politics. We shared our age, ambition and ruthless pragmatism. In later years my pal Brendan McGahon affectionately dubbed us the 'Kray Twins' (a reference to the infamous London gangster brothers) for the fear we could engender when we entered the party meeting rooms during heave periods.

Phil and I surveyed the situation. Not good.

'I am so fucked it's unbelievable,' I said. 'All my enemies are going to have a field day. But, unlike Dukes, I'm damned if I'm going to lie down and play dead.'

'What else can you do?'

'Throw my hat in the ring as a leadership candidate.'

Phil laughed. 'You're a divil,' he said appreciatively.

'I know it sounds crazy, but I think there must be at least a dozen sore heads that are not happy about the way Dukes has been treated,' I said. 'I haven't a hope of winning, but defiance might be tactically better than surrender. It might be no harm to put down a marker for the long-term future.'

Phil was up for the audacity of this and sussed out the mood music in the corridors to see if I could garner a credible showing. I issued a statement and briefed the media about my candidacy. I was thirty years old. Most parliamentary party members derided the notion that someone so young, without ministerial experience, could be a serious leadership contender.

'Fair amount of consumer resistance' was how Phil, ever understated, summed it up.

The alacrity with which former Dukes supporters now tried to lick John Bruton's arse was only surpassed by the *post hoc* emotional trauma and guilt many TDs suffered because they had shafted Dukes so brutally. The overwhelming desire was for a coronation rather than a competition. Universal appeals for unity were the order of the day. 'Enough of the bloodletting. Time for healing' was the mantra. I couldn't get any sort of campaign off the ground against that.

Apparently John Bruton and his closest supporters were incandescent with rage at the temerity of my rebellious lack of compliance with his accession to the leadership. He asked to meet me. Phil said I should agree, in order to negotiate a retreat on the basis of staying on the front bench. Bruton was in no mood for deals, seeing my antics as decidedly not in the party's interest. The best he could offer on the basis of my immediate withdrawal was a joint statement in which he would praise my work as the front-bench health spokesperson. I had no choice except to backtrack.

When he was putting together his front bench in early 1990, Bruton appointed me spokesman on transport and tourism. I was content to get out of health. Although it had been very good to me, my primary policy interests lay in economics, finance and business.

My relationship with John Bruton was civil and business-like, while devoid of warmth, friendship or trust. Anything he asked me to do I did willingly and with total commitment. As with Dukes's leadership, my sole objective was to become a minister and that could be done only by getting into government. Politics is a team game and I was a team player.

I vigorously applied myself to the same thorough research on all facets of the transport and tourism portfolio, as I had done with health, building up a network of contacts and files of information.

I also kept the home fires burning, paying particular attention to my home base in Enniscorthy. In the Wexford County Council election, I was re-elected with 1,740 votes (the quota was 1,675) in an effective vote-management exercise, with 38 per cent support. I became chairman of the Enniscorthy Urban District Council and revamped the town's Fine Gael branch by recruiting a group of postal workers because nobody knew an area like a postman did.

The change of leader provided no bounce for the party in the opinion polls. We continued to stagnate at 21–22 per cent. Haughey was ousted in February 1992. With the aid of the country-and-western set, Albert Reynolds defeated Bertie Ahern for the party leadership. By July, when Des O'Malley gave his public evidence at the beef tribunal – a commission of Inquiry of Dáil Éireann into malpractice in the Irish beef-processing industry, mainly focussing on Goodman International – deep tension was emerging between him and Reynolds and it looked as if this would force an early general election. Reynolds was itching for a chance to gain his own electoral mandate. Within the opposition parties, Labour's Dick Spring was maturing into a formidable political force. He was dubbed the 'real leader of the opposition'. His unprecedented success with Mary Robinson led to a rebranding of the party with a red rose. Labour had real middle-class appeal, as well as socially appealing credentials.

The same misdiagnosis that had done for Dukes was now being applied to Bruton: Jim Mitchell would describe him as suffering from a 'charisma deficit'. He was perceived as too right wing, a farmer-rancher from Meath with a silver spoon in his mouth. He was not televisual – people didn't like the look of him. It was part of a pattern: Fine Gael's triumphant return to power was always one new leader away. In fact, the party's problems were more deep-rooted: the Progressive Democrats occupying our traditional territory and the prospect of perpetual opposition because of

Fianna Fáil's capacity to coalesce with whomever would help them make up a Dáil majority. To this problematic reality were added two further negatives: the long shadow Garret FitzGerald cast over all his successors, and the professionalism of Dick Spring. He had put together a coterie of top-class advisers, such as Fergus Finlay and Greg Sparks. I believed the best Fine Gael response was to support our leader wholeheartedly, not to dump on him at the first available opportunity.

Throughout the summer of 1992, the mutterers were back in business. Bruton's response was to carry out a significant front-bench reshuffle in the autumn. My relations with him improved to the point that he appointed me spokesperson on agriculture, a promotion I relished and that was of great voting benefit to me in my rural constituency. He also reappointed Alan Dukes to the front bench, along with Peter Barry as deputy leader. This was the team that would fight the next general election.

I threw myself headlong into cultivating relationships with the farming organisations and the agri-media. Michael Berkery, general secretary of the Irish Farmers' Association, and Matt Dempsey, editor of the *Farmers Journal*, were particularly helpful to me in preparing new policy proposals. I attacked the incumbent minister, Joe Walsh, with gusto, accusing him of poor outcomes in the Common Agricultural Policy reform and GATT (General Agreement on Tariffs and Trade) negotiations, highlighting Fianna Fáil's lack of a European party alliance, like Fine Gael and the European People's Party.

Farm incomes were going through a tough time. As a former farmer, I spoke the farmers' language of enthusiastic advocacy (plenty of 'poor mouthing') and it went down well. Although my opposite number was likeable, he was perceived as being more interested in the food-processing industry than in farming *per se*. I travelled the country to as many rural constituencies as possible, happy whenever

I could to don wellington boots. Word got back to Bruton of my positivity, energy and endeavour. Incrementally, we were coming to trust each other more and get along together better.

The general election was held much earlier than anticipated on 25 November 1992. It was not a good national outcome for Fine Gael since our vote share declined to 24 per cent. In fact, it couldn't have been much worse, with the loss of ten seats in the lowest party tally since 1948. In Wexford we held up quite well at 34.5 per cent, a marginal gain over the 1989 result. I obtained 7,043 first preferences and was well clear of my two colleagues. This time Avril Doyle edged out Michael D'Arcy by 109 votes to win back her seat. His elimination on the fifth count pushed me over the quota with 10,716 votes. However, the result was a personal triumph for Brendan Howlin, who topped the poll with 10,338. The Spring Tide swept all before it.

My working life was transformed after the 1992 election, when I recruited a new Dáil secretary. My incessant constituency and policy research workload resulted in a high attrition rate and turnover of secretaries. My impatience and workaholic tendencies involved them in early-morning starts, no lunch break and late nights in the office. Tom Enright lost his seat in Offaly, so his former aide became mine. Geraldine Lannigan O'Keefe was superb, never saying no to mountains of typing, phone calls and printing. Without her indefatigable dedication and skill for a decade, I couldn't have kept my constituents happy, while increasingly shifting my time to front-bench and party business. Deirdre knew her as Wonder Woman.

If the poor election results were a blow to Bruton, worse was to follow. Despite there being no Dáil majority for Fianna Fáil, Dick Spring humiliated Bruton in a much-publicised post-election meeting in the Shelbourne Hotel, harbouring old resentments that related to bruising battles in cabinet. A 'rotating Taoiseach' was promulgated. Bruton appeared impotent. It seemed Labour was contemplating a crossing of the Rubicon. And that was what happened.

Labour switched from being relentless prosecutors and railing against Fianna Fáil to coalescing in government with them, with a combined voting strength of 101 TDs. This defied the historic dividing line and axis of Fianna Fáil versus the rest. While the head honchos in the trade unions (knee deep in the Social Partnership, which involved government, employers and the unions right up until 2010) loved it, traditional rank-and-file supporters recoiled in horror. Brendan Howlin became minister for health, and John Browne was reappointed a minister of state.

Total despair descended on Fine Gael. Our traditional alliance partner had forsaken us and done the unthinkable. Initially we didn't know whether to attack or befriend Labour, knowing we would never get into government without them. The scale of the Fianna Fáil/ Labour Dáil majority was so great that they looked like being in government for two terms. Despite our howls of protest and the fears of their own grassroots, Dick Spring was swayed by the prospect of a British–Irish government peace deal on Northern Ireland, with an IRA ceasefire and the prospect of spending £9 billion of European structural funds.

Fine Gael's oxygen pipeline was switched off. Permanent opposition beckoned just as Fianna Fáil seemed on the verge of becoming as much a part of the permanent government as the civil service. I felt I would never be a minister. Fearing a fresh wave of leadership woe, I called John Bruton and asked to meet him in the leader of the opposition's Dáil office where I had often sat face to face with Alan Dukes.

'John, I don't need to tell you that you're in trouble,' I said. 'The same spineless fuckers that drifted away from Dukes are turning Turk on you. My assessment is that you may just about survive the forthcoming post-election vote of the parliamentary party, but it won't be long before they try to take you out with a motion of no-confidence. I learned a lot from Dukes's mistakes. If you want my advice, assistance and total loyalty, it's fully available to secure your position.'

He stared at me as if I was stating the obvious. I moved as delicately as I could into finding out his precise thinking.

'First, I need to know that in all circumstances you will fight to retain your job. There is no point in preparing defences if you fold your tent like Dukes. We both have to live in the real world of politics. You must treat loyalty as a two-way street. What's good for you has to be good for me in terms of promotion now and in the future if we get into government,' I bluntly suggested.

Unlike Dukes, Bruton was highly attuned to and aware of his potential vulnerability. He readily agreed that he had to make preparations for battles ahead. He signified that he wanted to meet every member of the parliamentary party, all sixty-six TDs, senators and MEPs, on an individual basis to review the general election, and get their take on why the party had done so poorly.

Bruton was a typical Meath man: he had no intention of conceding. He knew that any leadership aspirations of mine were necessarily predicated on becoming a minister first. Nobody has ever skipped that particular phase of political career-building, because nobody would be a credible leader without the experience of running a department.

'Dukes's big failing was not to appoint key loyalists whom he could always rely on to the top jobs,' I went on. 'You need a woman from Dublin as deputy leader. I'm impressed by the gutsy characteristics of Nora Owen. She fits the bill perfectly: Dublin North constituency, female, perfect Fine Gael pedigree from the Collins dynasty, a member of the class of '81, feisty, pragmatic and tough. Now that Peter Barry has said he's retiring as deputy leader, there's a vacancy for Nora to slot into.'

He nodded.

'Another guy who really impresses me is Michael Lowry. He has a mighty base in Tipperary. As former county chairman of the GAA, he cleared all the debts on Semple Stadium in Thurles. Fine Gael has massive debts. He should be put in charge of resolving that headache. Phil Hogan needs to be promoted. You will not get better eyes and ears around the house and the party. He should be put in charge of headquarters, modernising the organisation and getting us ready for the next election. These are the types of people you need around you, not prima donnas who will be sycophantic to your face and then badmouth you in their constituencies, when the polls are shite. I'm talking about mates you'd bring into the jungle with you, carrying a machete and be certain they wouldn't stick it in your back. Make no mistake: the same people who took out Dukes are going to come for you within a year. They'll present you with white gloves, whiskey and a revolver. I can name right now those who will front up and those who will let you down and wobble when they're most needed. You could name them too – self-serving weaklings. First you have to see off the vote in a few weeks. If they were smart, they'd move now. They're not. Only Dukes will overtly seek to shaft you at this point. But he's a beaten docket for the leadership and will be perceived as personally bitter. If you don't prepare, you'll go under a bus down the road.'

Bruton used endless hardback, green-covered notebooks for all meetings. He wrote down everything I said. I'm sure he thought I was a clinical and callous bastard. He was probably right, but we had a common interest. That's all that's required in any power struggle. It's the strongest bond possible. He suggested we keep in regular contact.

From that moment on, over the next two years, Roy Dooney, Bruton's chief of staff and right-hand man, was constantly asking me to drop down to Dooney's office for a chat. We would have lengthy phone conversations. I grew to understand Bruton's eccentricities and insecurities. His public image and private persona were totally different. He was a great colleague: open, tough, humorous, self-deprecating and intensely hard-working.

Bruton survived the post-election confidence vote with minimal rancour, mostly from Alan Dukes, who was entitled to blow off some steam. The perceived wisdom among the leader's opponents was that this was the wrong time to make a putsch. Big mistake.

Bruton carried out a significant front-bench reshuffle, which he delayed until early March, subsequent to having a long chat with everybody on a one-to-one basis. Michael Noonan was demoted from finance to transport. Surprise, surprise, I was picked to replace him in this key economic portfolio. Over previous weeks, Noonan had gone on a solo run, calling for another devaluation of the Irish punt. He also let it be known that he would be taking up 'leadership positions' on issues beyond whatever portfolio he held. It was clear to me that, until he was leader, leadership heaves in Fine Gael would continue. While holding the most eminent party positions and playing the team game, Noonan always retained the dexterity to imply that the party could have done better under him. In all the internal strife, he was the only individual I thought was more Machiavellian than me.

Nora Owen was appointed deputy leader and spokesperson for foreign affairs. Michael Lowry became director of party finances and chairman of the parliamentary party, a role he was to revamp. Phil Hogan joined the front bench. Jim Mitchell was dropped and made chairman of the Public Accounts Committee, while Gay Mitchell was appointed justice spokesperson. Throughout this period, Bruton had his own tight group of close pals, most notably Enda Kenny, Seán Barrett and Richard, John's brother. Kenny was chief whip and Richard Bruton was a tireless policy wonk. However, Bruton did reappoint some whom we knew might revolt against him.

Owing to the change of government, the budgetary legislation and the finance bill had to be processed. I worked incessantly at my new brief. I relished the challenge of all aspects of fiscal policy, macro-economics, sector planning and taxation reform. I was so industrious in my approach to opposition finance bill amendments that I tabled more than three hundred, covering every conceivable angle of debate against the new minister for finance, Bertie Ahern. Included in this compendium was a cut-and-paste revision of an idea that was floating around for a tax amnesty to encourage previous tax dodgers to come clean and return what they owed to the exchequer. I proposed a 10 per cent rate. The front bench approved everything but, as it turned out, did not pay that much attention to the details.

All hell broke loose when the government proposed its own tax amnesty. Bruton led the charge in the Dáil. He thought it was immoral and utterly wrong. It wasn't long before Fianna Fáil and especially Labour, who were taking heat on the topic, highlighted my proposal. Bruton was apoplectic with rage. It was humiliating for me to have to backtrack, but the public, PAYE and the media mood was totally opposed to the amnesty. I ate humble pie with a soup spoon.

Apart from that débâcle, my profile soared on all economic debates. I developed brilliant expert contacts. I revelled in the opportunity to reply to the budget speech spontaneously, speaking for more than an hour live on television. I lambasted the Labour Party for their blatant hypocrisy towards Fianna Fáil and highlighted the grandiose offices of programme managers and advisers, which were enormously costly. I formulated detailed tax reforms and cuts to be financed through the abolition of the PRSI ceiling, which seemed to me to be anomalous, providing a lower marginal tax rate to higher earners. I wound up the strongest possible (and ultimately successful) campaign against the residential property tax, which was deeply unpopular in the middle-class suburbs. I was hawkish on controlling state expenditure and ensuring tight fiscal policy.

Throughout the next year, I was in Bertie Ahern's face at every opportunity. There was a Greencore share sale fiasco, involving Davy stockbrokers, which resulted in a special Dáil debate. After I had spoken, excoriating him, he mumbled that he just wanted to agree with everything I said. I couldn't get over it. But, then, Ahern was the most driven, ruthless, relentless, canny, manipulative, charming, confusing political operator I ever encountered. He was the professionals' professional. He looked around every corner for trouble and often defused it before it got out of hand. It came as no surprise to me that he was the only Taoiseach in the history of the state to win three consecutive elections. The consequences for the country were entirely secondary to his political requirements. As he saw it, his political interests *were* the national interest.

In 1993, Bruton decided to establish an external commission to analyse and review Fine Gael's identity, organisational structures and policies. This navel-gazing exercise could not and did not address the hidden agenda of those who constantly undermined the leader with what was termed the 'Bruton factor'. Eoghan Harris was drafted in to improve not just the image and communications of the leader but those of the parliamentary party. We were notified of the dates of Eoghan's media training course. I turned up suffering from a hangover on the second day. Eoghan was forcefully explaining the impact of the Provisional IRA campaign on politics in the Republic when I had the temerity to interrupt and say the North wasn't a big issue on the doorsteps in Wexford. I was taken aback when Harris erupted with rage, banging the table, berating my ignorance about the fundamental fissures in Irish life.

The polls continued to be abysmal for Fine Gael, despite Labour dropping from 23 per cent to 16 per cent. I was constantly on *Morning Ireland*, defending our line and particularly protecting

John Bruton. On a cold Monday in February 1994, the latest MRBI/*Irish Times* poll was the worst ever. Fine Gael was down to 16 per cent nationally and our core vote (before apportioning the 'don't knows') was a catastrophic 13 per cent. Bruton's own leadership rating plummeted to new depths. This prompted the decision of four members of the front bench – Jim O'Keeffe, Alan Shatter, Jim Higgins and Charlie Flanagan – to resign from their positions as spokesmen. They called a press conference on the Dáil plinth to state that they were tabling a motion of no confidence in the leader of the parliamentary party. This dramatic move shocked many colleagues, but for me it was not entirely unexpected. In fact, Bruton and I had planned for this day.

Bruton called me down to his office. Even though he had seen it coming, he was anxious, pacing up and down the room, pulling on his braces, tugging at his hair, emitting deep sighs.

'This is perfect timing for us,' I told him. 'It's the run-up to the Euro elections, we're making progress with our campaign against the residential property tax and right now we can call on forty party votes. Many are sick of the sniping and want this issue firmly dealt with. You will win.'

He took reassurance from my total confidence. We agreed our tactics. At the weekly front-bench meeting, before the four rebels could get into their stride and resign, Bruton sacked them and adjourned the meeting. The chief whip tabled a motion of confidence to pre-empt any negative motion. Michael Lowry set 15 February as the date for the crucial parliamentary party meeting. This was a proper knockdown, drag-out fight to the bitter end. Noonan and Dukes upped the ante by conducting joint live interviews from the Limerick studios on the Sunday lunchtime RTÉ radio programme *This Week*, openly committing to a savage attack on Bruton. There appeared to be a concerted conspiratorial plot, which I knew wasn't the reality: the pair were making it up as they went along.

In response, Bruton's closest supporters publicly fronted up. Nora Owen played a blinder. Bernard Allen and Gay Mitchell were unequivocally onside, backing the leader. I encouraged Bruton to use the vacancies on the front bench to encourage wannabes into believing that their prospects of promotion were imminent if the right result could be procured. I had positive conversations with Paul McGrath from Mullingar and Michael Creed. Some guys – Bernard Durkan and Donal Carey, for instance – love a battle, the more savage the better. Every few days, we would recheck our respective lists of definites and waverers. No bullshit escaped sceptical scrutiny by Phil Hogan and Michael Lowry. It was counter-intelligence at its most enjoyable, albeit with a frisson of fear attached to it. Bruton held countless hours of interviews with individual TDs, senators and MEPs, stressing his humility and a listening leadership. Each of us had to kill ourselves to persuade them that Bruton was their best option. Each of us had to debrief with the others to work out what point we had reached in our campaign. It was the learning curve to beat all others. Learning who was lying. Learning who was promising. Learning who was an ally. Learning how to plant fifth columnists into other candidates' camps to get a read on what they were at. 'I want you to find out about Josephine Bloggs,' I'd tell a fifth columnist. 'She's promised us her vote, but I need to know what she's telling the other crowd. Off you go now.'

Off they went, and back came the information. We discovered naked duplicity, and eventually decided that the only way to verify how certain key deputies, who had promised Bruton their vote, would act was to involve Liam Burke, a Cork City TD from the north side. His local nickname was the Silver Fox. He was a wily operator and the perfect choice if you wanted – and we *did* want – a double agent. He joined the enemy camp, gaining access to their lists, in order to see whom they had secured. This gave us a brilliant insight into what was really going on.

The meeting was held in the usual room at the National College of Art and Design, adjacent to Leinster House. The marathon drama went on for almost eight hours in a strained and uncomfortable atmosphere. Lowry said that legally we could have an open roll-call vote, but we would have a secret ballot. He appealed for calm and mutual tolerance. More than forty people spoke, with few surprises. It wasn't about Fine Gael's heart and soul of Christian democracy versus social democracy, nothing to do with idealism or ideology. It was about who held power in the party.

Enda Kenny proposed the motion and spoke first. Charlie Flanagan spoke first for the insurgents. I liked him. Sadly for his career, he always seemed to be on the losing side. Each opposing speech was prefaced with pained sympathy for Bruton, acknowledging his hard work and sincerity, before sorrowfully saying he was a liability.

Jim O'Keeffe, from Cork South-West, described 'the Kilbrittain factor' in his constituency, where a branch AGM had identified Bruton's faults: it was one of the group who had persuaded Dukes to quit.

In my own contribution, I presented a detailed analysis of the opinion polls, explaining that changing the leader would not fix the problems. In fact, having a fourth leader in a handful of years could only send out a message that we didn't know what we were doing. No Brad Pitt figure would come over the mountain to save us. We had to realise the problems posed by the Progressive Democrats, the post-FitzGerald context, and Fianna Fáil's grip on government. Unity of purpose was a prerequisite to progress. Let's play the ball, not the man. 'If John Bruton loses, Fine Gael will take a leap into the dark,' I concluded.

Most of the contributions were predictable. I was disappointed that Frances Fitzgerald, whom Bruton had promoted to the front bench, spoke and voted against him. I was less surprised about Theresa Ahearn, from Tipperary South, who also opposed him – she had been dropped from the front bench. Noonan made a rather tame anti-Bruton speech, unlike John Cushnahan, the Munster MEP, who let rip. Phil Hogan argued that no previous Fine Gael leader had been voted out in this manner and it was a bad precedent to establish. Peter Barry and Paddy Cooney, senior party elders, did not speak. Avril Doyle not only did not speak but left early to attend a funeral. The last speaker was John Bruton himself. He started off in a low tone, measured, but clearly emotional. He spoke about 'commitments in life' and how seriously he took them – to his wife and family and, most of all, to his party, Fine Gael. He emphasised that politics was about substance, not imagery. He was resisting this vote not just for himself, but to protect a future leader from a similar fate of being ousted for something as flimsy as an opinion poll. He got a big round of applause.

The tellers, Peter Barry and Michael Lowry, were sworn to secrecy. Despite this, I'm certain that Bruton won by 41 votes to 25.

I did not feel any animosity towards those who must have hated my role and pugnacity. In fact, I respected combative foes more than the lily-livered members who waffled duplicitous horse shite. Many a good laugh was had throughout the process. Phil Hogan really relished the combat. The more practice he got at in-fighting, the better he became at it, whereas I found the whole thing a depressing distraction from trying to get into government office. Any victory against colleagues is Pyrrhic.

Job done, move on to the next business. The new front bench was appointed; loyalty was rewarded. The European elections were held in June. Our target was to retain our four seats, one in each constituency. We readily achieved it, with more than 24 per cent of the vote, up 4 per cent on the 1989 Euro results. More significantly,

Fine Gael won a by-election in Mayo, with Michael Ring taking the seat vacated by new EU Commissioner Pádraig Flynn. Democratic Left's Eric Byrne won the seat of Dr John O'Connell in Dublin South-Central. Labour's alliance with Fianna Fáil was deeply unpopular. Back home, I got 529 votes (quota 340), helping Fine Gael to regain its three seats on the Enniscorthy Urban District Council.

Those results meant that the leadership issue was off the agenda, at least until the autumn. November saw two by-elections in Cork City, North- and South-Central constituencies. John asked me to be director of elections in North-Central. The candidate I wanted, Darragh Murphy, a bright young prospect, was nobbled at the convention by the incorrigible Liam Burke.

Liam was a legend on the doorsteps. He would bring a Dictaphone and speak into it in front of the householder. 'Memo to city engineer Paddy Murphy: repair to roof and chutes on number fourteen Coolpark Heights,' he would bellow. 'I raised this with your office already – still not done. This is totally unacceptable. Immediate works must be carried out ...' Some of the residents would think he was using a walkie-talkie to speak directly to the official. 'He gave them useless shower right jingo,' they would say, not knowing that there wasn't even a tape in the gadget.

It was a fully hands-on experience because I lived in the Imperial Hotel for three weeks. We waged an all-out negative campaign against Labour's opulence in office, hiring a satirical cartoonist to do adverts in the local press. Despite waves of leaflets and intense repeat house-to-house canvasses, Colm Burke could not win. The feisty Kathleen Lynch of Democratic Left romped home on Cork's North Side, as the leading anti-government candidate. Michael Lowry was director of elections in the eminently winnable next-door constituency, and Hugh Coveney comfortably won back his former seat in South-Central. The combined results of all the by-elections meant that Fine Gael, Labour and Democratic Left had a working Dáil majority. Fine Gael's relationship with Democratic Left had transformed through co-operating in opposition.

This precipitated a crisis for the Labour Party in government. Rows had been simmering over the summer months in relation to the publication of the Beef Tribunal report. The nomination of Attorney General Harry Whelehan as president of the High Court prompted a walkout from cabinet by Labour ministers on the day of the count. The attorney general's delays in processing the abuser Father Brendan Smith's extradition eventually toppled Albert Reynolds as Taoiseach, after which Dick Spring seemed on the verge of doing a deal with the new Fianna Fáil leader, Bertie Ahern.

Just when it looked like our chance of government had gone, with an imminent deal between Spring and Ahern, I made a serious miscalculation in an interview on *This Week*. Facing a further period in opposition, I became disillusioned in my ongoing defence of Bruton and the latest prospect of never-ending soulless opposition. I began to doubt my own stance. I was fed up with politics and internal rancour, and when the presenter asked me what would happen if we didn't go into government, I responded by saying that Bruton should be given 'time and space' in those circumstances to consider his future options.

Bruton rang me that afternoon. He had had a chat with journalist Vincent Browne, who had agreed that it seemed I was distancing myself from him and expressing disloyalty. I dismissed it as a misunderstanding.

By this stage Lowry was Bruton's closest adviser and confidant. He was the main man in the inter-party negotiations, especially with Democratic Left. This was the most incredible achievement in jockeying. Lowry was sorting out Fine Gael debts of £1.4 million; he was also the key party organisation player and a successful by-election director. His phenomenal personal progress derived partly from his pulling all the leader's strings but also from his lack of interest in a policy portfolio. It meant that from being a nobody two years earlier before I had advanced his talent, he had become the ultimate fixer and was the most ruthless guy in the party. He rang me after that conversation with Bruton, laughed at me for dropping myself in it, and told me he would see me right, whatever that meant.

Unbelievably, as Dick Spring crossed the floor of the Dáil to enter into negotiations for a Fine Gael/Labour/Democratic Left rainbow government, I was somehow off-side. 'You carried the ball from your own try line, dancing around every tackler, and now you've it right in front of the try line,' Austin Deasy sneered. On 14 December 1994 I waited in my office, unsure of my fate. It would be unprecedented for the finance spokesman not to be appointed to cabinet, but there is always a first, and I might have fitted that unenviable slot. After the Dáil vote, Bruton, as Taoiseach, went to Áras an Uachtaráin. No phone call, no tip-off. Time was moving on. Jesus wept. Was I going to be left out? I waited by my phone.

The phone stayed silent, but a loud knock came on my door and, when I opened it, two heavies from the Taoiseach's office stood ready to escort me to John Bruton's new office. I went in and sat down at a poorly lit side table.

'I want to appoint you minister for agriculture, food and forestry. Is that okay?'

I accepted with utter relief and gratitude.

'Under cabinet protocol, I need to ask you if you are a member of any secret organisation.'

I didn't know what he meant. The Freemasons or what? Either way, no, I wasn't. Nothing stood in the path of my becoming a minister. My thirteen-year Dáil wait was over. I had joined a party, got onto the local council, become a TD, retained a seat, secured a front-bench post, ascended to the top tier and had now got into government. It had been a veritable snakes-and-ladders contest, rolling the dice, climbing, regularly being bitten in the arse and falling down.

I had reached the cabinet summit at thirty-five years of age, despite endless setbacks. Power at last.

8: Yes, Minister

'Ivan, do you know anywhere that would be good to hide money?'

We were queuing in the antechamber of Áras an Uachtaráin to receive our seals of office from President Mary Robinson. Michael Lowry was in front of me and managed to whisper the question to me without fully turning round.

'For Christ's sake, Michael, this isn't the time or the place but, as it happens, no, I don't.'

The official ceremony began and I thought no more of the question. I know, I know. Here was a man about to be appointed a government minister who had as good as confessed to me that he had money to be secreted somewhere from the tax man and I had simply disavowed expertise in hiding money. No questions asked, no outrage expressed. No report made, then or later, to the Taoiseach. Condemn me by all means, but that's the truth of it. I'm a live-and-let-live guy, so Michael Lowry's problem, as far as I was concerned, was Michael Lowry's problem. I was concentrating on the formalities of taking power.

The sequence passed in a flash. You are given this metal seal for a matter of seconds as you shake hands with the president. You never see the item again. No memento or individual photograph, just a group portrait of the entire cabinet. Then a cabinet meeting in the Áras, where the first decision taken was to cut our ministerial pay. Then Nora

Owen, Phil Hogan and I headed off to the Taoiseach's celebrations in Navan. The next morning it was up early for an interview on *Morning Ireland* to highlight our leadership in self-sacrifice.

Next step was to meet the senior civil servants in what had been until recently Minister Joe Walsh's department. Senior civil servants have only one hope when administrative change happens: it is that their new minister has held office previously. Someone who has already been a minister does not have to be house-trained. They know about the routine, lifestyle, code of secrecy, loyalty to the system, appropriate behaviour, departmental pyramid structure, government procedures and distrust of all that is external. As the youngest member of the cabinet and a first-timer at the table, I was going to be a disappointment on all of those fronts. All departments of state have a pyramid structure. At the summit of the hierarchy, the secretary general can make or break any minister. My secretary general was Michael Dowling, a tall, quiet-spoken man from Killarney. His vast experience as a career civil servant included time as private secretary to former agriculture minister Mark Clinton, principal officer in the dairy division, and years of key negotiations representing Ireland in Brussels. So high was his standing among Eurocrats that other national delegations regularly sought his wise counsel. He was now within a year of retirement, facing the worst challenge of his career.

To help everyone get to know the new kid on the block, I toured all six floors, shaking hands. When I returned to my office, I found on the imposing desk a weighty black binder assembled by the ten heads of divisions in the department, a management group called the MAC. A veritable compendium, it covered what each one of the 4,096 departmental employees did in administering a £2 billion budget, including every farmer-related scheme and payment of premia, headage entitlements (for those in disadvantaged areas) and capital grants. It covered

FEOGA (Fonds Européen d'orientation et de garantie agricole) procedures and payments for the food industry, forestry schemes, rural development/alternative enterprises aid, animal and plant health controls. It spanned warble flies and ragwort, wandering animals and cruelty shelters, plus the entire panoply of the CAP and GATT (the world trade regulatory system) rules. I spent the next few weeks reading and rereading everything in that binder.

I was the political head, public face and advocate for the largest single sector of the economy – agriculture and processed food – with an annual output value of £8 billion. Agriculture accounted for 40 per cent of Ireland's net exports, generated 200,000 jobs, several hundred agri-businesses and various significant state agencies: Bord Bia, Teagasc, Forbairt, the Irish Horseracing Authority, Bord na gCon, Bord Glas, the National Stud and Coillte. I decided that no event, policy, development or controversy was going to happen without my involvement.

I had to make urgent appointments: my private secretary, special adviser, programme manager and two drivers. I had been approached in Wexford to transfer two local gardaí, Niall McCrea and Larry Byrne, as drivers. I knew they would be totally loyal and discreet, and was enthusiastic, although the proposal met with stiff resistance because the two men would have to be specially trained in Templemore and existing drivers from the special pool would have to be transferred. I persisted, and a couple of months later had Niall and Larry alternating behind the wheel of the state Merc.

I had Jimmy Deenihan from Kerry North as minister of state to carry out all the mundane functions I did not want to do. The standard advice was and still is to screw the minister of state by giving him or her low-profile responsibilities, like horticulture or animal/plant health – preferably as few as possible. I had no difficulty implementing this approach. Even in those areas that were specifically delegated, I knew I would have to negotiate the required funds from the Department of Finance. I didn't want anyone to be in any doubt as to who was boss. I was going to front up for any good news stories within the department's ambit. Jimmy was welcome to fill in for me on the tedious stuff. His constituency colleague Dick Spring knowingly acquiesced in my plan to suppress Jimmy. The only downside was: if the shit hit the fan on any topic, it landed on my desk. As it turned out, no minister for agriculture ever had so much shit hit their fan and Jimmy was lucky I kept him below the radar, where he was also below the line of fire. But that was much, much later . . .

One perk of being a minister was that Lily, my part-time local secretary, could be appointed full-time, working in my home, from which she could try to keep me linked to reality, now that I was not only in the bubble of Leinster House but shrouded in the layers of bubble wrap that come with ministerial office. You are ensconced with a diary of eighty hours' weekly commitments. Each year, the minister has to attend sectoral, state agency, farmers' and business representatives' events, including AGMs, award ceremonies, official dinners/receptions, cabinet meetings, Dáil sessions, monthly EU Agricultural Council meetings, foreign trade food fairs, rural constituency visits, plus horse, pony, livestock and machinery shows across the land during the summer. He or she officiates at every local exhibition, fair, book launch and opening. That's before they can even think of dealing with a multiplicity of demands from individual constituents, party members and personal associates, who 'need a quiet word' to sort out whatever problems they may have. All privacy evaporates.

The job of the agriculture minister was intensely important to Fine Gael. One third of party members were farmers. The best-attended backbench committee meetings were those held every fortnight at Agriculture House on a Wednesday night. My political guys were under orders to look after and prioritise problems that party deputies and senators brought up. I set out to tour every rural constituency on Friday of each week, meeting and listening to agri-business, local media, farmers' organisations, marts and party activists, while also presenting certificates, cutting ribbons and smiling. Always smiling.

Of course, that level of non-stop activity meant that time for thinking, analysing, listening and reflecting went out the window. A minister's most important function is to exercise sound judgement on the big decisions. The distraction offered by an overstuffed diary can make them fall short, through exhaustion. I failed to grasp, through lack of experience and unbridled enthusiasm for the role, that I should not say yes to every invitation. On the other hand, senior civil servants are superb operators and I relished virtually every moment of working with them, quickly realising that the way to get the best out of them was to leave the ways and means of solving a problem up to them, having outlined the problem and desired outcome.

I was in a hurry to get things done, to personify political power in action. During the Christmas break, before my political appointees were *in situ*, I called in Dermot Murphy and Danny Carroll, who had respectively been Joe Walsh's information officer and programme manager. At a brainstorming session we drew up three new initiatives: a charter of rights for farmers, setting performance targets for every customer-service component of the department; a new mega international food fair in Dublin, bringing in buyers from all over the world; and an ambitious twenty-year strategy to develop the forestry sector since we had only one third of the average European land-use in afforestation. I had an overarching sectoral vision: improve on farm efficiency (30p per gallon variation in milk-production costs), retain the maximum number of farming families, and add value to processed food. But, of course, the *realpolitik* of being a minister is responding to the conveyor belt of uncontrolled events that explode in front of you.

My first problem was a collapse in pig prices in late 1994. What to do? Call in the IFA and draw up a list of actions: a European Union storage scheme, which saw the EU buy up surplus stock, reduce levy deductions on pig slaughtering and launch a new pig-meat marketing plan. Within weeks, all requests had been delivered. I discovered the concept of 'the package', a series of measures presented as an all-encompassing resolution to the agri-media. This was my continual approach to the in-tray of problems that required a political response.

Next up? Horrendous flooding, particularly in south County Galway, in early 1995. The ministerial prerequisite is to be part of the crisis, so I manned a makeshift boat with RTÉ's Jim Fahy, his camera crew and the local Fine Gael TDs, delivering pictures for the lead item on the nine o'clock Sunday-evening news. Visibly shocked at the fifteen feet of water under which farms were immersed, I exuded heartfelt sympathy and promised immediate government relief. The February budget delivered a £2 million cash scheme of fodder aid. In each crisis, I was on the spot, identifying with the distressed, using the power of office to deliver. Great stuff, I thought. Let's have more of this.

The sea ferry companies Pandoro, Stena Sealink and Irish Ferries had received complaints from concerned organisations, like Compassion in World Farming, about the cruelty to animals when being transported by sea, and they announced that they would no longer carry livestock on their ships. The trade in live animals within the EU was important to producers and essential to exporters. I summoned all three ferry companies to high-profile meetings.

My officials drew up new rules on stocking densities on board, prior approval of route plans, journey times and rest periods, adequate ventilation, the hiring of trained personnel and accompanying vets. We argued that the provision of these safeguards for the animals should allow the business to resume. Since the issues were transnational, I raised with the EU Commission and Council the need for European regulations. I travelled to London to meet the British agriculture minister, William Waldegrave, to seek a common approach. By the end of March I had signed the statutory instruments into law.

Then I encountered my first experience of official systemic secrecy. Separate from animal sea transport within Europe was the larger trade of exporting live adult cattle to third countries, such as Egypt and Saudi Arabia. Unknown to me, in October 1993, 264 of 1,067 cattle had died aboard a boat travelling from Greenore to Al Mokha, a port city on the Red Sea coast of Yemen. This was due to conditions at sea and the intense heat, causing injury and stress to the animals. The *Irish Times*, through Seán McConnell, got hold of the story, which was initially denied by official sources. He actually travelled on one of the boats, publishing a daily diary that was deeply upsetting to animal lovers. I was furious at the cover-up and that I had not been made aware of the full facts. I announced in mid-April the suspension of all live exports beyond the Mediterranean and that we review the approval arrangements. By the end of October, we had put in place welfare stipulations whereby vessels had to meet new criteria to ensure the safety of animals, as well as restrictions on travel in stormy weather. My approach was always to confront problems head on, rather than sweep them under the carpet. This did not go down well with the network of farm organisations, business operators and officials, who preferred to maintain business as usual. Their disregard for and cavalier attitude to public opinion worried me, not least because I feared being left carrying the can of political responsibility.

The biggest hassle from farmers in that first year related to an income crisis in the sheep sector. From Easter onwards, the price of finished lambs dropped to unsustainable levels. At the May EU Council meeting, I procured a special scheme to take 1,000 tons of sheep meat off the market; this was the overhang of the previous year's unsold lambs. I actively sought and obtained an additional top-up of eight pounds per animal to the annual ewe premium scheme. By autumn, it was clear that it wasn't enough.

The IFA ran a strong campaign in Wexford, where sheep farming was significant. 'We hold Ivan Yates personally responsible,' the IFA's statement said.

Ireland was seeking reform of the entire method of calculating the European sheep subsidy. No other member state supported us. On the plane over to Brussels with my top officials, I explained that what we had achieved was insufficient for 48,000 Irish sheep farmers. 'This is a big political problem for me. I don't care what you have to do, but by the end of the year, I need a package. I know I was happy after the May deal in Brussels, but my arse is out the window on this one.'

Bart Brady, who dealt with all the EU business, stated that nothing further could be done. Michael Dowling, the department's secretary general, said nothing, but listened intently. Over the following months leading up to the December EU Council meeting, he came up with an ingenious solution whereby the Rural World payment, previously made only to sheep farmers in disadvantaged areas, such as the west of Ireland, worth another five pounds per animal, would be paid to every sheep farmer in the country. We claimed this as an incredible victory because it applied only to Ireland, with total additional cash of £26 million. My senior advisers were miracle workers.

My constant message to farmers? I was unequivocally their champion. Each budget and estimates announcement day, I would proclaim my achievements of tax concessions, additional agricultural reliefs, allowances and extra spending. I wasn't playing to the general gallery, rather seeking to cement my place as a memorably effective minister for agriculture.

My bureaucrats' ingenuity wasn't confined to finding solutions. They also minded my back. My private secretary, Peter, came into my office one day with a bundle of yellow Post-it notes. 'Minister, you know the way you come in at 6 a.m. and devour all the departmental files on your desk? Well, I think some of the notes you write and initial could come back to haunt you. I don't think it's wise to leave your fingerprints around like this. May I suggest you use these in future? That way your points can be dealt with and your role erased by discarding the note.'

'Ingenious,' I said.

My senior staff could also stop things happening through neat political footwork. One afternoon, Michael Dowling sat down for a chat in my office. 'Minister, the Horseracing Board need to rationalise the number of racetracks in the country. There are twenty-nine in total and they propose that six should close.'

'Michael, stop right there. You know how passionate I am about horseracing. There is no way on my watch as minister that I could stand over any track closures.'

He explained the need to reduce costs and went through the losses incurred by the six racecourses. Ballinrobe, Tipperary and Navan were on the list. We agreed a strategy that would enable us to scupper the plan by passing the file up the line to the Taoiseach. The Navan racecourse was right in the heart of John Bruton's Meath constituency. I alerted Roy Dooney, Bruton's chief of staff, to the negative local impact this would have on his boss. I suggested a memo from Bruton expressing his alarm might be appropriate. Within a week the plan was aborted, never to be resurrected.

I received many phone calls from the Taoiseach about the updated position to decentralise a European veterinary research station to Grange in County Meath. On the margin of every trip to Brussels, we would lobby Commission officials to expedite the reluctant transfer of Eurocrats to this proposed new facility. Repeated delays resulted in many missives from the Taoiseach's office. Conversely, any time I had good news of progress, I contacted him personally.

Playing the Department of Finance is a vital skill for a minister and a department to develop. Our point man for this relationship was Assistant Secretary General Tom Arnold, an absolute gent. Phil Hogan had been appointed minister of state at Finance. We compared notes on our induction process during the early weeks. Then, on Budget Day in February 1995, disaster struck. Hogan's personal political assistant was a raw recruit. Unbelievably, he faxed the full budget summary to a journalist at the *Evening Herald* in the morning before Ruairi Quinn's Dáil speech, which was against every rule, protocol and tradition. All hell broke loose. Quinn was understandably furious. Bruton took advice from the new government press secretary, Shane Kenny, and Attorney General Dermot Gleeson, and Phil was forced to resign. Wrong call, I felt, and still do. John Bruton should have held his fire. Life in government is attritional. You have to absorb some blows, rather than overreact to every hitch, and this was undoubtedly an administrative hitch. Many, if not most, media storms abate after a few days. I was devastated for Phil and spent the evening in his office. It was terrible, painful and a waste of political talent, albeit, given his career since then, a temporary waste of talent.

One of the solid positives of my own role was that no minister for agriculture had ever lost his seat in a subsequent general election, largely because of the special support those ministers received in securing re-election through good-news decisions.

I got the same treatment and it had an almost weekly pay-off. All files relating to County Wexford in departmental headquarters at Agriculture House were treated with special significance and political sensitivity. During my time there, positive discretionary discrimination was the rule of thumb. Brendan O'Donnell, the chief executive officer of Bord Glas (the Horticultural Development

Board) and formerly Charles Haughey's private secretary, came to tell me he had received a request for funding from the annual Enniscorthy Strawberry Fair, a shop window for the soft-fruit industry in the county. Did I share his concern that we should support this local voluntary endeavour? Did I what! Does a cat drink milk? He soothingly proposed that £15,000 per year should come out of his budget, with a suitable local press conference so that he and I could announce the subvention triumphantly.

Bord na gCon received a proposal from the Enniscorthy greyhound track to redevelop its privately owned grandstand facilities. The management felt that over the years the track had been treated as a Cinderella for investment, with priority going to state-owned tracks. I had lobbied hard for a VAT reduction on greyhound feedstuffs and for dog stud fees to be tax-exempt, and supported Bord na gCon's requests for increased capital locations. When Kevin Heffernan unexpectedly resigned as chairman, I nominated dynamic businessman Paschal Taggart for the post. An 80 per cent grant was speedily approved for an investment of £100,000. Again, a local press conference heralded the good news and I performed the official opening in July 1996.

The racecourse outside Wexford town had been in decline for many years, despite the enthusiasm of the local committee and the energy of the manager, Michael Murphy. Plans were drawn up for a new grandstand that would cost £500,000. A local contractor was engaged, resulting in early completion. To appropriate fanfare, I cut the ribbon with a radiant smile. I had worked hand in glove with Denis Brosnan, long-standing Irish Horseracing Authority (IHA) boss and Kerry foods supremo, to obtain a £15 million government capital fund to provide a long-term plan to upgrade nearly all horseracing tracks. This was matched by private investment in a deal with Ulster Bank, resulting in a total investment of £30 million. It was no coincidence that Denis had been a classmate in

Killarney, at St Brendan's Christian Brothers School, of Michael Dowling, secretary general of my department.

These constituency projects were relatively straightforward, unlike the procuring of the Tour de France cycle race for 1998, the bicentenary of the 1798 Rebellion, which was profoundly significant in County Wexford, owing to the bravery of the slaughtered pikemen. I received a request to meet Pat McQuaid, the head of the Irish Cycling Federation. The meeting would be private and in Wexford. Ireland was experiencing a golden era of cycling success with Sean Kelly and Stephen Roche. I sat down with Pat in the bar of the Ferrycarrig Hotel.

'Ivan, I have a proposal you might be interested in. The largest annual television audience for a sporting event is for the Tour de France. Unlike the Olympics or the World Cup, it's held every year. Every second year, the opening three-day stage commences outside France. If I could obtain one million pounds of state sponsorship, we might be able to get the 1998 start in Ireland. It would be a wonderful opportunity to promote Irish food and drink. Is there any way Bord Bia could come up with six hundred thousand pounds? If so, we might get the last stage to start in Enniscorthy, which would be a huge economic boost to the area and a shop window for local tourism.'

This was worth approximately £300,000 to the Irish Federation and there would be the prestige associated with hosting such an important event. Pat was also approaching Minister for the Environment Brendan Howlin, another Wexford deputy, for similar funding through his department via the local authorities. I liked McQuaid's forthright style and ambition. I called in my senior officials and found £600,000 for the project through An Bord Bia, the food agency. The race authorities agreed the detailed route for the three days. After day one in and around Dublin and day two in the Wicklow mountains, the race would recommence in Enniscorthy on day three, ending up in Cork, before the cyclists took the ferry back to France. I was thrilled at the prospect of such an event being hosted in my home town.

Then, out of the blue, McQuaid rang me to say a problem had developed. Because the race had to go through Carrick-on-Suir, the home town of Sean Kelly, it would have to start in Wexford, rather than Enniscorthy. I expressed dismay and disappointment and said I would have to get back to him.

'Pat, I'm very sorry,' I told him, in a telephone call a week later. 'The board of the food agency has taken a minuted decision not to support the Tour. I did my best, but it's fallen through. I was disappointed that Enniscorthy couldn't have benefited. I'm not sure what you can do.'

To my pleasant surprise, Pat rang back a week later. 'Ivan, you won't believe it. Those fuckers made a mistake in the road measurements. When it was rechecked, it was found that the race could indeed start on day three in Enniscorthy.'

'That's fantastic news, Pat. Maybe I could work something with our overall departmental budget, via Bord Bia, to get the cash. Leave it with me. I appreciate that Enniscorthy is back on track.'

By the time of the race, June 1998, I was no longer minister. I didn't actually care that I wasn't invited to the official event. Pulling the stroke for my backyard was craic enough.

Equally convoluted and protracted was a proposal emanating from a meeting with Ruairi Quinn in the Department of Finance. He explained that there was a chronic shortage of office space and meeting rooms in Leinster House for burgeoning parliamentary activities. Instead of a huge new construction project, he'd had the bright idea to take over the six-storey adjacent Agriculture House, which would have to be vacated by all the department officials. A tunnel was to be constructed linking the buildings.

I discussed this with my senior officials, who responded with outright opposition. They explained that they had thwarted a previous proposal by former Taoiseach Albert Reynolds, who had announced decentralisation of six hundred of their jobs to Cork. I told Ruairi the idea was a non-runner. He met me again, this time with Brendan Howlin. If I could push the idea through cabinet, overruling departmental management and trade union opposition, they suggested, 350 jobs would be relocated to Johnstown Castle, Wexford, which had been given to the state in 1944. The notion adequately sugared the pill for me. An *aide-mémoire* was drafted by Finance and the Office of Public Works (OPW).

I manfully apologised to everyone in the department, outlining the unsuccessful battle I had fought. Sadly, it was a *fait accompli.* Subsequently, when I was on business in Portugal, the story of the project was leaked. A lead front-page story in the *Irish Independent* depicted it as a major political stroke by me, with a furious response from staff representatives.

In January I performed a sod-turning and signing ceremony at the castle with Hegarty Construction for a £7 million contract and unveiled a massive rock with a foundation inscription wording, leaving no one in any doubt about who had delivered this economic windfall, even though late 1998 was the completion date. Despite initial resistance, through promotion incentives and inter-department transfers, a full staff complement works there, and it is also the headquarters of the Environmental Protection Agency: the annual public payroll was then to be worth £10 million annually to the local economy.

Early on in my time as minister, I was brought to see the acutely overcrowded office in the local District Livestock/Veterinary building in Enniscorthy. A new building was promised, using an out-of-town site, at a cost of £1.5 million, when the local Chamber of Commerce lobbied me strongly for a town-centre site so that staff would continue to buy lunches and do their shopping in town. This was becoming a vote loser, rather than a winner. I pleaded with the lads in Dublin to reconsider, but to no avail because the job had gone to contract. Remarkably, all ended happily when I was informed that there was a problem with the title deeds, so the OPW could now go ahead with an alternative urban site. The Lord moves in mysterious ways.

My biggest domestic headache was the urgent need for manufacturing jobs. We announced food expansion projects at Yoplait, Nutricia and Irish Country Meats across the county, along with new factories – the Mexican Tortilla Co. in Wexford and Integrated Packaging in Gorey – but there was nothing to fill the vacant 'advance factory' – built and paid for by the IDA, on a speculative basis, but remaining empty until a suitable tenant could be found – in Enniscorthy. Despite all my private pressure on the IDA, nothing materialised. I returned from a three-day trip to New Zealand, severely jet-lagged, on a Friday to hear of another major job announcement in Waterford. I had been promised that my own town was the top priority in the south-east region. I went ballistic and when RTÉ's regional correspondent, Michael Lally, rang me for a comment, I let rip at the IDA. He suggested I come down to him in New Ross to do a recorded television-news interview, highlighting that Wexford had the highest unemployment statistics in the region. In the recording I accused the IDA of neglect, false promises and geographical bias.

On the Monday, George Shaw, the Taoiseach's private secretary, rang. This was never good news. The Taoiseach was looking for me urgently. We spoke on the phone. He said that it was unacceptable for a senior minister to attack a state-sponsored body publicly. I should immediately apologise to Richard Bruton, the relevant enterprise minister, and meet to repent face to face with Kieran McGowan, the IDA boss. Ouch. My tail was firmly between my legs. What was good home-town optics was bad politics. I rang Richard and duly met Kieran in my swanky office.

He couldn't have been nicer, suggesting we devote patient persistence to procuring an international medical-devices business. Within months Angiodynamics, a New York-based firm making cardiac stents, were announced as factory tenants, with prospects of at least a hundred jobs. Ecstasy. Photo calls and ribbons followed. Kieran McGowan had been correct when he said we should wait for a sustainable venture: the plant has blossomed into the area's largest employer, after a management buy-out as Clear Stream, thanks to entrepreneur Andy Jones. Today, through C. R. Bard, it employs 280 people.

Investor confidence in the Irish economy was taking off, with 7 per cent growth in 1996. Urban-renewal designation, approved for Enniscorthy by the previous government, was starting to ignite, with several million pounds being spent on the construction of new offices, two hotels, a cinema, shops, apartments and town houses. The long-awaited £25 million public swimming pool and the modernisation of St Mary's Christian Brothers' School were going to tender. Vast infrastructural investment on housing, a new town square, library, fire station and Garda barracks was showing results.

The build-up to the 1998 bicentenary planning was foremost in the mind of County Hall officials in Wexford. The events they sought to host that year included the Fleadh Cheoil, the National Ploughing Championships, the All-Ireland Drama Festival, and a world sheep-shearing contest. An interpretive heritage centre for 1798 in Enniscorthy, costing £2.3 million, was to become a lasting centrepiece. A grant of £1.6 million was required from Bord Fáilte. I pestered tourism minister Enda Kenny relentlessly, but kept getting the message that EU operational funds were vastly oversubscribed. I hosted a summit in my office with Bord Fáilte officials, county manager Seamus Dooley, and political apparatchiks. I berated the negativity we had encountered, abusing them freely. Eventually we prevailed. Irish public administration is intensely political.

With my secretary Geraldine as a constant source of harassment and Tom Tynan as my political enforcer, each project was dragged over the line. I held press conferences and seminars, whooping up the extravaganza of this Klondike of more than £25 million for my home town. I took repeated political ownership of the visible physical transformation. In April 1997, as a prelude to the general election, we distributed to every household in the county, through An Post, a £200 million summary of political deliverance, covering all state spending.

Brendan Howlin and I worked as a pincer movement of pressure on our respective party colleagues. Wexford was the only constituency with three ministers. Boy, were people going to remember it.

The most fun I had was in building my relationships with the agri-media corps, whose view on my performance, I knew, was critical. A new trend had emerged in the media, whereby specialist correspondents were interviewed on radio and television to give their analysis and verdict on the controversy of the day. Their endorsement or favourable spin, since the media spoke to the media, was worth far more than self-praise. The key people were Joe O'Brien of RTÉ; Mairead McGuinness, editor of the *Farming Independent* and the weekly *Ear to the Ground* programme; Willie Dillon, *Irish Independent*; Seán McConnell, *The Irish Times*; Des Maguire and John Shirley of the *Irish Farmers Journal*; Ella Shanahan and Eric Donald of *Farm News*, RTÉ 1.

My public-relations team comprised Dermot Murphy, his sidekick Noel Molloy, occasionally Neil Ó Mailloir, appointed Fine Gael press officer in 1996, and my programme manager Michael Miley, who had been public relations officer at Teagasc. A grey-haired, chain-smoking man in his fifties, who had been a long-standing Fine Gael supporter and sheep farmer, Michael knew how the system worked and was a master of the dark arts of spin.

My team's job was to brief and spin on my behalf, leak as appropriate, glad-hand, set up events, then ensure that I got all credit for good news and no blame for bad. We held regular press conferences in the department, with open-ended question-and-answer sessions. When we issued free EU beef to hostels and voluntary organisations, we had the agri-media in to eat it, prepared by a top chef. At that time, many editors were asking if a full-time agriculture correspondent was justified. My job was to supply the current correspondents with enough stories to protect their posts.

We had great craic manufacturing news headlines from Brussels with RTÉ's Tommie Gorman, the ultimate professionals' professional, who encouraged me to ham up the punch lines. After I had delivered a sheep compensation package, he told me that the IFA weren't happy.

'If Jesus came down off the cross, the IFA would still not be happy,' I said, knowing it would bounce me up that night's news list.

It was Tommie who told me on one visit to Brussels that, according to his news editor, we were way down the list for the nine o'clock news – always a huge priority for me. This was at the height of the Bishop Comiskey controversy. Brendan Comiskey had departed to America to be treated for alcoholism. Tommie indicated that my positive sheep-sector story for that day was going to be well down the list for the bulletin unless I was to make a comment on Comiskey. I nodded and the camera rolled.

'I don't like to kick a man when he's down,' I said. 'He's done a lot for ecumenism in County Wexford.'

It was perfect: it didn't commit me to a position, but genuinely relayed my sensitivity and sympathy, and allowed my own story in at an earlier stage of the bulletin.

Of course, keeping stories *out* of the news was sometimes important, or at least controlling how they unfolded. One day, the guys in the greyhound section of the department briefed me about an Irish dog, a Derby final winner at Shelbourne Park, that had allegedly failed a subsequent drug test although the results had not been published. Now the owners of the runner-up were suing the greyhound authorities for compensation on the basis that their dog had been the rightful winner. It was a mess that had been covered up. Now that I had been told about it, I knew I would become part of the cover-up. My officials proposed to handle it through legal settlement while continuing the policy of concealment. I was livid. I could see the political risk for me because the story would inevitably get out.

I summoned Michael Miley and Dermot Murphy to my office. We agreed that the only option was to leak the story without my fingerprints on the leak. The following Sunday, it was a lead item on the front page of the *Sunday Independent*. Perfect for me because I couldn't be accused of any cover-up conspiracy. The department officials, especially the secretary general, were irate. I agreed that the leak was awful and that an urgent inquiry would have to be conducted as to its source. Inevitably, the investigation ran into the sand and the culprit was never revealed.

Figures in state agencies became partners in public relations. For example, I travelled with Michael Duffy, chief executive of Bord Bia, to trade fairs and exhibitions all over the world, promoting Irish food and drink, and he made sure that the agri-media corps were wined and dined in the best restaurants. To cover the horseracing media, Dermot ensured that Val Lamb, *Irish Field* editor, and Colm Murray of RTÉ were always given VIP treatment. Matt Dempsey of the *Irish Farmers Journal* was perhaps my closest external confidant and adviser.

What are the perks of being a minister? For starters, the government jet is the last word in luxury, with Army Air Corps crew operating from Baldonnel, supplying the best food, drink and space. I didn't always get to use the jet. It didn't matter, though, whether it was a scheduled flight, the government jet or the clapped-out Beechcraft two-seater in which I once travelled to Portugal: I was constantly terrified, suffering mid-air panic attacks, even though I took more than three hundred flights as a minister, and I still suffer from a disabling fear of flying.

I tried to keep trips abroad as short as possible, including one to New Zealand, where Jim Bolger was prime minister. His predecessors hailed from Craanford, a village near Gorey, and he had been on a state visit to his parents' home a few years previously. I was told of our countries' extensive mutual agricultural links so I decided I must conduct a reciprocal visit in the autumn of 1995. I wasn't prepared to be absent for more than a week, so I went for three days – a jet-lag disaster. Michael Dowling and I flew to Dublin, Heathrow, Los Angeles, Auckland and Wellington non-stop, with a maximum layover of two hours. Despite medicinal alcohol, I was unable to sleep on a flight because of nervousness, so Michael kindly procured sleeping tablets from Denis Brosnan. They didn't work either.

We were driven to the home of the agriculture minister in the mid-afternoon. I explained my exhaustion and need to collapse into bed. I fell into the deepest sleep of my life. The arrangements were that the prime minister and his wife were due for a private dinner at the house that evening. I awoke to bright daylight and no sound.

'Oh, sweet fuck, I've slept it out, into the next day. They probably didn't like to wake me. Jesus, I've missed Bolger. What a diplomatic embarrassment.'

It transpired that I had slept for only an hour, but the guilt, oddly, stayed with me like a hangover.

If rubbing shoulders with the good and great floats your boat, read on ... Dr Michael Smurfit invited me to a private dinner at his K Club. His firm, Woodfab, was having problems procuring enough timber from Coillte at the right price. I always insisted, when embarking on such commercially sensitive conversations, that I would bring along my Sir Humphrey Appleby (Michael Dowling) to avoid subsequent misrepresentation. The encounter didn't yield any progress on the problem, since there was a ferociously competitive tender process for limited timber sales. The most memorable feature of the night was that Smurfit drank different wine (Petrus, I think) from us out of his own decanter. Bad manners, methought, even if what we drank was top-notch vino.

Dr Tony O'Reilly also requested that I visit his mansion, horse stud and pedigree Charolais breeding farm at Castlemartin for a day. The ultimate debonair multi-millionaire cool dude, telling sporting anecdotes and business war stories, O'Reilly was delighted with our department's handling of a food project in Dundalk for Heinz, but railed against Richard Bruton's treatment of the insolvency of the Irish Press Group.

John Magnier is one of the most impressive men I have ever met. Michael Dowling and I visited the Coolmore stud, then had dinner at Magnier's house. It was amazing how he harnessed people's skills, from his father-in-law, the iconic trainers M. V. O'Brien and Aidan O'Brien, to wealthy investors as partners over decades, transformed stallion productivity (in both hemispheres), obtained access to the best mares through foal sharing, and bought back his own stallions' progeny at sales to boost median prices. Magnier is one hell of a smart cookie. He is well matched by his mate J. P. McManus, whose charity banquets and golf fundraisers at Adare were unmissable, although I do not play golf. The post-dinner auctions were incredible. On one occasion a signed U2 poster from the Fly tour was on display in the foyer. Interested bidders could place a note on it, signifying their higher bid. A pal of mine wrote '£500', plus his name. After the meal this lot was wheeled out for open bids. It sold for £150,000.

Stan Cosgrave, top equine vet and boss of Walter Haefner's Moyglare stud in Maynooth, is a Fine Gael stalwart and tremendous fun. He and Walter were forever drawing up twenty-year breeding plans for the stud, even though they were over seventy and eighty years respectively, the definition of cheerful optimism. One day, as minister, I was invited to the Aga Khan's Ballymany stud on the Curragh before the running of the Irish Oaks. Stan beckoned me over and asked me, in a whisper, to lobby His Excellency for cash sponsorship for a new building extension at the RACE facility – a training centre for young jockeys, often from disadvantaged backgrounds – in Newbridge.

'He's a bit tight. We've been trying to tap him for years, but no go,' Stan told me. I duly *plámás*ed the Aga Khan for an hour, suggesting how much my government would appreciate his aid and how the new building could be named after his star filly of that year, Ebadiyla. A few weeks later an ecstatic Stan rang me. 'You won't believe it! We got a cheque for a hundred grand! You're a genius.'

I didn't think I was a genius, but I did think I was doing pretty well. And then the horror began.

9: 'We're rightly bolloxed now'

Three missed calls from Dermot. That could only mean trouble. Dermot Murphy was information officer with the department. He was modest, cute, shrewd, but most of all loyal. I rang him.

'What's the problem?'

'Oh, Minister, not sure, really, could be serious. I've been deluged with media calls … not just the ag lads, but news correspondents too.'

'Okay, shoot.'

'In the House of Commons there was a right rumpus today. In short, their health secretary said that the UK has ten new cases of CJD. But there was much worse news. British scientists now claim a link between BSE and CJD. Widespread panic. Looks like beef could be off the menu. We need a response immediately – the usual stuff, plenty of reassurance, "nothing proven as yet, no need for alarm".'

'For fuck's sake, this could change everything. If punters believe eating a burger or a steak will kill you with a debilitating brain disease, we won't have a market. Consumption will collapse. Okay, get our vets to put out their scientific response and we can assess the story in the morning.'

So began, on 20 March 1996, the worst food crisis ever in either Britain or Ireland. The worst disease up to then – foot-and-mouth

– was not transmissible to humans. A link between CJD and BSE changed everything. Within forty-eight hours British beef had been removed from supermarket shelves, McDonald's had dropped all beef products, consumption had declined by 90 per cent and the key markets of Italy and Germany had folded. Europe gazed, horrified, at TV news bulletins showing – again and again – footage of a cow reeling and collapsing to the ground with bovine spongiform encephalopathy, an incurable brain condition, commonly called mad-cow disease, while hearing, for the first time, that Creutzfeld-Jakob disease (CJD) had similar symptoms in humans, was terminal and linked to the consumption of infected beef.

Ireland's first case of BSE appeared in 1989. Up to 1995 the disease was merely a problem, presenting me with lots of soft media opportunities. Nothing too serious, me sampling any amount of Irish beef, with the greatest of smiling, complacent confidence. Such superficiality would no longer suffice. We now had to ascertain the scientific facts. We knew that the original source of the disease was bovine animals eating meat and bone from dead animals. Carcass brain tissue and spinal-cord material was rendered down to a powder, which in turn was used as a source of protein in animal feedstuffs.

A few years before 1995, meat and bone meal had been banned as a feedstuff for cattle and sheep, in the belief that this would stop the spread of the disease.

'There has never been a case of BSE in Irish steer cattle,' we told the world, and it was partly true, but only *partly* true. Animals were slaughtered at around two years old, when they had not lived long enough for the prion carrying the disease to develop in their brain. Only older cows had been infected. Our policy was to slaughter the entire herd once a case was found. As we removed and destroyed the animals that would have eaten the same feed, we maintained that we were eliminating the disease.

The fallout from the British government's handling of the BSE crisis was catastrophic for Ireland. We were the largest beef exporters in the northern hemisphere – nine out of every ten animals produced was exported live or in carcass form. We were 100 per cent self-sufficient in beef. No other EU member state came close. Ten per cent of Ireland's GNP was generated by the beef industry, with seventy thousand people directly depending on it for their livelihood.

Differentiating between Irish, Northern Irish and British beef was complex when it came to a Sunday joint. The buzz word was 'traceability' – tracing the food from the fork back to the farm of origin. No credible systems were in place to determine this, and there was no instant solution. Household consumption of beef was only a minor part of the market. Historically, Ireland had depended on EU support, through the Common Agricultural Policy, to maintain a pricing structure for commodity production. CAP reform, led in the early 1990s by EU Commissioner Ray MacSharry, meant switching financial assistance from the product to the producer. Subsidies were to be dismantled for exports and replaced by direct income aids to farmers, through various premia. Beef mountains from intervention were to be scrapped. Just when Ireland needed the biggest safety net ever for an unwanted product in a collapsed market, none existed.

Beneath the secretary general in the Department of Agriculture, which then employed four thousand staff, were eight assistant secretaries, each with division responsibility: animal health, crops, rural development, EU affairs, forestry, finance and personnel. John Malone was the assistant secretary in charge of all livestock matters, including responsibility for animal breeding, meat processing, marketing and prices.

The BSE crisis continued to worsen at even greater speed. The EU Standing Veterinary Committee banned UK beef products.

...yself, aged one (bottom), ...th my parents John and ...ary along with my siblings ...hristine, baby Valentine and ...y oldest brother John, in ...61.

...e family farm at Blackstoops, ...st outside Enniscorthy, bought ... my great-grandfather John F. ...tes in 1890.

Captain of the hockey team (middle, centre), at Aravon primary school, 1973.

First time on the stump.
On the campaign trail
with Garret FitzGerald in
1981, alongside running
mates Michael d'Arcy and
Louise Hennessy.

Left, a youthful Avril
Doyle (back), who became
a running mate and
constituency colleague.

At 21, I was the youngest deputy when I entered Dáil Eireann in 1981. Here I am on my first day, with my mother Mary and Dean Griffin at St Patrick's Cathedral, Dublin.

The John Bruton-led rainbow coalition of 1994, pictured at the Áras.

The day itself was a bit of a disaster, but happily the marriage survived! Myself and Deirdre on our wedding day, 1985.

And then we were six. Myself, Deirdre and our family of four, in 1994.

One of my proudest achievements as Minister for Agriculture was to launch the Charter of Rights for Farmers in 1995. Pictured here at the launch with Taoiseach John Bruton, alongside IFA President John Donnelly (left), and ICMSA President Tom O'Dwyer (right).

'Who's in charge here?' I was Minister for Agriculture when the BSE crisis struck in 1996, decimating the Irish beef industry. The months of strain would eventually take a serious toll on my own mental and physical health. Tensions reached an all-time high in Killarney where the EU Agriculture Council of Ministers had convened, and angry members of the IFA stormed a police cordon to gain entry to the hotel.

Meeting Pope John Paul II at a UN food conference in Rome in 1995.

Out with the begging bowl again. Myself and
secretary general Michael Dowling doing busines
in Brussels with EU Agriculture Commissioner
Franz Fischler (left), 1996.

With Enda, former office
mate in the '80s and cabinet
colleague in the '90s.

In races pose. I was ten when I placed my first bet, and Lester Piggott was riding the favourite. So began my odyssey of over forty years as a gambler.

The demise of Celtic Bookmakers in 2011 signified a dark time in my life, when I lost everything. A year in Swansea gave me a lot of time to think. And drink. But life goes on . . .

You never truly lose everything though . . . and you come to know what really counts. With my wonderful family, l/r: Sarah, myself, Ciara, Deirdre, Andrew and John.

With my Newstalk Breakfast co-presenter Chris Donoghue. Deep down, we love each other.

Key third-country markets – Egypt, Saudi Arabia, Iran, Libya – closed to Irish exports. Consumer concern led to other meat – poultry, pork and lamb – replacing beef. Confusion reigned about eradicating the disease. Price/income prospects for farmers and processors looked perilous. Oh, and Ireland was just about to take charge of the EU presidency of the Agriculture Council of Ministers from July to December 1996.

John Malone, who had the pivotal departmental job of looking after all the country's livestock sectors, was ashen at our first crisis meeting in the Montrose Hotel, where I was being briefed before appearing on RTÉ's *This Week*. Not only was he ashen, but he had a shaving gash on his left cheek. As a former departmental information officer, he knew we must have a coherent message to convey that we were on top of the crisis. No one in the department had ever experienced anything like the enormity of this disaster.

Since the first priority was to eliminate the disease, we decided that the spinal cord and the spleen of all bovine animals should be removed from the food chain and destroyed. They had been used to make burgers, gelatine and tallow products. This immediately brought me into direct combat with two critical interests: meat factories and the cabinet. I had already had a major clash with Larry Goodman, Ireland's biggest beef baron. The fallout from the Beef Tribunal was that the Department of Agriculture took the political hit for nefarious fraud and illegal malpractice by beef processors in blatant abuses of the EU intervention system (which created a floor price through the acquisition and storage of meat stock). Ireland now faced, on my watch, huge EU fines because of criminal fraud.

In the Dáil in 1996, under questioning from Des O'Malley about the department's regulatory failings, I had stated that I 'would shed no tears if Larry Goodman was no longer in the beef industry'. At every opportunity, meat factories seemed to operate like a cartel in simultaneously reducing prices with every piece of bad news about EU subsidies or markets closing. What was bad for farmers could be very good for meat-factory profits. I distrusted their operators, many of whom had started as cattle jobbers.

They mutinied in the face of my ban, which meant meat factories would have to bear the cost of removing and destroying specified risk material (SRM). They shut down all their facilities – effectively paralysing the industry. They blamed me for the stand-off and demanded state compensation to reopen. On Easter Tuesday we convened a summit in the department of all the beef processors. Panic was setting in among farmers with cattle ready to slaughter. On the fifth floor of Agriculture House, as the meeting opened, processors made clear their view that they had me over a barrel. They demanded a state subsidy to compensate them, knowing that I couldn't allow the stand-off to continue indefinitely.

We negotiated a formula whereby the taxpayer would compensate for the loss of SRM by paying a storage subsidy on the waste material until it was decided what to do with it. This deal was subject to government approval. I had to bring to cabinet a memorandum setting out the scheme and its costs. This was to become a familiar ritual in the months ahead because I had to go with a begging bowl to government colleagues in a tight fiscal situation. Dick Spring and Proinsias De Rossa, the other party leaders in the rainbow government, were not dependent on farmers' votes, so extra agriculture expenditure was a low political priority for them.

Cabinet procedure was surprisingly regimented, almost legalistic. Each time you sought new expenditure, you had to go right back to a square-one dialogue with the Department of Finance. A file would then be prepared for the government secretary's office and the Taoiseach's office to get it onto the cabinet agenda. A process of observations from other departments, called 'obs', ensued. Each chair around the cabinet table is rigidly retained by a specific person and I sat beside the attorney general, Dermot Gleeson. Each Monday the cabinet agenda would be circulated, with bulky files on each item. A minister's job is to represent his or her department at the cabinet table. Debate was chaired by the Taoiseach, who sat opposite the Tánaiste and minister for finance. The format provides the basis for turf wars. Cabinet members change from politicians to advocates for the brief provided by their department's mandarins.

Before the weekly cabinet meeting, each of the three party leaders met to clear the agenda. This short-circuited debate. Because the most senior civil servant, the government secretary, sat beside the Taoiseach, kept the minutes and advised him on procedural issues, there was little informal political discussion – as there would be at a front-bench meeting. My memories of the cabinet table were of stern, dour sessions, truncated debate and tension generated by rigid formality.

Thankfully, each memorandum and *aide-mémoire* on new controls, compensation packages for farmers and diplomatic initiatives were all approved. But any cabinet progress in this crisis had to be set against what Tom Tynan, one of the best men I had working for me, had said to me before BSE moved into disaster mode.

'Ivan, you've got to realise your popularity as agriculture minister is directly dependent on the price of cattle in Tuam mart this week. Forget all that fancy PR and make sure you deliver real results in the pocket. That's the only bottom line that matters.'

Back in the days when I was Fine Gael opposition spokesman on agriculture, I had met Tynan, a Kilkenny man, who was then the dairy sector executive within the IFA. When I became a minister, I chose him as my special adviser because he knew farm politics inside out, and was able to develop relationships with key players and serve as my eyes and ears. A strong recommendation of my closest political friend, Phil Hogan, Tom was invaluable in good times and bad.

In the context of BSE, my ratings were due for a sharp descent, possibly free-fall. Cattle prices were set to drop by 16 per cent in 1996, to little more than eighty pence per pound. The previous November, export refunds had been cut by 25 per cent, as agreed at the GATT negotiations in 1992. These payments amounted to more than £700 per animal to third countries to import excess EU beef. No Irish beef had gone into intervention in 1995, because intervention had effectively ended. Now Libya banned the importation of live Irish cattle, followed by Iran and Saudi Arabia. We were up the creek without a paddle.

And so began months of intense lobbying of my fellow agriculture ministers in the EU Council and Franz Fischler, the EU agriculture commissioner. We had to instil an understanding of Ireland's unique dependence on beef exports at political, diplomatic and administrative levels. We had 1.7 million animals due for slaughter and sale each year. My foreign travel was incessant: regular trips to liaise with the supportive German minister, Jochen Borchert (a Christian Democratic Union colleague in the European People's Party), streetwise French minister Philippe Vasseur, the UK's Douglas Hogg and Spain's savvy Luis Atienza. These guys were the big hitters around the EU Council table since they each had ten votes in determining a qualified majority while Ireland had only three. Along with my departmental honchos, I charmed and cajoled the bejesus out of them.

The scale of Ireland's beef industry meant that mass exports of live animals and carcasses to non-EU states was of pivotal importance, so my trips to Libya, Russia and Egypt were interspersed with their veterinary delegations and ambassadors visiting Ireland to assess our control and eradication plans. Such was our dire necessity to sell beef, we could not be picky or choosy about government regimes with whom we had to deal. Colonel Gaddafi's administration was the *bête noire* of the Western world. A no-fly zone was in place over

Tripoli, so I had to fly in through Tunisia to meet the minister responsible for live cattle imports, an army general who arrived in his green military uniform, beret and dark glasses. At the start of the meeting, he parked his large belly and revolver on a small table in front of us.

As with similar revolutionary regimes, such as Iran, we would open proceedings by referring to 'our shared heritage', meaning as countries who had gained their own independence and fought against imperialism. On corporate investment trips to the United States, I was equally effusive about our commonality through emigration. When in Rome, do as the Romans do.

All these diplomatic initiatives, however, were not enough to meet Tom Tynan's criteria for sustaining credibility. The farm organisations, particularly the IFA, went on the warpath. In the previous eighteen months as minister for agriculture, I had created a stick to beat myself with by becoming the most energetic champion of farmers at the cabinet table and in Brussels. I had trumpeted improvements in Ireland's tax code, a special compensation package for sheep farmers and a charter of rights for farmers in their dealings with the department. Farm incomes had reached the highest level ever. I hadn't been behind the door in claiming credit for every piece of good news. Now expectations were raised that I could resolve the BSE crisis and protect the threatened income of Ireland's beef farmers.

I had no control over the price paid to beef processors at the factory gate. By late April 1995, I had secured from the EU Commission a full reversal in the 25 per cent reduction in export refunds of the previous November. This was worth seven pence per pound. Emergency intervention was reopened, with successful Irish tenders accepted. A floor price had been created to prevent Armageddon.

Between Easter and the end of June, my primary focus was to secure an income compensation package and it came through at a Council of Ministers meeting: £86 million for Ireland in a national envelope of cash with an unprecedented element to deal with special cases of animals that did not go through meat factories, such as live exports and heifers sold to local butchers. Ireland got proportionately more than any other EU state. But was it enough? Hell, no. It only whetted the appetite of farm leaders to extract additional compensation when Ireland took over the EU presidency. All summer an intensive lobbying campaign by the IFA's army of storm troopers put me under pressure to achieve more. John Bruton's brainwave was that I would do a national tour of Fine Gael public meetings in early September to highlight our strategy in town-hall-style format, with face-to-face encounters with farmers. So I did battle in Tullamore, Cootehill, Ballinasloe and Charleville. Thousands attended, bombarding me for hours with questions on all aspects of the beef sector. The autumn is always the most difficult and precarious period of the year for cattle prices because a glut of animals is ready for slaughter at the end of the grazing season. Trouble was looming. It arrived the day my private secretary, Corkman Peter Hanrahan, the soul of discretion and loyalty, arrived into my office.

'Minister, Seamus Healy needs to chat with you. He's been on to me a number of times. He's here now.'

Seamus Healy was assistant secretary with responsibility for animal health and veterinary issues. He dealt with all the administrative implementation of recommendations from scientists.

'Okay, I'm busy, but I can have a quick word if it's that urgent.'

I liked Healy. We shared an interest in cricket. He wore thick glasses, chain-smoked and had aged visibly over the BSE months. He came in, sat down, started to talk, and within twenty minutes I was apoplectic. I could not believe what I was hearing. The entire edifice of my public pronouncements on the safety of Irish meat was to be undermined.

'We have something of a problem,' he began. 'You will recall our regular briefings at the end of each month as we release the latest confirmed cases of BSE, their geographical county of origin and arrangements for depopulation of that herd and cohort animals. Over recent weeks, it emerged that some of the positive cases are cows aged less than four years. The essential factor here is that they were born after the ban on feeding meat and bone meal to ruminants. At first we were puzzled about the basis of this. Was there another means of transmission of BSE? It seems on further epidemiological analysis that these animals may have eaten meat and bone meal.'

I was shocked. 'I don't understand. How can this be? I know what happened with angel dust [illegal growth promoters] has been unbelievable, in terms of flagrant abuses by a few individual rogue farmers, jeopardising an entire industry. But given what was happening in Britain, surely farmers didn't disregard the ban. Anyway, the department must have had an inspectorate in animal provender facilities to ensure the regulations were implemented.'

'Well, it seems there may not have been sufficient dedicated staff for this purpose. The vast majority of animal-feed manufacturers rigorously segregate feed rations for ruminants from those for pigs and poultry. It may have been that on certain farms where there were mixed enterprises – having cattle, pigs and poultry – they let the odd bag of meat and bone meal get mixed up in the feedstuffs for different species . . .'

'Hold on a second. Are you seriously fucking telling me that all I said at home and across the world about Irish beef being safe is a load of bullshit? That we don't know for how long our animals have actually stopped eating meat and bone meal? That BSE may not yet be near to eradication? There's a huge credibility issue here and I'm the one who is going to carry the can for this fuck-up. This is unbelievable, unacceptable and I want to know what the hell you're going to do about it.'

'This was before my time in this job,' he quietly pointed out. 'I came to you as soon as I knew of the problem. We're going to propose to you revised regulations, which will ban meat and bone meal entirely – to all species. In other words, this product will no longer be available. All meat and bone meal will be exported or incinerated as a waste product. We should have the regulations by way of statutory instrument prepared shortly for your signature. I suggest we just get on with the further ban without too much fanfare. We suspect that only a small number of isolated feed plants or farms may be involved. We'll tighten inspection controls on the ground. We should not overreact. Media coverage could be damning.'

We did exactly that: kept the head down, introduced the additional ban and hoped that the number of cases of BSE had peaked. At least I knew that now the control systems through the ban on Specified Risk Material and the elimination of meat and bone meal from the food chain would eradicate BSE in Ireland. Two later additional measures were restrictions on knackeries (processing fallen animals used to feed local dogs) and a uniform implementation of the regulation of smaller butchers' abattoirs by the department, instead of by local authorities. In the fullness of time, all this eliminated the disease.

One of the highlights and significant organisational events of an EU presidency is the hosting of the informal council. Previously it was just a perk for the agriculture and the Economic and Financial Affairs Council (ECOFIN – finance ministers) that was approved, since it was a costly shindig. Michael Dowling prepared a detailed file in advance, which surprisingly concluded that the only place it could be held was in his own native Killarney. Apparently Wexford didn't have what was required.

I had previously attended informal councils in France, Spain and Italy. They had involved a jamboree of boring banquets, photogenic farm visits, involving local artisan food produce, endless drinking and a ritual council meeting on an esoteric topic.

The three-day event took place at the Europa Hotel, on large private grounds outside Killarney. The IFA took the opportunity to hold a demonstration on the final day, Tuesday, when the council met to discuss, among other things, my request for an extra £30 million of top-up payments for Irish farmers. We got down to business around a large rectangular table in the amply sized conservatory of the hotel, with glass windows looking out on the Lakes of Killarney. I was impatient to get the compensation resolution agreed, because Commissioner Franz Fischler, Minister of State Jimmy Deenihan and I were due to host a press conference immediately afterwards. The schedule was tight because we were due to visit the Listowel racing festival in the afternoon.

The debate among ministers dragged on endlessly. I particularly recall the Swedish and Spanish ministers droning on with contributions that I thought were irrelevant to our compensation issue. Then, unusually, Dermot Murphy appeared in the meeting room and handed me a note. 'Security alert,' it read. 'IFA troops have broken through Garda cordon at perimeter and are about to storm the hotel. Need to wrap up meeting ASAP. Media circus.'

I handed the note to Michael Dowling. He dispatched one of our delegates to investigate further. The delegate returned to whisper that matters were deteriorating; the gardaí had lost control of the situation, which was becoming increasingly ugly, volatile and unpredictable. I asked Dermot to do something dramatic. He didn't disappoint me. An electronic button was pressed. Steel shutters loudly rolled down around all the glass walls. Then a garda in full riot gear stepped inside the meeting room, for all to see. I interjected in the debate and explained that there was a 'security crisis' and we had to end the meeting immediately. I asked that the agenda items be agreed. This was done with alacrity and alarm.

We proceeded to hold a press conference, with all the ministers photographed munching Irish burgers in the presence of representatives of the Irish Creamery Milk Suppliers' Association, the other major farm organisation. At this stage I had a better assessment of the problems outside the front of the hotel. It seemed it had been a wet day and many of the protesters had sought shelter in the adjoining pub. Some were the worse for wear. The gardaí were unprepared for their disgruntlement at being out of shouting distance of the council meeting, and the protesters simply ran through lines of despairing gardaí to surround the hotel foyer. They were determined not to allow the ministers and the commissioner to depart without confronting them.

Furious at the way the event had been hijacked, I explained that we had secured agreement to further compensate farmers. I appealed to them, through a megaphone, at the request of the gardaí, to allow our visitors to go to their various destinations. 'Women and children are afraid and upset inside the hotel,' I added. This was picked up by the TV news and regarded as an over-dramatisation of the situation. In fact, the wife of Douglas Hogg was visibly upset, fearing that the demonstration would turn into an anti-British riot.

Eventually the protesters dispersed. Fischler and others scarpered by helicopter. The day's events allowed me to remind subsequent EU Council meetings of the type of pressures, even potentially violent abuse, that I was under because of our unique dependence on our beef sector. It was never fully appreciated by the IFA or by the demonstrating farmers that we had used an informal council to extract extra cash for farmers, running counter to normal procedure.

Four weeks later, Michael Dowling came to my office. 'Minister, we need to discuss the current visit by the Russian delegation of vets and officials. They are not entirely happy. As you know, they are importing a hundred thousand tonnes of our beef. Given that there is a live export animal ban everywhere except Egypt, which may not last, it is critical that they continue this trade.'

'I thought this was under control. I'm due to meet them for dinner this evening. I'm happy to do whatever. I've already been to Russia this year. What's the problem?'

'They've been reviewing the geographical and regional breakdown of BSE cases and are wondering if we could isolate beef from those areas with the higher incidence. They have highlighted the counties of Cork, Tipperary and Monaghan. It's imperative that we avoid a total ban. Maybe we could show some flexibility by not including beef from those counties. They are seeking a new veterinary protocol to sign, which would ensure future exports. How would you feel about that?'

'Michael, for the love of Jesus, will you give me a break? This is nonsensical. It is impractical to segregate carcasses or cuts of meat after the animal is killed and the ear tag removed. Either way, with so many animal movements occurring during the animal's lifetime, this is not operationally feasible. I have never heard anything so ridiculous. It makes no sense at all.'

'Minister, I agree, but what choice do we have? If this is what they want, albeit that it has no scientific basis, we may have to agree in order to sustain the business, maintain cattle prices and not be dependent on intervention. I've spoken to the beef guys quietly and they think they can possibly manage to implement a version of the Russian requirement. Nothing has been agreed as yet. Perhaps you should think about it over the next few days.'

When we had concluded the meeting, I called in Michael Miley and Tom Tynan.

'We're rightly bolloxed now,' was Tom's immediate reaction. 'For Chrissake, people have never forgiven Michael Collins for his six-county partition of Ireland. You're proposing to repartition the twenty-six counties. How do you think the Fine Gael TDs in those counties are going to react? They'll accuse you of protecting Wexford, your own constituency, which also has a high incidence rate.'

We agreed to try playing hardball with the Russians. The choice for me was between the totally dire or the utterly dreadful. The delegation was leaving Dublin airport in a few days. They refused to speak to me, regarding it as political interference because they were scientists. We agreed to the revised protocol, excluding the three named counties, and faced into the inevitable mayhem. Opposition politicians and farm leaders were at one in condemning my handling of the situation – caving in to ridiculous demands. An emergency debate was sought in the Dáil and the Senate. Local politicians and media in the affected three counties took grave offence at my arbitrary action. The protocol was without precedent.

I clung to the defence that without Russia's importation of 100,000 tonnes of beef the entire sector would collapse. In early 1997, the Russians added a further five counties (Cavan, Meath, Wexford, Donegal and Limerick) to the ban. There was no furore then, because people realised that the restriction had little practical impact. Pragmatism and expediency were justified in the end, but the politicisation of the row would come back to haunt me. In my absence and without my knowledge, my PR machine and political proxies exaggerated my personal role in the alleged arm-wrestle with the Russians at Dublin airport, claiming that I was personally present in face-to-face talks, which was untrue and led to quips about my powers of bilocation.

This side show was to become entirely eclipsed by one of the most profound personal events in my life, which happened at 2.10 p.m. on 23 October 1996. That Wednesday was my thirty-seventh birthday. I had attended the usual departmental and Dáil business. For some weeks I had been feeling strangely unwell. My daily and weekly work routine was chaotic: managing all aspects of the BSE crisis; regular departmental work; different constituency visits on most Fridays, with umpteen engagements; unprecedented amounts of constituency work every weekend, with hundreds of individual problems; endless air travel and unceasing flak. I wasn't eating properly, drinking a gallon of coffee every morning in lieu of breakfast, followed by sandwiches at my desk. I stayed in the Mount Herbert Hotel (now the Sandymount Hotel), instead of having my own apartment. I would eat a late-night room-service meal. After a bottle of wine I would fall asleep, but wake in the middle of the night and fail to get back to sleep. I was first into the department, even before the cleaners and porters. All my life I had successfully solved problems by applying energy, analysis and focus to them. I was totally up for the challenges of being a cabinet minister and was determined to make a success of it, but something outside my control was happening. In the front seat as a passenger in the ministerial Mercedes, I would feel the road was coming up to hit me in the face. I would get headaches right on the top of my head, almost in my scalp, that were unlike any normal headache, even a migraine. I dismissed my symptoms as tiredness and stress, which would pass, telling no one other than Deirdre.

That Wednesday, as usual, I worked through lunchtime in my office. I looked out of the window from the fifth floor of Agriculture House. The autumn leaves were dropping off the trees onto the square below. The radio was beside that window. The room was palatial – a plush carpet, beautiful paintings, ornate timber panelling, with a wonderful desk. The big black security phone was at the side, to be used only for calls from the Taoiseach.

I was listening to *Liveline* on RTÉ Radio One. Marian Finucane was the presenter and she was interviewing John Donnelly, the IFA president, who appealed to his entire membership to attend a national rally to protest about my and the government's handling of the BSE crisis. I switched the programme off, sick of listening to the same shite. I returned to my desk and lifted my gold-plated Cross ballpoint to resume work.

Only to find that I couldn't. I couldn't think, I couldn't function, I couldn't write. I tried to pull myself together and get on with my duties. I couldn't. I was scared. I took a few deep breaths, which I often found worked if I had a mental blank in a radio or television interview. In this case, it didn't. I was simply paralysed. When Peter Hanrahan knocked on the door and entered, I managed to put down the pen and explained that I was really ill. He could not have been more sympathetic. Peter had constantly chided me for working crazy hours and not pacing myself. He arranged for my driver to collect me and bring me to the hotel to rest. Later I spoke with Deirdre at home, explaining how terrible I felt – no energy, no ability to act. The Duracell bunny had stopped.

Phone conversations ensued with our family doctor Michael O'Doherty, who recommended that I see a GP he knew in south Dublin. I attended Dr Donal McCafferty, who concluded that I was suffering from nervous exhaustion. My own terror was that I would join the ranks of close relatives who had suffered bouts of severe mental illness. Dr McCafferty reassured me that this was unlikely, given my age and circumstances. He prescribed antidepressants and complete rest for a few days at home. All appointments were cancelled, even my clinics. I lost a stone in weight over the next week.

But ministers cannot get sick, especially those in the eye of a very public domestic and international storm. The next week I was due to chair a pivotal EU Council meeting in London to reform the imbalance in the beef sector. The Commission and the presidency had jointly formulated proposals for an extensive cull of calves and young animals to reduce the post-BSE structural beef surplus. It was called the 'Herod' scheme. New measures for EU-approved beef assurance schemes, with full traceability, and national quota reductions/reform were up for approval. This was a crucial meeting. My absence was not possible.

On Sunday I met Peter at Dublin airport. On that one and

only occasion, I was late and we missed the flight. We had to get another flight to London and that night I was unable to sleep. I could see that Peter was worried about my health. The two-day meeting was attended by one of the largest ever media scrums from every member state. At one session I could feel the room spinning from my top table seat. I had to concentrate hard just to hear and understand what was being said around me.

Peter and I and other officials were staying in a hotel two hundred metres from the official venue. We had to cross a viaduct that arched above a busy four-lane motorway. Early one morning, I walked to the meeting alone, ahead of the others. I hesitated. I stopped and looked over the wall at the juggernauts thundering below, and such was my despair that I gave serious consideration to jumping. But I was too cowardly. I wanted to escape and get some respite but lacked the courage to take it through suicide. Somehow I completed the session, which was a success, achieving landmark EU BSE controls and the prospect of market stability in the medium term.

I maintained all my public, ministerial and EU commitments until the end of December. In November I met Northern Ireland's three MEPs in Belfast at their request. They wanted their beef industry to escape the UK ban and be classified with that of the Republic. The Rev. Ian Paisley interrupted the start of the discussion.

'I refuse to sit down with you as a minister in the South. I won't be seen to be associating with you.'

I was about to tell him where to stick his posturing when I realised he wasn't finished.

'But I will meet with you as an EU president.'

Such semantics paid off, because the following May the Northern Ireland ban was lifted while it wasn't until August 1999 that Britain's nightmare ended. Despite the continuing closure of certain markets, the worst had passed. Beef prices were maintained at floor level above eighty pence per pound. My outward façade concealed my inner desperate anxiety and ill health. At one point I felt I could not continue. I asked to meet the Taoiseach privately. I explained my sickness and offered my resignation. John Bruton was sensitive and compassionate, outlining a health problem he had had and how he had overcome it. He dismissed any thought of me quitting and offered his full support to lighten my load. I'll never forget his warmth and genuine consideration.

Around the second week of January, I had to return to Dr Donal, who prescribed a stronger antidepressant called Seroxat. 'Don't worry, we're only starting on the possible cocktails of medication,' he told me. 'You're on the mild stuff so far. I'll get you through this.' I used to pick up the tablets from a pharmacy in Donnybrook rather than Wexford, to avoid any gossip.

My attitude to the BSE crisis did not publicly alter. However, privately, I was determined not to let anxiety over the crisis get to me ever again.

Only in retrospect can I see the wood for the trees. Total farmer income compensation amounted to £133 million. The EU beef-sector reforms removed one million calves (only 19,000 in Ireland), restoring market balance. Meat-labelling schemes achieved traceability and ensured future food safety. The years 1995 and 1996 have been unsurpassed to date for record total farm incomes. And Fine Gael even gained eight Dáil seats in rural constituencies in the June 1997 general election.

Back then I was under siege but adamant that I wanted to get off medication, so I asked Dr Donal about alternatives. He referred me to a psychologist named Peter Colquhoun, who was to change my outlook on life. And my perspective on what I had always seen as a happy childhood. In my initial dialogue with Peter, I explained what a success I had been in Aravon: in my final year I was head boy and captain of the hockey team. I had done well in my studies and was well prepared to go on to St Columba's.

Peter began to peel back the layers of my self-protection, forcing me to come to terms with a much less happy childhood than I had chosen to remember. It was painful and rigorous. I was convinced that he had reached everything, but at the end of my period of therapy, he advised that one or two incidents I had not dealt with were likely to surface out of the blue. While this might be upsetting, it would be like a boil bursting in my head, giving me permanent release. That was precisely what happened.

It occurred during the week I was in England filming with the Mint Productions crew for the programme *Who Do You Think You Are?* We were travelling by train from Oxford, where I'd visited the University Museum, to Cornwall, with me looking out of the window at the scenery. Unbidden, my mind went back to Aravon, and myself as an eleven-year-old boy, half naked in front of Mr Mansfield, the headmaster who dealt with sex education. I could remember viscerally just how mystified and troubled I was and how abusive the situation had been.

I went back to tell Peter about this recovered memory, realising that the vulnerable, scared child I had been had come back to bite me emotionally in adulthood. Peter concluded that this abuse and other childhood miseries had turned me into an utterly driven person, with addictive (even compulsive) tendencies. I had always had a low boredom threshold, needing life to be all about action and distraction.

Peter's insightful advice helped me to learn to detect when things were about to spiral out of control, and how to take a breather at those points and calm down. Thanks to him, I realised that preoccupying myself with work and play was a way of keeping on the run from pain. But you can never outrun unacknowledged past hurt.

10: Losing the Faith

The summer of 1997 allowed me to catch up with normal life. By now Deirdre and I had four wonderful kids, aged between nine and four, Andrew, Ciara, Sarah and John, all going to the local primary school in Enniscorthy. It was the best of times, beyond bottles and nappies, to enjoy them growing up together. Deirdre and I started to take proper holidays with them in Britain and the west of Ireland. Meanwhile, I was starting to benefit from psychotherapy, which gave me a greater awareness of how driven I had become in my addiction to work.

John Bruton and I met to chat about life in the 28th Dáil, review our time in government, plan a future party strategy and discuss the imminent appointments to the new opposition front bench. The venue was a quiet restaurant in Baggot Street, behind Government Buildings. It was no routine chat. I was determined to convey my loyalty to him as leader and, at the same time, the waning of my political passion. I was falling out of love with politics.

'John, I need you to know that I'm a changed man. There was a time when politics was my all-consuming passion. Over the past year, I've been reflecting on what I want out of life. I didn't get the ego or power trip out of being a minister others do. Aspects of the stress with BSE were no fun. There was a time I harboured ambitions to be party leader, but that's now firmly off my agenda. I think it's a shit job and ministerial life is grossly overrated. Whatever happens in the coming years, under no circumstances will I be seeking your job. The extent of my commitment to politics is to work to re-elect the rainbow government and you as Taoiseach. I want to repay you for having faith in me by appointing me minister. But that's it.'

Bruton wanted to switch me out of agriculture to another economic ministry and make me overall director of party policy. I met separately with Mark FitzGerald, Garret's son, telling him of my end-game intentions, and to encourage him to stand for the Dáil and eventually seek the leadership. I took on the role of spokesperson for public enterprise, opposite Mary O'Rourke, who to me was much more suited, as a former teacher, to education, welfare or health than commerce.

Writer Roddy Doyle, speaking once about his fourteen years of teaching at Greendale Community School in Kilbarrack, in north Dublin, said that for the first nine years he loved it. The next three years, he endured it, as an obligation, a job and a salary. The last two years he hated it. My own experience as a Dáil deputy matched that pretty exactly. From 1981 to 1997 was terrific; during the years leading up to the local elections in June 1999 I performed as a professional politician, discharging my duties routinely and assiduously. It was a paid job, no longer a vocation.

In the constituency, I was enjoying enhanced pre-eminence within Fine Gael. Michael D'Arcy was in his mid-sixties, facing the autumn of his political career. Avril Doyle was switching her attention towards the looming European elections as a candidate in the Leinster constituency. The intensity of competition for the three of us over seven elections was abating. The flip-side was that the burden of party chores, such as fundraising (a Fine Gael constituency executive needed £30,000 to pay for a general election, separate from the costs to a candidate on the election trail) and attending branch, district or constituency executive meetings, fell increasingly on my shoulders.

I had good fun harassing Mary O'Rourke and there were plenty of scraps on TV debates and in the Dáil. I obtained a leaked copy of a consultant's report into rail safety and berated her about the lack of track and signalling investment, the serious consequent risks to passengers. When the chairman of CIÉ resigned, O'Rourke maintained that she had first heard of it on morning radio while sitting in the bath. I accused her of 'dropping the towel' in her subsequent remarks about him. I shared the concerns of private operators, like Ryanair's Michael O'Leary, who zoned in on her lack of business acumen and her pandering to the unions.

I derided a proposed mega-tunnel for an underground Luas line, calling it a 'black hole' that could cost more than £400 million to build. The scheme was eventually shelved. I poured scorn on the Bord Telecom/Eircom public share flotation, which burned the fingers of ordinary investors. With the help of Seamus Mulconry, I launched policy documents on bus competition deregulation, integrated public-transport initiatives, the Dublin Transport Authority, and a major drive to provide comprehensive e-government across all departments and services.

Meanwhile, Gaybo retired, Ruairi Quinn replaced Dick Spring as Labour Party leader, TV3 was set up, the Nice referendum defeated, blue flu was endemic, asylum-seekers flooded into the country, Bishop Comiskey resigned, the full horrors of clerical abuse were revealed and Mary McAleese became president. Bertie Ahern was planning to be the first outgoing Taoiseach to be re-elected since 1969. Opinion polls reflected his increased credibility, reputation and authority. Ahern's success with Tony Blair in procuring the Belfast Agreement and ratification by plebiscite, North and South, was truly historic. The 1997 to 2002 Fianna Fáil/Progressive Democrat government did well. Rocketing investor confidence, a reduction in unemployment, the prospect of joining the single euro currency and rapid economic growth led to its increased popularity. Ahern's masterly management of consensus with the social partners rendered the Dáil irrelevant to national decision-making. The opposition was powerless and neutered because the key decisions on budgetary matters were negotiated in a trade-off between pay moderation and enhanced net pay through tax reductions. Partnership ran through most facets of public policy.

Nineteen ninety-eight was an unforgettable year in County Wexford as it hosted the events to celebrate the bicentenary of the 1798 Rebellion. The Fleadh Cheoil, National Ploughing Championships and the Tour de France went well. Beyond the special commemorations of Vinegar Hill Day, the establishment of the Wexford Senate and the battle of Oulart, virtually every parish decided to have its own ceremony. Costumed pikemen in hobnailed boots marched up and down at crossroads; and the removal of blankets from inscribed rocks led to endless speeches by local historians about 'equality, fraternity and liberty'. This became a Sunday ritual. Sunday: the only day of the week when I used to be sure of spending time with my family. The litany was unending: Ferns, Tintern, Bree, Carrick-on-Bannow, Bunclody, Cranford, Killanne, Horetown ... No one wanted to be left out. I became black sick of it, and resentful that public life meant there was no personal control of my diary.

The local and European elections in June were the political highlight of the next year. Avril Doyle duly topped the poll in Leinster with 67,881 votes; we all enthusiastically supported her one-way ticket out of Wexford politics, paving the way for my easier future re-election. I was obliged to stand again for the county council and urban district council elections and topped the poll respectively with 2,235 and 622 votes. The Enniscorthy district Fine Gael tally of 4,915 surpassed Fianna Fáil's 3,398, a turnaround from the 1980s, but we still lost a seat on the town body.

A friend of mine, Pete Lennon, a former local bookmaker, had time on his hands and each day we would go around the outskirts of

Enniscorthy in a slow house canvass, most unlike the hectic pace of a general election. I confined myself to the town territory. Nationally, Fine Gael got 28 per cent of the vote, with seven extra councillors. It was a reasonable performance in the context of prevailing economic prosperity. I was now back on the treadmill of monthly council meetings, with associated thorny issues of choosing locations for a proposed incinerator and Traveller halting sites.

In the run-up to my fortieth birthday in October 1999, I started to take stock of my life. My kids were about to enrol as boarding pupils at Newtown School in Waterford. This was going to set me back in gross earnings around £10,000 per child per year for the next umpteen years. My TD's salary was fine, but there was no prospect of extra cash. Deirdre was a full-time mum. Could I make more money in business than in politics? My own company, Celtic Bookmakers, which I had started as not much more than a hobby in late 1987 to indulge my passion for gambling, was starting to take off. I checked my TD pension situation and was surprised to find that, once I had served twenty years (June 2011), I would be at the maximum point on the scale, 50 per cent of salary. If I stayed as a TD any longer, I would not get any extra money.

Life in opposition was soul-destroying and the chances were that Fine Gael would be there for several more years, owing to the growing mainstream support for Bertie Ahern. The endless routine of constituency work, party meetings, fundraising, clinics and funerals had started to get me down. Despite the warmth of personal contact, I found the repetitive work increasingly futile: all parish pump, no novelty.

It was actually getting worse. A crystallising moment for me occurred at the annual two-day gathering in September of the parliamentary party in Athlone. Jim Miley, the Fine Gael general secretary, and his sidekick, Terry Murphy, hosted an organisational session on TDs' re-election. They were telling us to work on two new personal initiatives on the ground in constituencies: first, we should assemble databases of voter groups (such as teachers, nurses and publicans) for regular mail shots; second, we were advised to spend up to one day per week knocking on doors in different parts of the constituency, leaving a calling card with contact details and times of clinics. For me this was the ultimate prostitution of life as a community and social worker. I wasn't a political Jehovah's Witness. It may have been sound advice, but I wasn't prepared to do it.

At a deeper level, I reflected on my twenty years as a public representative. Through my early years, I knew exactly what I believed in: profitable private enterprise in an Ireland Inc. context, believing Irish people could not live by consuming what we produced. I believed in incentivising hard work and taking risks. I believed in efficiency in public services, symbolised by the implementation of one-person buses (eliminating bus conductors, despite strikes and resistance). I was for tackling head-on vested interests that increased costs to the consumer or taxpayer. I wanted a consensus approach to reconciliation in Northern Ireland. The Ireland I believed in was a secular state with liberalised laws facilitating personal freedom and, above all, a society founded on a meritocracy of opportunity, rather than cronyism.

I had become so professional, pragmatic and adept as a politician that I believed only in my career. Principles or beliefs could be suppressed to suit the circumstance. In opposition, you simply opposed the government parties. Your job was to deride and nit-pick at their incompetence. Like Alana McCree's dog, we went a little of the road with everybody and ended up not advancing at all. Cowardice, cute hoorism and caution were rewarded, while courage was deemed to be naïve. In a mad scramble for the centre ground of Irish politics and political correctness, blandness ruled. Focus groups replaced individuals with convictions. The media happily bought into this group-think.

The life of a Dáil deputy began to seem pointless to me. It was impossible to make a difference where the garnering of local votes took precedence over all else. In truth, I was burned out. It was about me as much as the system. Survival, by holding on to your seat, was what mattered most. If you're a one-dimensional person, whose sole *raison d'être* is politics, that's fine. I wasn't. Increasingly, with more than half of my life over, I found that, with most passion spent, I was left with drudgery.

Yet I had responsibilities to the dedicated supporters and party workers who had invested so heavily in me over seven successful general elections. I could not just abandon them. Their hopes and expectations of me were that I could go all the way to the political summit. How could I sell them short? Conversely, I felt it would be more dishonest and hypocritical to pretend I was still that thrusting politico when I knew inwardly I wasn't. What use was I to anyone as an embittered cynic?

I spent months agonising as to the best course of action. I skived off duties such as by-election campaigns, inventing plausible excuses. I sought advice from mentors like John Lynch and my bank manager, Frank Casey, in Enniscorthy. I met up with Shane McCauley (former Oireachtas Committee clerk), who said everyone went through the boredom factor in their job. 'Imagine what it's like for a dentist looking into mouths every day,' he told me.

Most pals could not begin to fathom how I could even contemplate repudiating a great prospective tilt at the party leadership in the years ahead.

I made up my mind. I met John Bruton privately in June 2000. We were beyond the midway point in the lifetime of the Dáil; he was planning another reshuffle, focusing on the team for the next election.

'John, I've decided that I'm not going to stand at the next election. This has nothing to do with your leadership, the party or any grievance of mine. I've just had enough and want to pursue a career in business, spend more time with my family, get a new life, take on new challenges and be my own boss. I'd rather you didn't reappoint me to the front bench. I want to quit.'

He was taken aback. 'No, Ivan, this would be a huge mistake for you. You cannot go ahead with this.'

I realised that not only was he concerned that I should do the right thing politically for myself, but also that he perhaps feared my departure would be interpreted negatively by his enemies in the party. My disillusionment with politics could be interpreted as disenchantment with his prospects of winning the next election.

'I understand your situation and medium-term desire to get out. How about you fight the next election? I'll appoint you to cabinet and after a year or two you can step down and then go. We would all be winners. We can have this private arrangement between ourselves.'

He dissuaded me from opting out, although I thought the plan crazy because people would suspect something was amiss for me to walk out of cabinet for personal reasons. I felt I owed him and the party, so I backed off with my exit strategy. He transferred me to the environment portfolio. I knuckled down to learning all about the brief, organising a seminar for all the voluntary NGOs to make submissions on environmental sustainability, recycling, climate change and the green agenda. My intention was to incorporate their best ideas into a cohesive Fine Gael policy agenda. However, with each passing week, I began to regret not standing my ground with John Bruton. The selection convention for Wexford was held towards the end of that year. Michael D'Arcy and I were joined on the ticket by Eddie O'Reilly, a school principal in Wexford town, formerly the party's general secretary and Avril Doyle's election agent. Amazingly I began my acceptance speech by saying, 'I had given serious consideration to not standing in this election ...' That was hardly inspirational talk to rally the troops. I was unhappy, indecisive and felt trapped. Phil Hogan, now the most astute, streetwise, power-hungry guy in the party, rang me.

'We're on again.'

'What are you talking about?' I asked, confused.

It was November 2000. The mutterings of discontent against the leadership were resurfacing.

'The bold Austin Deasy has tabled a motion of no confidence in Johnny baby. I think he's on a solo run.'

We quickly assembled a council of war in Bruton's office. I was dispatched to pour scorn on this crazy and disloyal venture, confidently predicting that Deasy would get six or fewer supporters and accusing him of being a serial opponent of three successive leaders. The meeting passed off without much rancour, no front-bencher proffering support for Deasy's motion. I was a teller for the counting of votes. Bruton won, but with twenty-four votes against him. I was shocked, sensing that the game was up for him. His sell-by date was looming. The next heave couldn't be resisted. Since 1997, I had received numerous private approaches to throw my hat into the ring, but told well-wishers of my pledge always to back Bruton. Now there would be no hiding place for me if he was removed. In late January, I did a lengthy profile interview with Ann Marie Hourihane of the *Sunday Tribune* in which I categorically stated that I would never be a contender and openly envisaged the day when I would leave politics. No one believed me. They couldn't figure out what I was up to, but assumed I was up to something other than what I was saying publicly.

The *Irish Times* opinion poll the next week put Fine Gael as low as 19 per cent and the boys made their move. This time, they attacked with an orchestrated full-frontal assault, led by Michael Noonan and Jim Mitchell. I did all I could, publicly and privately, to back Bruton, but I reckoned the best result would be thirty-six for and thirty-six against. I told Neil Ó Mailloir (the Fine Gael press officer), Roy Dooney and John Bruton that I would announce my departure if he lost. At that stage I was fed up with the in-fighting. We had enough problems combating the government without more blood-letting. I was sure the public would not reward more internecine strife. If the members wanted to rush like lemmings over a cliff, I was opting out. If Bruton was defeated, my deal with him was null and void. I would be free.

The meeting lasted for a handful of hours and a bitter, score-settling session it was, with things said that made it impossible for certain speakers ever to serve under Bruton again. He was determined not to resign. Phil Hogan, Nora Owen and Richard Bruton were the main defenders. I spoke in a veiled way about defeat for Bruton meaning the end of a network of personnel that had carried the party to some success. Noonan went for the kill and won by thirty-nine votes to thirty-three. It was game over for Bruton and his cohorts. A new leader was to be elected the following week.

John Bruton held a stoical late-night press conference at the side of the front Dáil courtyard, flanked by loyalists. I stayed back but gave interviews in the aftermath stating that I wouldn't be a candidate and I wouldn't serve on the next front bench if I was asked. This was probably perceived as rash sour grapes at Bruton's defeat, but my considered plan was to revoke my election candidacy in Wexford and announce my retirement from politics. I needed to handle it as diplomatically as possible with my key workers so that I left with the minimum acrimony.

I hastily convened a meeting around our home kitchen table with Bernie and Breda, and Lil O'Connor, my most loyal confidantes. We agreed that I would issue a personal letter to 700 party members on the following Monday night, before announcing my decision by press release a day later. Councillor Jack Bolger called unexpectedly to my house. I explained that my departure was non-negotiable. He was angry with me, and he was not alone. Party stalwarts were furious, dismayed and resentful. I was beyond caring. I was certainly beyond being persuaded to change my mind.

The news leaked to journalist Gene McKenna, who put it on the front page of the *Irish Independent*. I went into hiding at my mother-in-law's house in rural Wicklow, unavailable to confirm or deny my intentions until the letters had reached constituents. I thought a single interview with Seán O'Rourke on RTÉ radio at lunchtime the following day would suffice. But in Irish politics, most of the time, people don't resign even when it's obligatory, so when someone resigns for no reason there is a lot of curiosity. Neil Ó Mailloir organised a press conference at the RDS. It was an unusual experience, attending your own political execution, after years of exceptional toil. I just wanted to get it over with. I was pursued for potential ulterior motives. There were none. 'Knowing my luck,' I said, 'the new leader will soon be Taoiseach and Fine Gael will be in power for the next ten years.'

I didn't believe it for a second. I felt a sense of loyalty to the political network, which had been very good to me, so I didn't rip into the fundamental flaws of a political culture obsessed with local politics, cronyism, nepotism and insiders too often dedicated to the protection of vested interests. I couldn't turn so quickly on a system of which I had been a part for two decades.

Michael Noonan asked to meet me in his office before the leadership vote. I sat down in front of him, faking bonhomie. I began by congratulating him and wishing him well in the task ahead.

'Ivan, I really want you to reconsider your decision to step down,' he said. 'If I am leader, and it's looking like I will be, I can't contemplate the appointment of a front bench without you. Your energy and talent will be badly needed for the challenges ahead. I had always intended a senior post for you.'

'I'm flattered and appreciative, but my decision isn't impulsive. It's been on my mind for some time.'

As he became more persistent, I did the boyfriend/girlfriend routine – it's me, not you – barely concealing how much I was enjoying his discomfiture. I blamed him more than anyone else for all the leadership heaves, disloyalty and unrest towards Dukes and Bruton. He passively – and sometimes not so passively – pushed the notion that the party's main problem was the personality of the leader. I felt he and his cronies would pay a high price for their dual agenda of outwardly representing the highest echelons of the party, but privately grumbling about colleagues' failings. My sense was that the party would suffer a serious meltdown under his leadership, although I had no idea about the scale of it.

The meeting, on 9 February, saw no long speeches. There were proposers' and candidates' contributions only. Enda Kenny stood against Noonan. Jim Mitchell stepped aside in a typical back-room deal to be deputy leader. He and Noonan described themselves, ludicrously, as the 'dream team'. To me they epitomised the unprincipled politics of expediency. I voted for Kenny as a friend. He was always easy-going, likeable and inoffensive. His candidacy had no realistic prospect of victory. His pitch was west of Ireland advocacy, plus he appealed to the disaffected pro-Bruton camp. Heretofore he had not displayed any leadership ambition. I put his transformation down to his wife Fionnuala's political acumen. Noonan subsequently screwed Kenny by sacking him from the front bench. It was an unnecessarily small-minded humiliation.

Noonan did not have a proper grasp of the party's need for finance, professional organisation or campaigning. I rated highly his political manipulation skills, tactical nous and one-liner sound-bites, but there was damn-all depth of conviction to back it up. As the months went by, my worst fears were realised. No sustained bounce for the party happened in the polls. Noonan's big idea was a self-imposed ban on corporate donations to Fine Gael. I couldn't believe it when his front bench proposed compensation payments from the taxpayer for former taxi plate holders, who were suffering losses because of deregulation and competition. A similar bailout was promised to people who had bought shares in Eircom and seen their value plummet. These populist strokes badly backfired and were rightly ridiculed. Labour refused to do a pre-election deal and Fine Gael suffered its worst election defeat since 1948, gaining only 22 per cent of the vote. It was a catastrophe. Eleven of the front-bench members lost their seats, including Alan Dukes, Jim Mitchell, Nora Owen, Jim Higgins and Alan Shatter. The casualty count was twenty-three TDs. Not only was Fine Gael going into opposition with only thirty-one deputies, but oblivion was being predicted. Noonan, who at one point suffered a custard-pie drubbing on his tour and led a lifeless campaign, resigned the leadership forthwith. Fianna Fáil and the Progressive Democrats waltzed back into office with an enhanced majority.

Succession planning was under way from the moment of my announcement. I wanted to stay out of it, since I felt they were the party's seats (including councils), not mine. The general election was expected to be held in June 2001. I stopped carrying out my normal TD functions at clinics, funerals and party meetings. I had experience over the years of retired politicians acting as hurlers on the ditch, proffering unwanted advice – 'In my day, this was how we did it.' I was determined to stand well back from the race to replace me. I resigned from my county and urban district council seats and allowed the normal selection convention process to evolve. Paddy Kavanagh, my director of elections in the 1997 campaign, got my seat on the urban district council and Oliver Walsh was co-opted onto the county council after a hot contest with Paddy.

Paul Kehoe was a twenty-eight-year-old county chairman of Macra na Feirme and the Enniscorthy Fine Gael district executive.

He and Paddy Kavanagh fought a dour struggle to replace me on the Fine Gael Dáil election ticket. The rules of the party decreed that since a selection convention had already occurred, another could not be held. So, instead, a delegate ballot of 380 members was organised with the result kept secret, going directly to headquarters. Michael Noonan quickly announced that he had chosen Kehoe as leader and this had been ratified by the national executive. Those who were displeased with this outcome blamed me. The reality was that, sadly, my formidable election team was deeply divided on who should succeed me. Tireless and loyal workers were now openly bad-mouthing each other.

Kehoe was the only successful Fine Gael contender, with 7,048 first preferences. As a newcomer, he probably benefited in that he could not be blamed for anything, unlike Avril Doyle (3,940 votes), who, commandeered to replace Eddie O'Reilly, returned from Brussels, failing badly. Michael D'Arcy also lost, ending his career. The party's vote slumped disastrously. The political cycle had gone full circle: up to my arrival, Fine Gael had had just one seat in the constituency, and after my departure it had just one seat in the constituency. It was the end of an era in County Wexford politics – no more D'Arcy, Doyle and Yates as a ticket.

I was overwhelmed by the hundreds of letters I received from constituents and party supporters across the country. For all that I have decried the demands made by clientelism, it has to be balanced against the genuine kindness of people, many of whom never asked me to do anything. John Bruton penned the warmest letter, and local papers, voluntary organisations and other public representatives were exceptionally generous.

It has been said that every political career ends in tragedy. Not mine. I got out on my own terms with a reasonably unblemished record. I could do what I liked when I liked – an unbelievable transformation and liberation. Many former politicians have severe withdrawal symptoms. I didn't. Mostly I missed the friendships and camaraderie of close colleagues, whose humour, skulduggery and self-deprecating cynicism were great craic.

What did I not miss? Nutters, mostly. One example was the burly man in his late fifties who came into my clinic in Enniscorthy: Cecil Humphreys. He was a bachelor farmer living alone on the outskirts of the town. He claimed that the Land Commission had confiscated a farm from his father in the 1940s, under Dev's regime. I dutifully took notes of his allegations, while expressing mild reservations about getting the land back for him but promising I would write to the minister for agriculture. The ministerial reply established that the land had been lawfully acquired but Mr Humphreys wasn't taking no for an answer. He called again to my clinic and berated me for not trying harder. He began to accuse me of being part of a conspiracy against him. I apologised and suggested that he contact another TD or see a solicitor. A month later I was at home in our dormer bungalow, watching Ireland's dramatic penalty shootout in the World Cup last 16 match of Italia '90. It was the decisive David O'Leary goal. I heard outside the front door this almighty repeated crashing sound. I went upstairs and looked out. Humphreys was in his tractor ramming my car off the driveway, down a steep bank, through a wire fence and into a field. I rang the gardaí, explaining the bizarre situation. By the time they arrived, Humphreys had destroyed my car and departed. He was duly arrested and appeared in the local district court. I had to attend and sit close to him. By this time I had learned from his neighbours that he was a dangerous headcase. The hearing was adjourned, and at subsequent hearings, Humphreys accused the judge of being part of the same conspiracy to steal his land, and he physically attacked him. He was committed to the local psychiatric hospital.

Being free of men like Cecil Humphreys was one advantage to being out of politics. Another advantage was the absence of 'doorstepping', as happened on a sunny May afternoon in 1987. I answered a knock on the front door and found outside Tom McCaughren, RTÉ's high-profile crime/security correspondent, thrusting forward a microphone while holding a letter. He had with him a cameraman and a sound operator. I could see that the red light of the camera was on. They had parked their car on the avenue and had sneaked up to the house on foot.

'Deputy Ivan Yates, the Prison Officers Association [POA] has accused you of political interference in the promotion process within the prison service. They have a copy of a letter here that you wrote to the minister for justice. Did you make these representations? Is this your letter? Do you think it's appropriate for appointments to be done on a political basis?'

I was stunned. Any hesitancy or vague response would smack of guilt. This was a set-up. I examined the letter, which McCaughren had obtained at the POA annual conference in Wexford that morning. It referred to a Mr Joe Martin from Hempfield in Enniscorthy. It looked like the type of letter that I would write and it was a photocopy of Dáil notepaper. But I couldn't bring Martin to mind.

I said I would have to check out the matter and made the point that, whatever about my representations, the minister would have acted properly. After they left, I hurriedly rang my office to check my files for any person named Martin. There was none. We rechecked repeatedly, but still found no trace of any contact. My filing system wasn't foolproof, so I decided to ring Joe Martin a few days later.

'Hello. Are you Joe Martin? My name is Ivan Yates. I have become embroiled in a serious media controversy with the POA about getting you a job in Shelton Abbey prison in Arklow. Can you tell me, have we met? Did I get you the job? What's the story? We've no trace of you on our files.'

'Well, am I glad to hear from you. I've never met you in my life, but I hear you're a good TD. I live in Enniscorthy and work in Shelton. I got promoted off my own bat, without any help from anybody, despite begrudgery. I want my name cleared as well as yours. This is all a pack of lies.'

Extremely angry at being wrongly accused and determined to clear my name, I contacted my solicitor, Tony Ensor (ex-rugby international), in Bunclody. He suggested that I speak to his neighbour and friend Derek Nally, the well-respected former secretary general of the Association of Garda Sergeants and Inspectors who now operated as a private detective. We met, and he said he would speak to a senior official in the Department of Justice to ascertain what was on the appropriate file. He reverted to me with the good news that no scintilla of contact between me and Joe Martin existed and his promotion had been kosher. I arranged for our justice spokesperson, Seán Barrett, to table a written Dáil question to the minister for justice, Gerry Collins, to confirm my innocence. When the POA would not retract its allegations, I decided to sue the Association for defamation in the circuit court and also issued proceedings against the *Sunday Tribune* and journalist Fergal Keane, who ran a story on the front page to the effect that the POA stood over its claims after my denial. This was tantamount to calling me a liar. We settled the case on the basis of a full unreserved public apology in my local papers and the *Sunday Tribune* in October 1989, plus a donation to charities and legal costs.

I learned so much from my time in politics. I honed the skills of flattery, charm, persuasion, fake sincerity, even manipulation. I learned to understand the media, its agenda and impact; how lobbyists, vested interests, unions and spin doctors subtly wielded influence. For years later I would wake up in a sweaty panic at night with the recurring nightmare of someone's problem I had forgotten to deal with. In the dream, a Dáil usher would say that the constituent was at the Kildare Street gate looking for me.

When I started out, politicians were generally perceived to be pre-eminent patricians. When I left politics, they were deemed to be parasites. The chant, after successive tribunal revelations of sleaze and corruption, was 'They're all at it.' Public resentment of high salaries, expenses, pensions and perks will not change and has some justification. Let's face it, no private-sector employer would hire many of our Oireachtas members to do an important executive job.

Ireland Inc. was flying high when I left politics: record economic growth, lower taxes, vast numbers of new jobs, house prices rising by 30 per cent per year. There was no better, more opportune time to launch myself into a full-time business career. I aimed to build a significant and indestructible betting business, and was well on the way at that point. But, then, I had started gambling when I was ten.

11: Rascals and Rogues

I was lying on the sofa in the sitting room during the middle of my summer holidays from boarding school. My older brother John was fifteen and I was ten. While at Portora Royal School in Enniskillen, he and his mates would sneak off to bet on racehorses in the local bookmaker's. He was reading the racing page of the *Irish Independent*, sitting on the floor, his back up against the seat of the sofa.

'What's that mean?' I said, pointing over his shoulder.

'This is the name of the horse, followed by the trainer. Then there's the jockey. To the left is the previous form, showing how the horse has run. Beneath the runners are the probable odds for each horse.' John went on to outline the usual type of bet you could do, either a win or an each-way wager (equal stakes for a win and a place). I was immediately gripped at the prospect of making money so easily and, having studied the runners in a flat race at Leicester, I decided to place my first bet. Lester Piggott was riding the favourite. I would have one shilling to win on it. I fancied another horse to finish second. I wanted to put sixpence on, each way. John arranged to place the bet at the local branch of R. Power on Templeshannon Quay in Enniscorthy, right beside my father's shop and wool business. Dad was the landlord of the property. The bookie's was run by Bill Winters, a white-haired old man with thick glasses. John came back with my docket, which was a carbon copy of the handwritten bet. This was so exciting – except for the wait. In 1970 the only way you could get the result of the race was in the next day's newspaper.

To my delight, the result was exactly as I had anticipated with my main selection winning and my other horse finishing second. To my dismay, I got less than two shillings back because the odds on the second horse were less than enough to recover the losing win stake on the 'place' part of the bet. I was disgusted and vowed to learn a lot more about this game. So began my odyssey of more than forty years as a gambler. At Aravon School I devoured the racing pages of the *Irish Times* every day.

I became very friendly with Johnny, the school's handyman, who filled the coal stoves and maintained the buildings. We would chat for hours about horses. He became my 'runner', placing my bets, because I was not allowed out of the school and I was too young, anyway, to be in betting shops.

Horses became my heroes. An early favourite was Alangrange, a three-year-old, trained by Seamus McGrath and ridden by George McGrath. He kept improving and ran up a sequence of six wins, culminating in the Irish St Leger run at the Curragh in September 1970. I followed the horse's every run and unexpected victory. My first big win came at Cheltenham, on the festival's first day. I got Johnny to place a one-shilling treble. The last horse was called The Ghost. All three horses won, with The Ghost at 4/1. Johnny was thrilled and mimicked a ghost the next day, delivering me a pound note and a handful of coins. I was hooked on every aspect of horseracing: studying the form, weighing up the factors surrounding each race, deciding how much to bet, eagerly and nervously anticipating the result.

In 1971, Geoff Lewis was to ride Mill Reef in the Epsom Derby. I read all the previous Sunday's newspapers, which tipped him to win. He duly did, in Paul Mellon's black and gold colours. I listened to Peter Bromley's thrilling commentary on BBC Radio 2. The same connections brought off a double with Altesse Royale winning the Oaks the next day. I idolised Brigadier Gerard, who ran up a huge sequence of wins, including the 2,000 Guineas at Newmarket in the same year. That Christmas I treasured a book on him and his owner-breeder John Hislop. I became a devotee of Lester Piggott and Vincent O'Brien, backing their horses whenever I could.

On Easter Monday 1972 we were having afternoon tea at Nana's house. I sneaked into the kitchen to listen to Michael O'Hehir's vivid radio commentary on the Irish Grand National. It came alive as Dim Wit quickened to land my one-shilling each-way wager – such a thrill. Bula was my hero over hurdles, winning the Champion Hurdles of 1971 and 1972; I learned all about the horse, his trainer and jockey. Tom Dreaper, trainer of the legendary Arkle, retired in 1971. His son Jim took over at the tender age of twenty. I was his biggest fan and idolised horses like Good Review, Coleridge, Black Secret and Lough Inagh. In later years he would train Ten Up to win in consecutive years at Cheltenham, culminating in the Gold Cup in 1975. Brown Lad won three Irish Grand Nationals at Fairyhouse in 1975, 1976 and 1978, under a huge weight.

I loved following young horses that had the potential to reach the top, graduating through their bumper (two-mile flat races for new horses), maiden and novice hurdles, reaching their pinnacle in steeplechases.

One of my best friends at Aravon, Tim Bradford, who went regularly to race meetings, asked me one weekend if I'd like to go to Leopardstown with him and his father. Would I what! It was Fantasy Land: the beauty of the rippling equine muscles, the smell of the horses in the parade ring, the glorious colours of the racing silks worn by the jockeys, the tension of the grooms in the pre-parade ring saddling up, the roar of the crowd in the grandstand at the climax of the race, the thud of the horses jumping and landing at high speed, the buzz of the betting ring. I couldn't get enough of it.

Mr Bradford wore a trilby, smoked a pipe and worked in Gallagher's large tobacco firm as company secretary. He heavily backed a winner at 5/4 that day and I was impressed to death.

At St Columba's College I befriended lads with racing connections. Captain Christy, the winner of the Cheltenham Gold Cup in 1974, was owned by the parents of a chap in my dormitory. I envied the fact that he was allowed out whenever the horse was running. I also got to know my classmate Paddy Cooper, whose father, Tom, was one of the top bloodstock agents and was buying the most expensive horses, with the best American pedigrees, for the legendary Vincent O'Brien and his various owners. I once asked Paddy which was the most exciting two-year-old his father had bought for them. 'My dad says watch out for The Minstrel' was the answer.

I backed this horse, with his chestnut coat and distinctive four white socks, every time he ran. He was beaten in the 2,000 Guineas but won both the Epsom Derby and the Irish Derby in 1977. My first visit to the Curragh coincided with The Minstrel running in the green and turquoise colours of Robert Sangster. During the summer months horses looked even better in their gleaming coats. Any horse carrying the rug with the initials MVO'B separated me from my cash, especially when Pat Eddery took over as stable jockey to Vincent O'Brien.

In later years I became an enthusiast for his horses, such as Roberto, Thatch, Lomond, Alleged, Artaius, Apalachee, Golden Fleece, Storm Bird and El Gran Señor. I backed quite a lot of bad ones as well.

Throughout my early adolescence, I was too young to be allowed into a betting shop, so I would engage assorted adults as runners to get down my bets. I got to know all the betting shops in Enniscorthy: Powers, Corcorans, Paddy Breen (a crafty old codger) and my idol Pete Lennon, who seemed to offer odds on everything that moved, displaying them on boards around the walls in bright marker colours.

In the racetrack betting rings, I would seek out bookie Paddy 'Pro' Doyle from Enniscorthy. He wore a trilby and had a distinctive deep, husky voice. Instead of giving me a ticket to record my bet, he would say, 'Down to Ivan.' It made me feel like a trusted regular.

During the autumn and winter of 1973, I would bring my one-shilling pocket money each week to his shop to back Leeds United to win the Division One football championship. Under Don Revie, the club had been close to victory in the two previous seasons. At the weekends, I would check the results and marvel at the feats of Bremner, Clarke, Giles, Harvey and Hunter. They won the title that season. I duly collected a little bundle the following May. Another touch I pulled off, some years later, was in the Eurovision Song Contest. I recorded all the entries, and played them over and over again until I was sure that Bucks Fizz, representing the UK and singing 'Making Your Mind Up' was a certainty to win. I backed the group and collected a tidy sum.

I begged my mother during our holidays in Mayo to bring us to the races. I hadn't the patience for more rod fishing on the lake because I was catching damn-all. She kindly accompanied us to Tuam races on the Friday, after the three-day Galway race festival. The following year she brought us to the Galway races. It was a Thursday, the Galway Guinness Hurdle day. The crowds were so enormous that it was impossible to get a place in the stand. I backed a horse ridden by Ben de Haan in red colours. I was jumping up and down behind a throng of people to get a glimpse of the finish. He won. I was in seventh heaven. At twelve years of age, I vowed I would always come to this race meeting if I could. Annual repeat winners, like Spanner and Pinch Hitter, are still etched in my mind.

As I moved into my teens, I became more selective, betting on only one horse a week, guided by the adage 'A short-priced winner is better than a long-priced loser.' Backing a horse at 33/1 meant likely losses rather than rich pickings.

Handicap races give more weight to the better horses to slow them down, thereby equalising the chance of every horse in the race. Novice chases were characterised by more fallers than races for more experienced horses. I veered away from betting on those races, which were usually sponsored by bookmakers.

I knew then that, whatever I did as an adult, horseracing and gambling would be a huge part of my life. My passion was for the magical mystery of horse and jockey galloping towards the finish. Elation or despair made life stimulating. Racing offered something to look forward to and plan for, through endless hours of studying the form and analysing each race. Gambling was the difference between life lived in black-and-white or in Technicolor.

My ambition was to visit at least once every one of the twenty-seven racecourses in Ireland, North and South, and all sixty in Britain. It took me forty-two years to achieve it. I could write a separate book on the unique character, atmosphere and locality of each venue and how the track variations suit certain types of horse (front-runners or hold-up horses, which make a late run).

Throughout the 1980s I would try to get away in the springtime to as many point-to-points on Sundays as possible. I would relish following the amateur jockey Ted Walsh on whatever he was riding, usually the hot favourite. The facilities were non-existent in a mucky field, but I loved being so close to the horses and fences. All my holidays were geared towards going racing. I would take in the adjoining greyhound track in the evenings. I even went hare-coursing one winter, but found it distasteful and the betting too limited.

My most indulgent week of racing was at Easter 1983. Deirdre and I stayed in a bed-and-breakfast on Dublin's North Circular Road, travelling to the Fairyhouse Festival for each of its three days. Remarkably, I made money every day, thanks to backing the winner of the bumper in the last race. We then got on the Wednesday-night ferry to Liverpool, docking in the early morning, checking into a small hotel and going to the three days of the Aintree Festival. My banker bet of the entire week was Dawn Run in the Page Three Hurdle on Friday. This mare was a spectacular front-runner in the famous red and black colours of Mrs Charmaine Hill. I couldn't countenance defeat for her and backed her in the betting ring at 3/1. To my horror, she went out in price to 10/3. I backed her again. To my consternation her odds drifted to 7/2, so I put the last notes in my wallet on her at that price. She led from the front and romped home under Tony Mullins.

With my winnings I went to a local auction that night and bought a certified mounted horseshoe belonging to the legendary Red Rum – I'd backed him every year in the Grand National. It still stands proudly on a mantelpiece at home, with the maroon and gold ribbons of his racing silks.

The Aintree Festival, often regarded as secondary to Cheltenham, is my favourite jump meeting of the racing calendar because of its top-class horses, relaxed atmosphere (on Friday, Ladies Day, inebriated women wear the equivalent of shoelaces and a smile, despite the cold weather). The city facilities of Liverpool are cool. However, the Cheltenham Hurdle was always my favourite betting race of the year. See You Then won a hat-trick in 1985, 1986 and 1987. I had my maximum stake on him in each of those two last years. I lost heavily when a hot favourite whipped around at the start of the same race, losing twenty-five lengths, in controversial circumstances.

One Wednesday morning I was in Leinster House on the way to a parliamentary party meeting. In the main foyer, I met Charlie McCreevy and Brendan McGahon, TD for Louth. They were waiting for a lift to bring them to Down Royal races that afternoon. It was a long journey and they would be gone for the day.

'Ivan, why don't you come with us?' Charlie said. 'My pal Aidan Walsh is about to pick us up. Forget the party meeting and live a bit.'

I hopped into the back of the blue Mercedes. Aidan was a wool merchant and had bought my late father's business. Charlie regaled us with political and racing stories on the journey up. As we neared the track, close to the Maze prison, he explained that a horse called Seán Ogue was running in the first race, a maiden hurdle. The horse, trained by his good pal Michael O'Brien in Kildare, had no form, was a complete outsider – and a no-hoper to a regular onlooker. Such was the secrecy about backing this horse that Charlie said he would have to wait in the car until the race started and the betting was over. If he was spotted on the course, his connection with Michael O'Brien would lead to the horse being fancied. I had only about a hundred quid with me. Charlie gave me three hundred to back the horse for him and I was told to take any price to as low as 5/1. Aidan and Brendan were also getting cash on with the bookmakers. The horse was mostly 20/1, with the occasional 25/1 for a place. I got the signal to start backing it, fifty pounds each time. The odds started to tumble – 16/1, 12/1, 10/1, 7/1, 5/1. Then the race was off.

Seán Ogue galloped off in front and stole ten lengths at the start. Coming into the finishing straight, he was still in the lead. But the 6/4 favourite, trained by Arthur Moore, was cruising up on the outside. All our bets were to win, not each way. Our horse got the full whip treatment from the jockey. A photo finish was called. The nag clung on for a hard-fought victory. We regrouped in the bar. Joy unconfined, whoops of delight. A real touch was landed – Charlie was secretive about how much. We stopped at several watering-holes on the way home, reliving the drama of the coup in the race.

For a racing aficionado the year is punctuated by highlights in the racing calendar. From October to April, it's the return of the National Hunt perennial superstars, kicking off with the Listowel autumn festival, through Fairyhouse in December, the pulsating

Leopardstown meeting for four days after Christmas and big early-year Sundays, culminating in the highlights at the Cheltenham, Aintree and Punchestown festivals. True National Hunt fans wrap up well and have a drop running from their frozen noses. No weekend in the cold, dark and dreary months is not enlivened by top-class TV racing on Saturdays at the likes of Ascot, Sandown Park or Newbury in Britain or Sunday fixtures in Ireland at Naas, Navan and Gowran Park.

Along with the stretch in the evenings in April come the delights of flat racing with Group racing and classics for three-year-olds. The promise of potential world-beaters implodes or blossoms. Each spring is full of new hope for owners and trainers, who dream the dream. It's then a feast of fun through a series of spring and summer festivals, including the Newmarket and Curragh Guineas, Chester, York, Epsom, Royal Ascot, Newmarket's July course, Glorious Goodwood, York again, Doncaster, interspersed with all-age Group 1 races, followed by autumn meetings to establish the champions for each season. I have always found it easier to back winners in lesser tracks and lower-grade races.

Punters, through the intensity of their bets (irrespective of the size of their stake), get the same vicarious pleasure as the horses' owners during the race. In a few seconds, their horse can go from cruising to victory or defeat. Distress signals from jockeys pushing and driving, with no quickening response from the horse, spell disaster.

Bookmakers call it 'the bug'. You either have it or you don't. Two-thirds of the population are unmoved: they don't get it. But for those of us who are smitten, whether we're eight or eighty, the same exhilarating pleasure is sustained. Never mind the disappointments – you can, after all, explain them away. The psychology of losing means you continue to reinforce your original opinion even after defeat. Talking through your pocket, you blame the jockey, trainer, ground conditions, the run of the race or just bad luck.

Part of the buzz of winning is the vindication of your opinion – so important in punter banter. Every race has a winner. Unlike football or any team sport, there are no draws or replays, although the occasional dead heat can happen. The most important factor in picking winners is the form book. Some horses are simply better and faster than others. However, the amount of rainfall and its subsequent effect on the ground is the biggest single variable in a horse's performance. Tracks are either left- or right-handed, which can suit certain runners. Each horse has an optimal race distance. Stables can run in and out of form.

When you have weighed up all the above, you decide which horse is the proverbial 'good thing'. The problem is that the best horse doesn't always win the race. Here are examples of how I have lost money: horse falls, unseats rider, gets brought down or runs out; jockey gets tactics wrong by being too far back to catch up, misjudges the pace of the race, runs too free, mistimes the finishing kick, mistakes the winning post or the number of circuits, gets stuck behind a wall of horses, takes the wrong course; trainers can err by not having horses fit enough, sometimes can run them too quickly after a tough race, haven't schooled them to jump well enough or are unaware that a filly/mare is in season; horses can be ailing from various breathing (wind) problems, can burst blood vessels, have respiratory infections, injure a tendon, ligament or back muscle during a race, suffer a virus, boil over with anxiety and sweat up before a race. Tack problems can arise if the saddle slips or the bit slips out of the horse's mouth.

Frequent post-race failures are explained away by the statement that 'The horse has become a bit of a thinker.' This means that the animal has copped on to the fact that it doesn't have to try: it will still get fed. Some horses improve greatly with experience, while others become 'dodge pots', refusing to race or even start. Horse training is an industry for excuses. The day you stop forgiving is the day you quit the game. All horses can be inconsistent. Racehorse owners on average recoup less than a pound for every six they invest in buying the horse and paying all its bills. Breeding from proven winners and bloodlines does not ensure ability. As one trainer once said to me, 'Elvis Presley's brother couldn't sing a note.' Expensive purchases don't ensure success.

But it's the very improbability of pulling off a winner, knowing all that can go wrong, that makes the venture so beguiling and intriguing. It is a mug's game, but it's great craic trying to succeed at it. The pursuit of sustained profit from punting is illusory for ordinary racegoers. If you can keep your losses to single-digit percentages and bet only what you can afford to lose, there's lots of enjoyment to be had. Controlling your stake is the single most important discipline for a punter, no matter how convinced you are that a particular horse is a certainty. It is crucial to be consistent in your betting patterns because, statistically, your luck will even out. The only guaranteed way to make money is consistently to back selections at a longer price (i.e. bet on 3/1 shots at 6/1), which can be done only with inside information, being able to anticipate market moves.

The quickest way to the poorhouse is to follow tips. Take responsibility for your own cash. Conversely, good-quality information is invaluable. Such as: the horse needs the run; has improved a lot at home beyond previous public form; the stable lads are backing another horse in the race against their own. The live betting market on the racecourse is a veritable stockmarket as to a horse's chances on the day. Secrecy from those closest to the horse is paramount, to the extent that certain rogues will deliberately put out the opposite information to procure better odds, downplaying its real chance. Even worse than no info is the wrong info. The second fastest way to the poorhouse is to chase your losses. If you have a losing bet, forget about it. There will always be another day.

The culture of the racing fraternity is unique, with a language all its own: also-ran (down-the-field loser), banker or nap (guaranteed winner), jolly (race favourite), ringer (fake substitute horse), cheek pieces/visor/blinkers (varying degrees of horse headgear), knock (not pay), on the nose (back to win), on the bridle (horse cruising in race), drifter (odds lengthening), lay/play (oppose/back), tongue tie (helps horse breathe during race), hot/cold (horse or trainer in form/out of form), screamer (shock result), rag (complete outsider), black type (highest quality races), ante-post (betting market in advance of race), bar (horses not quoted in the betting), Bismarck (horse that will be beaten), boat race or penalty kick (one-horse race), kite (cheque).

On-course betting parlance is even more marked. It has its own currency: monkey (£500), grand or bag of sand (£1,000), ton (£100), pony (£25), deuce (£200), nifty (£50), score (£20). Odds terminology can be bizarre when numbers have names: neves (7), rouf (4), both spelt backwards; bottle (2), carpet (3), double carpet (33), hand (5); top of the head (9/4), up the arm (11/8), ear'ole (6/4), levels (1/1). The traditional tick-tack hand signals between bookmakers are now virtually redundant. A 'penciller' and 'runner' are a bookie's staff. A heavy loss is called a nosebleed. A high-roller mug punter is known as a donor. A bad trainer 'couldn't train ivy to go up a wall'. A bad tipster could 'stop a clock or a train'.

Bookmakers call themselves rooks (an abbreviation of crooks). 'Rails bookmaker' means those in the most prominent pitches. 'End of the line' bookmakers are in the worst pitches. A 'tanker' is someone who underwrites a racecourse bookie's financial operation; if there's a lot of them around at the meeting, you may hear the expression 'more tankers than the Gulf of Oman'. Life on track is all weather, harsh and often hungry.

The business of bookmaking comprises making a book of odds that reflects the bookie's profit margin. The true odds of an event outcome reflect the real probability of each variable. For example, if you toss a coin, there are only two possible outcomes: heads or tails. The probability can be calculated as a percentage: 50 per cent heads, 50 per cent tails. This equals evens or 1/1 odds. In an absolutely balanced soccer match or three-horse race there are three possible results: home win, away win or draw; any of the three horses. Again, you can calculate the percentage by dividing the number of outcomes (three) into 100 to give you the percentage chance of each: 33 per cent, which equals 2/1 odds. If you take in £10 on each option (total £30), you pay the winner £30 (the stake plus £20 winnings). This is a perfectly balanced book.

The fundamental problem for track bookmakers is that usually only one or two horses/greyhounds are actually backed in a race, so they don't obtain a balanced book. They are basically gambling that the favourite will lose. Their daily profit or loss, like that of the punter, depends on the results. The life and cash flow circumstances of bookmakers and punters oscillates between Cloud Nine ecstasy from winnings or Skid Row despair from losses. The interaction between racing and betting means that there is an incentive for skulduggery. Significant investment is made by the racing authorities to safeguard the integrity of the sport, but it cannot alter human nature. As the fearless racecourse layer Davey Hyland once told me, 'Ivan, it's like this. Not everybody involved in racing is a rogue, but every rogue at some point in their life gets involved in racing.'

When I was a bookmaker between 1988 and 2010, many horses lost me a fortune. Istabraq's first win in the Champion Hurdle of 1998 was a crushing blow, costing me more than £300,000. Irish bankers at Cheltenham regularly were stood for €500,000 at the height of the boom – meaning that we'd have to pay out on those liabilities in the event of them winning. My worst ever personal result was on a Heineken Cup rugby match between Munster and Leicester. It was the last match before the redevelopment of

Thomond Park, where Munster had a 100 per cent win record for twelve years. A hurricane was blowing down the pitch and against them in the second half and they lost 13–6.

My unluckiest loser came when Frankie Dettori was nearly killed in a plane accident in June 2000, just before Royal Ascot: I had backed him to be top jockey at the meeting. His enforced absence did not procure me any refund. That year he was due to ride one of the best horses I have ever seen – Dubai Millennium – which destroyed the field for another Group 1 devastating victory.

My most nerve-racking wager was on Jamie Spencer to be flat champion jockey in 2007. After several months of ups and downs, he had to win the last two races of the season at Doncaster in November to tie with Seb Saunders in a dead heat pay out. To my delight, Jamie made it.

My most memorable wins? I needed cash to pay the kids' boarding-school fees. I lumped on Manchester City, under Kevin Keegan, to win the Division One championship at the start of the 2001/2002 season at odds averaging 3/1. Thankfully they won a record number of games and points to clinch promotion to the Premiership. I was a nervous wreck, constantly on the website checking the latest team news. Goals from Shaun 'The Goat' Goater did the business. In the run-up to the 2006 All Ireland hurling final we needed to buy a new family car because the old one was clapped out. Cork were reigning champions and up against an emerging Kilkenny team. My pal Phil Hogan rang me. 'Kilkenny will not be beaten on Sunday. I've never seen anything like the hyper-commitment and intensity of preparation that Brian Cody has put into this team. You can bet your life on them to win.' I did so. It paid for a nice Volvo S80, which is still going strong. I call these exceptionally rare investments – or liabilities – 'boneshakers'. Enormous self-discipline is required to keep outlays and liabilities under control, irrespective of how adamant an opinion you have.

Nowadays I have come full circle. For twenty-two years as a bookie, I couldn't enjoy the best horses because I desperately needed them to be beaten for the sake of the business. Now that I am no longer in the trade, I have rediscovered my youthful love of equine superstars – Big Bucks, Frankel, Quevega, and Sprinter Sacre. I call them ATM machines because they always win. For me the allure of the racing pages makes life tingle. I buy, read and enjoy the *Racing Post* and the *Irish Field* before any other periodical. A regular flutter helps many a senior citizen get through the day or long, boring week. Moral guardians often don't understand this lifestyle.

While I know (to nod, say hello and wish good luck to) most top Irish trainers, I always assumed that any share in a nag would be with my long-standing close friend Jim Bolger. He and his wife Jackie have been dinner guests, at home and in restaurants, for thirty years. Jim is one of the most outstanding self-made men County Wexford has ever produced. His training and breeding of internationally successful horses span many decades, including premium classic winners. He started with nothing. His feats with Give Thanks, Park Express, Park Appeal, Finsceal Beo, Teofilo and New Approach are truly spectacular, given the finite resources at his disposal. A non-smoking Pioneer, Jim is a tough disciplinarian, mentoring dozens of youthful men brilliantly, including Aidan O'Brien and Tony McCoy. He is a generous, unassuming, lucid family man and a loyal friend.

My own horsey enterprise began when I was attending and sponsoring a Cheltenham preview night at the Goat Grill pub (Charlie Chawke's famous establishment in Goatstown) in March 2007. After several pints and informed horsey banter on the panel, I chatted with racehorse trainer Paul Nolan during the interval.

'Paul, one day I'm going to buy a horse, but I only want to get involved in a good one. If you ever come across something exceptional, let me know. I'm in no hurry. Wait for the right horse.

Money isn't an issue.' False bravado: I was bluffing. Nevertheless, my flourishing business, Celtic Bookmakers, would buy the horse.

Ten days later I had a call from him.

'Ivan, we're after coming across the horse you want. We've been watching this fellah work in Colin Bowe's yard in Kiltealy. He's exceptionally promising. Colin trains a lot of point-to-point horses and says this is the best he's had for some time. He ran yesterday in a point-to-point in Tipperary and fell unluckily at the last fence, when he had almost won the race, having been badly hampered and making up an ocean of ground. He's really well bred by Bob Back, out of a winning mare at Cheltenham called Hidden Ability. He is owned and bred by the famous P. J. 'Jockey' Doyle, who's living in Gorey. The name of the horse is See U Bob.'

'How much, Paul?'

'Well, that's the problem. Because he ran with such promise yesterday, a number of agents are trying to buy him. The top owners, like Graham Wylie in the north of England, are interested. So are Eddie O'Leary [brother of Ryanair's Michael] and other agents. I've offered eighty thousand euro, but they want a hundred.'

'Jesus, Paul, that's a bit strong for me. I don't think I can afford that, even though the business would be paying for it and would own the horse as a marketing venture. Can I think about it? I'll call you back tomorrow.'

That evening I went for my regular 100-length swim in the pool at the Ashdown Park Hotel in Gorey. When I was back in the changing room, my phone announced five missed calls from Paul and a voicemail message to ring him urgently. Half-dressed, I rang him.

'I was trying to get you, Ivan. We had to make a decision on the horse. They had decided to sell him today. We bought him for a hundred grand. We just couldn't let him go. It's the most exciting, best potential horse we've come across for years. If you don't want it, I'll try to find another owner.'

'Paul, that was quick. I understand the score. Okay, I'll certainly take a half-share in the horse for fifty grand. If you could get another joint owner, that would suit me perfectly. I've never done this before and I don't want to make an eejit of myself or get ripped off at every turn. If I had another experienced owner with me to show me the ropes, it might be better for everybody.'

'Okay, I hear what you're saying. I'm off to Cheltenham this evening and I'll contact you when I get back. I'll see if I can find a partner for you.'

I was really busy with the business over the next few days of Cheltenham, hectically managing several million euro of bets and liabilities. On the following Friday night, Paul rang and suggested that I come out to look at the horse in his stables at Toberona, just outside Enniscorthy. It was late and dark. He showed me round other stable stars, then brought me to see Bob. He looked magnificent.

Because Cheltenham had been very profitable for the business, I offered to buy the horse outright. Paul said he had procured another half-share owner, John Brennan, who had owned many successful top-class horses over the years. I knew his parents well as Fine Gael supporters from Ballywilliam, near the Wexford/Carlow border. John, too, was prepared to buy 100 per cent of the horse. I arranged for him to call to our house for lunch over the St Patrick's holiday weekend. John interviewed us. He was full of warnings.

'The most expensive way to get into the racecourse for free is as a racehorse owner. You need to know that you have to write off this investment right now. The best any owner can expect is for the horse to win back the costs of training and racing. Your capital outlay is gone on the day you buy.'

I felt that I would never again get so close to horse ownership and that a 50 per cent risk was prudent in every respect. We did the deal. John kindly agreed that the horse would run in Celtic Bookmakers' newly registered racing colours of green, red and white. It was settled with Paul and his brother, assistant trainer James, that the horse would be given time to develop by not running again until the following winter and meanwhile being put out for summer grass. He was only a five-year-old and needed time to mature physically. The following autumn he was brought back into training, with the aim of running in a bumper race before Christmas. The word from the stable about the horse's work levels was exceptionally pleasing. Eventually he was entered to run at Fairyhouse on their big December Sunday card in the last race, the bumper.

Sadly, Deirdre's father, Cam Boyd, died after a long illness and was buried on the day Bob was to run. The lads suggested that they proceed with the race as a gentle introduction, even though Deirdre and I would be absent. When the time for the race came, the funeral was over. I rang the race commentary line. Des Scahill's voice told me See U Bob was last in the early stages. However, he made up a lot of ground and ran on well to finish fourth. I hadn't backed him. Everyone was delighted with the run.

The next run was at Gowran Park in February. Deirdre and I met up with John Brennan for a few drinks before the bumper. Despite odds of 16/1, Paul and James Nolan quietly fancied the horse. I had no bet. John was beside me in the grandstand as the horses were walking around at the start. 'This horse could win a Gold Cup one day, according to what I'm hearing from James,' John said.

I was not a little sick when the horse ran abominably. He never raised a gallop and was well beaten, some seventy lengths back from the winner. The ground was atrociously wet, almost unraceable, but there was no denying that this did not augur well. I was devastated, but not surprised. I had listened to so many owners' sob stories over the years, telling me of bitter disappointments and false hopes with potentially great, but ultimately moderate, horses. The following week Paul rang me to say they had discovered that the horse had a bad abscess in a tooth and that this probably explained his abysmal run. They weren't giving up on him, but we would wait for good dry ground to show what he could do.

Saturday, 19 April 2008 was a day I will never forget. Bob was entered to run in a bumper at Cork racecourse, just outside Mallow town. Since this horse's last run, I had got to know James quite well. With each phone call, he was more upbeat about Bob. They had a number of top-grade race winners in the stable at the time. I told them I would prefer to be given realistic assessments rather than false expectations and bullshit. James suggested that I might back the horse. I travelled down with my great pal Michael Sheil, a semi-retired racecourse bookmaker. I told him I was going to get stuck into the horse: if he didn't deliver today, I wouldn't back him again. He had his doubts.

I felt everything was in Bob's favour: drying ground; different tactics (this time he was going to make the running); it looked a less competitive bumper race, since the main meeting was on at Naas that day; and the form of his initial Fairyhouse race was working out well: horses that had finished behind him in that were now emerging as winners. I arranged for my son Andrew, who was at university in Swansea, to back Bob anywhere he could in the UK. I used some of my industry contacts to back it sporadically and quietly throughout the morning. The initial early prices of 25/1 and 20/1 shortened up to 5/1. We arrived at the track in mid-afternoon; Bob's race was the last on the card. I didn't back the horse there and his starting price odds drifted to 7/1. John Brennan and Paul were in the parade ring before the race. I didn't tell them I had significant money each way on the horse. I couldn't see him being unplaced.

I was shaking like a leaf in anticipation as the race started. To my consternation, one of the country's top trainers, Noel Meade, had the really well-fancied 7/4 favourite, Go Native, in the race. Meade had just trained the last three winners at the meeting. This was supposed to be his most fancied runner. Just my luck to run into a top newcomer, with my cash down. Barry O'Neill was the amateur jockey on board Bob, claiming seven pounds off the horse's official weight. As agreed, he shot off in front, with a twelve-length lead throughout the first circuit. There is a long, flat finishing straight at Mallow. Nina Carberry, on the favourite, tried to close the gap, but Bob tenaciously kept finding more. He galloped relentlessly and romped on to win by eight lengths. I roared him home. I was delirious with joy. It was one of my most exhilarating experiences ever and exceptionally profitable.

Drinks and a hearty meal in Clonmel were enjoyed by all. John believed in instant celebrations. I delivered gifts to the trainer and jockey the following week. It seemed the Nolans' hopes for the horse might be vindicated when Go Native came out the following week and impressively won a high-class bumper at the Punchestown Festival. However, we came down to earth with Bob's next race at the Curragh in a hot winners' bumper race in early May. It was a mostly flat race card, the €30,000 prize money the main attraction in running him. I only had a few quid on because he was taking on the best horses on ground that was too soft. He led from the front, but ran with the choke out (too freely) and was easily passed in the final straight, tiring, to finish unplaced. We all agreed to put him away for the summer, with a view to bringing him back for a campaign over hurdles in the autumn.

Bob next ran on my birthday, 23 October 2008, at Thurles in a maiden hurdle, ridden by ace champion jockey Ruby Walsh. The lads told me not to bother going to the races because he would be given an easy introduction to racecourse hurdling, by being settled in the back to learn a steady jumping rhythm and, with luck, run on into a place. He wasn't fully fit and would improve a lot for the race. That afternoon, I was a guest panellist on an outside broadcast with George Hook at a newly launched office block at the Beacon Quarter in south Dublin. We were due to go on air at 4.30. The race was off at 4.20, so I arranged to listen on the mobile-phone commentary line. A bookmaker friend of mine, John Hackett, texted me about the horse's chances: 'Zero. I'm not backing it. There'll be another day.'

As expected, Bob was on a tight rein at the rear of the field throughout the race. As the final half-mile approached, he started to improve and was staying on nicely for a place. Jumping the second last, he hit the front and, to my horror, because I had not backed him, won easily by three lengths. I was in equal parts shocked and annoyed. This was not in the script, even though he was 4/1 favourite in a bad race. I knew that he was well capable of winning a maiden hurdle, but maybe not better hurdle races. I had missed the boat of getting on him in a winnable race, for which he would no longer be eligible. This was not streetwise for a gambler, but he wasn't ever bought to land a 'job' (gamble). My deflation was counterbalanced by the Nolans' enthusiasm that this was even more evidence of how good See U Bob might be. Everyone wants to dream the dream of having a wonder horse. I wanted to live it.

The dismal frustrations of ownership became all too apparent in time. Bob had a poor run back at Cork in a competitive conditions hurdle in November, where he was held up and failed to quicken in heavy ground, finishing fourth of six runners. There was no real explanation available, other than the ground conditions. We decided to give him a break until there was better ground in the spring of 2009, concluding that perhaps he needed a longer rest period between races. My preference was not to be overambitious with the horse. Instead of running in ultra-competitive novice hurdle races, I pressed the Nolans to run him in a handicap hurdle, which he would have a reasonable chance of winning.

Our next day out, this time with all the family – they had warmed to his cause, having initially been dismissive – was at Leopardstown on the big Hennessy Gold Cup day, 15 February.

It was a €25,000 hurdle, where Bob was due to be ridden by Alain Cawley, the stable's retained jockey. I almost never bet in handicaps, especially these sixteen-runner lottery affairs. Bob was held up at the back of the field and came with a thrusting run on the outside around the last bend. He rallied throughout the home straight, finishing fastest in a photo finish, with five horses flashing by the line in a bunch. The camera angle in most photo finishes, especially at Leopardstown, favours the near side. After a tense wait, Bob was declared the winner by a nose. Happy days, but again private frustration with myself for not backing him at the lucrative odds of 12/1. James, Paul, the travelling head lad Tommy Woods and the entire entourage in the winners' enclosure were thrilled.

His next run was in a valuable Fairyhouse handicap hurdle at the Easter Festival meeting. It was the feature race on the last day, a Grade B race worth €90,000. The ground had dried out. In the stable, confidence was high again. I had a reasonable bet on, each way at 7/1, not to miss out as I had in the horse's most recent wins.

See U Bob finished last. My disappointment was doubled a few days later when I was telephoned to be told that the horse had been distressed after the race and had had to be examined by a vet. The diagnosis was unclear. I vowed not to back him again, irrespective of his chances. I was finding myself in bits each time he ran, out of concern for his well-being. Even for a few days before the race, I would get anxious and feel relieved if he was a non-runner. Instead of looking forward to him racing, I was almost as afraid as you would be for your child, who might have an accident crossing a dangerous road. I had never expected ownership to turn out like this.

Remarkably, given the health scare, the horse next ran in Killarney one Sunday in May, in an equally competitive handicap hurdle. Deirdre and my daughter Ciara went along for the day with Michael Sheil and John Brennan. Despite the previous problems, See U Bob went off in front and rallied really gamely to hold on for victory by a neck, under a great ride from Alain Cawley, at odds of 12/1. It was a Lazarus-style performance relative to his lamentable previous race.

Nobody could explain the horse's form. But nobody cares when a horse wins a prestigious Grade B race, worth €50,000. His next most ambitious target was the Galway Guinness Hurdle, one of the year's top races. His odds were 25/1. The kids went for the day out. I had gone beyond trying to fathom when or where the horse might even run well, let alone win. As it happened, he jumped poorly and finished well down the field. We put him away for a steeplechasing campaign later in the year.

All horses have their official birthday on 1 January. For this 2010 season See U Bob was rising seven years old and approaching his optimum performance period. The expectation from a breeding perspective was that he would be most effective as a steeplechaser, rather than as a hurdler or a bumper horse. I felt he was utterly inconsistent, could not be relied upon, yet on any given day he could unexpectedly win. He ran on 18 January at Thurles in a two-mile beginners' chase, ridden by Alain again. This time he was up against a Willie Mullins/Ruby Walsh long odds-on (1/3) hotpot Kempes, a top-class horse and the winner of eleven races. Bob was 4/1 second favourite. In a thrilling finish between the two, Bob led at the last fence and rallied to win by two and a half lengths. It was his best ever performance. While I was absent, I was delighted for my son Andrew, who had gone for a most memorable day out with his mates and Deirdre. More than anyone else, Andrew had been the driving force behind me in buying the horse. Unknown to me, he had urged Paul to talk me into the purchase. Andrew was the animal's greatest cheerleader.

Bob followed this up with a valiant second to another good horse of Willie Mullins's, Citizen Vic, at Leopardstown on the last day of February 2010. These two runs gave him a rating of 145, so he was in the top twenty novice chasers in Ireland that year. That meant he was too highly rated to be competitive in handicap chases, since the weight he would have to carry would be too much for him. From now on it would be difficult to place him in a winnable race. Paul wanted to run him at the Aintree Festival in the Grade 1 Magul Novice Chase on Grand National day. Privately, I had serious reservations. I felt he would be completely out of his depth and wasn't entitled to be in such an elite race. I much preferred a weak conditions novice chase at Navan, but all the kids, as well as Deirdre and John Brennan, wanted a big day out. It was a privilege to have a runner in such an important race, and at my long-standing favourite annual jumps event. See U Bob finished seventh of seven finishers, but was not disgraced at being behind by thirty lengths because the other six were superb horses. I feared jumping at such a fast pace over the big obstacles would unnerve him forever. I believe he became a lot more deliberate at his fences subsequently, losing vital ground in races.

Bob's last run under our ownership was in a three-runner novice chase at Punchestown in May, where he jumped poorly and finished second. I met Paul before the race and explained that, owing to external circumstances, we could no longer afford to keep the horse on the balance sheet. This was nothing to do with Bob or his training. We offered John Brennan the chance to buy out the horse entirely, but he had so many other horses in training that he declined. Instead, Paul arranged to sell See U Bob for the same price that we had bought him, less five grand for luck, to J. P. McManus, the legendary Limerick racehorse owner.

I was delighted and appreciative that the horse was, first, going to stay with the Nolans (as JP's first horse with them) and, second, that he would be superbly cared for, by being in elite ownership. I really wanted the horse to achieve greater success. He did go on to win a Grade 2 race, the Webster Cup, at Navan. Sadly, he then lost his form completely. In 2012 he was switched to Jonjo O'Neill's stable in Britain. I saw him race at Chepstow, feeling emotional. I watch his every run, remembering with nostalgia his best days. He eventually rediscovered some useful form.

I freely admit that the ownership venture was the most extravagant and irresponsible indulgence of my life. Deep down, I knew it was financial folly, but I wanted, for once, to dream my impossible dream. As it turned out, Bob won five races for us and earned a gross £70,000 in prize money. Instead of a loss, the company made a marginal profit on him. This doesn't begin to explain the delight, joy, dismay and disappointment he gave us. I loved the horse and his narrative. I don't expect to repeat the experience, but would advise anyone similarly interested in racehorse ownership to do it on a joint venture, partnership or small-syndicate basis. It reduces the financial exposure and enhances any celebration on the good days.

12: Poacher Turned Gamekeeper

Politics was my vocation, profession and career, but my entrepreneurial DNA had begun to assert itself as far back as the 1980s, when I had set up Celtic Bookmakers as a small business. Paddy Mahon, who bought ewes for us, once said, 'The Yateses were always more interested in the pound than in power,' and he was right. Coming up to my thirtieth birthday, after four general elections and six years as a backbencher, I was ready for something new, and a vivacious little bald man with a trimmed moustache helped to point me in the right direction.

I first met Pat Boland, the man who made it possible for me to enter the betting business, in his betting shop, Metro Bookmakers, in Spencer Street, Castlebar, in August 1986. Several years older than me, he had emigrated to work in London as a barman, although he eventually got the sack because he was furtively consuming large quantities of the proprietor's alcohol. Pat had a serious drink problem and returned home broke and broken.

With the help of AA, he got his life together again, marrying Maureen and fathering three daughters. Pat was an irrepressible serial entrepreneur. His first retail shop was Rings and Things in Crossmolina, importing cheap jewellery from the London market, which he bought with cash. It was tat, but he was able to sell it as proper gear in rural obscurity. A most hilarious character, he treated financial disaster (usually mine, rather than his) with droll humour. Regarding me as a classic privately educated toff, he set about completing my education. He could have taught Gillette lessons in sharpness. On holidays in Mayo, when Deirdre went shopping I would sneak away for a few pints and bets, usually backing Henry Cecil-trained odds-on favourites to snare a few hundred quid to pay for the holiday. I liked Pat's shop. When I paid the 10 per cent betting tax, he pushed it back over the counter to me.

'You're that young guy Ivan Yates, who's going to be Taoiseach one day. I've seen you on television. You're a class act. Usually I'd send a car for punters who back favourites, but you only seem to back winners.'

Pat's charm, flattery and affability were overpowering. I said I wanted to build on a lifetime of gambling, to have a poacher-turned-gamekeeper career beyond politics, and Pat became my mentor, teaching me the rudiments of the bookmaking business: how to obtain a property lease, install the race commentary and results service, obtain betting-shop equipment, recruit and train staff, negotiate discounts, handle the Garda and Revenue licensing procedures, cope with innumerable fraud and cheating features on both sides of the counter. He also opened my eyes to the underbelly of life in Ireland and the darker, more devious characteristics of human nature. Pat was extremely well read, devouring Sunday newspapers on Mondays when he got them for free, after a newsagent pal had returned the mastheads to the distributor. Pat was exceptionally tight, without being mean. His motto was 'Where there is a little, take a lot; where there is a lot, take it all.' Whenever business was not going well, he would buy the most expensive new car so no one feared they mightn't get paid out in a bet. He was the best man ever to spot a sinking ship and to reach the lifeboat, while simultaneously assuring all around that everything was okay.

On a Thursday morning in November 1987 I met him in Bartra House, a coffee shop in Ballina – I was going to spend the rest of the day working in his Crossmolina Metro betting shop. Throughout our conversation, he kept looking over my shoulder at a man sitting in the corner, catching his eye, nodding to him and giving him a thumbs-up sign.

'Pat, who *is* that guy you keep gesticulating to?'

He leaned towards me and whispered, 'The local Customs and Excise officer for the betting tax.' I ended up doing what I always ended up doing with Pat: shaking my head. I quizzed him as to the basic economics of each of his betting shops: gross percentage margin, property, staff and other running costs, target levels of betting turnover per week, profit-and-loss data analysis.

His answers were anecdotal, rather than factual, because he did everything on a secretive, unrecorded cash basis. Profit was based on what cash was in the till at the end of the week.

'Ivan, you'll never be short of money again, once you get going,' he assured me. Although later I discovered, painfully, Pat's notional 30 per cent gross win (margin between bets taken in and money paid out to customers) to be completely wrong – the industry norm was 14 per cent and smaller independent operators usually garnered only 10 per cent – I could not have set up Celtic Bookmakers without his practical assistance, advice and introductions to people like Johnny Birrane, who became an ace exchange operator and layer. Pat personified for me the contrast between the excitement, glamour and risk-taking of the bookmaking business and the repetition, boredom and frequent pointlessness of a TD's life.

I needed a site outside my constituency but within fifty miles of my home, so that I could get to it as required. I narrowed the options through a study of towns and their betting shops in the neighbouring counties of Waterford, Carlow, Kilkenny and Wicklow. I would call to each betting shop in a town and place a small bet at the same time over consecutive weeks. Each betting slip had on it a printed docket number, time and date. This meant I could compare each week's number and calculate accurately the total number of bets they had taken in over the previous seven days. If I applied an average stake of five to eight pounds to each wager, I could estimate the total turnover in the shop. This is called 'test docketing' and provides reliable local market research so one can identify the busiest outlets. While painstaking and time-consuming, it gives an excellent feel for the competitiveness, head count and betting dynamics of each shop.

Tramore is a traditional seaside resort and residential town adjacent to Waterford city. In the late 1980s, it satisfied all criteria as a suitable location for my first betting shop. An hour's drive from Enniscorthy, it struck me as a quiet backwater that wouldn't attract unwanted attention. It had only two betting shops, both owned and run under the name R. Power, the operator who had rented my father's property on the quay in Enniscorthy. Highly respected, honourable and with deep pockets, the firm was, nonetheless, somewhat old-fashioned, without many of the innovations and upgrades I saw elsewhere, especially in Dublin and Cork. My plan was to establish a foothold, so R. Power would ultimately close the weaker of their two shops.

Having exhaustively sussed out the town, I decided to open a new betting shop in the upper part of Tramore, close to the pubs and residential estates. Rita Barnett owned and ran a fishing tackle and bait shop on the ground floor at 34 Main Street. It was a tiny shop, with a small backyard, including an outdoor dilapidated staff toilet. Rita was resolutely not prepared to enter into any lease beyond two years and nine months because she feared any tenancy beyond three years would give me long-term rights. She wanted to be able to get rid of me. I agreed to that and to her monthly rent of three hundred pounds, payable in advance. She would pay the rates.

One of the few things Pat didn't and couldn't advise me about was anonymity, one of my key objectives in setting up the bookmaking venture. If it was a disaster, I didn't want my name associated with it. Neither my mother nor Deirdre had any interest whatsoever in being a bookmaker, vaguely disapproving of those seedy dens of iniquity. So I had to find someone who would front the operation for me.

Willie Tector, one of my most loyal canvassers, was a knowledgeable punter who lived in Campile, close to the Ballyhack ferry that ran every hour across the estuary to Waterford, so he could readily travel to and from Tramore. Out of work at the time, he was happy to be the licensed bookmaker, tenant on the lease and named account-holder for all suppliers on the basis that he would have no financial exposure. My solicitor, Tony Ensor, drew up an agency/assignment agreement and an employment contract between Willie and Deirdre, whose name was to be on all bank accounts. Celtic Bookmakers operated as a sole trader in the name of Deirdre Yates, with Willie Tector as the licensed bookmaker. We had the beneficial interest of all associated with Celtic Bookmakers, despite it being in Willie's name. Willie now had a job at a time of economic recession that paid £120 a week, his PRSI and travel expenses. He duly applied for and obtained a bookmaker's licence.

Large British bookmaking chains, such as Coral, Ladbrokes and Mecca, were expanding into Ireland at the time, so I figured a company name with an Irish flavour would help my brand. Hence Celtic Bookmakers.

Once we had premises, we installed what all bookies had: a live audio link to the racecourses, providing the betting odds, race commentaries and results through the Extel Exchange Service. Jackson & Lowe provided daily, by post, printed sheets for each race and a single display race sheet for a staff member to write up all the day's results.

I agreed an all-in cost of seven hundred pounds, plus 10 per cent VAT, to fix up the shop, the work to be completed by 19 December. A local painter and metal sign-maker did the external work. Carpets were fitted; an electrician installed the Extel system and TV aerial. We signed contracts with the ESB and Telecom Éireann.

We then hit a hitch. The existing local bookmaker, R. Power, lodged an objection under the 1931 Betting Act to the Tramore Garda superintendent that a third betting shop in the town could not be justified. We countered that Tramore's population had increased to six thousand and that Power's, running the only two shops, had a monopoly. We produced statistics showing the ratio of population to the number of licensed betting shops in other towns. Because I was legally committed to loads of signed contracts from suppliers, I was prepared to appeal to the district court if I had to. Thankfully, I didn't have to. Our application was approved.

We recruited a local girl, Vivienne, the daughter of a Fianna Fáil councillor. Neither she nor Willie had worked in a bookmaker's before, so they spent a full week in Pat Boland's shop in Crossmolina, familiarising themselves with the rudiments of the business.

I borrowed five thousand pounds from my mother and used my personal savings of about two thousand to finance the set-up. I approached my local bank, AIB, at Slaney Place, Enniscorthy, for an overdraft and a thousand-pound revenue bond, which Customs and Excise officers required to cover betting duty (10 per cent paid by the customer on all bets) in the event of a default. The bank agreed to an overdraft facility of six thousand pounds, on condition that it would hold a charge over our home. I hoped that the overdraft would not be needed and that we would generate positive cash flow. Pat maintained that once the money started rolling in, there wouldn't be any loan requirements. While my maximum pay out was ten thousand pounds, I asked Pat to lay off (bet back with another bookmaker) any liabilities beyond three thousand.

I planned to open on St Stephen's Day 1987, timed to coincide with my availability during the Dáil Christmas break. It is one of the peak betting times of the year. Pat promised me that rogues and fraudsters wouldn't try any sharp practice on the first day. Instead, they would wait to assess our vulnerabilities. I greatly feared a big pay out and not being on top of liabilities on multiple combination bets. At the other end of my anxieties was the fear that we wouldn't have any customers because punters might not believe they would get their winnings from a rookie outfit.

I needn't have worried. There was a hidden pent-up demand in the town for a new bookmaker to create a choice, real competition and better value. We were knocked over by the level of business that presented itself on our first day. At each race start time there were queues of people handing in bets and cash. We weren't able to keep up with the results at Kempton Park, Leopardstown, Limerick and Down Royal. We were still manually processing each bet, so bets weren't settled on time when they were presented for payment, and we were wide open to every type of fraud and malpractice – betting slips were tampered with, people tried to collect on a losing horse – visibly out of our depth, but customers seemed to like us. It took us hours, with the help of a Ceefax teletext, to record results and process all the wagers, successful or not. Mercifully, nearly all the favourites and fancied horses lost. The largest pay out was eighty pounds at 7/2, amounting to £360. I went home at ten o'clock that night, carrying plastic bags bulging with banknotes. I poured them out onto the sitting-room floor. We had won more than two thousand pounds. I was on a high and hooked on being a bookmaker.

In the early months of 1988, we overcame most of the business's teething problems. We set up daily bookkeeping and filing systems for all winning bets, from cash reconciliation and from the recording of costs. Gradually, as Willie and Vivienne became more proficient, we eliminated human errors. After the peak holiday period, the number of race meetings reduced to a couple per day or fewer, if poor weather caused abandonments.

The overall management of the business was relatively simple: we started with a cash float of a thousand pounds, took in each day's bets, paid out on winners or each-way successful bets and were left with cash at the end of the day. Winning bets collected on days subsequent to the day they were struck were called 'late pays'.

This was a great business: no stock purchases or inventory, unlike most retailers; no credit, because punters paid for their bets upfront; industry odds in our favour and favourable sports results meant net profits. Every Sunday I would travel down to the closed shop. (It was many years later that Sunday racing was introduced.) I would check every bet. The handwriting of each punter became familiar to me. I would recheck the cash balance to ensure there were no cash-handling mistakes. I engaged a local accountant in Enniscorthy and a pal of mine, Eugene Doyle, to oversee our accounts ledgers and take care of the monthly PAYE/PRSI payroll red tape. He even got me an employment incentive-scheme payment for £720 on Willie's pay costs, since he had been on the live register and eligible.

By Easter I was hungry for more. A review of eighteen weeks' trading showed a turnover of £70,000, with a gross profit of £14,000 before running costs of £7,000 were applied, leaving a net operating profit of £7,000. Projecting forward for a full year, if I could obtain an 18 per cent gross margin and keep annual costs per shop to £23,000, then on a turnover of £4,000 per week I would be able to pay for the shop within a year and have a cash surplus of more than £10,000. I saw considerable benefits in having a second shop. A different locality might mean a better spread of bets. Extending my central costs over more shops made economic sense: this was a perfect business for economies of scale.

Each week I would travel the N11, to and from the Dáil, to check out the betting shops in Bray, Wicklow and Arklow. Wicklow town had only two shops, both situated beyond the heavy footfall area on the main street. At this stage, I knew precisely what I wanted in a site location. It had to be close to pubs, parking, maximum footfall and preferably near to banks. I spotted a small jewellery shop for sale, in a perfect position.

I made a written submission in May 1988 to the local AIB manager, Brian O'Connell. I felt I could easily achieve the target weekly turnover of £4,000 with this pitch. The lock-up unit was small, and could be bought for £15,000. I requested a term loan over five years. I agreed to give them a personal guarantee, security of the shop in Wicklow and a charge on our house. By mid-May, the loan was approved.

When it came to property dealings, I relied on a former mate from St Columba's, Adrian Haythornthwaite, who had set up in partnership as an auctioneer in Wexford town. 'Ivan, a shop property is either spot on or spot off,' Adrian said. 'Saving money can be penny wise and pound foolish in the wrong location. In negotiation, always know your walk-away position in advance. Make your offer and then shut the fuck up. Close your mouth. Do not reopen it. Let there be a lengthy silence. No matter how long the pause is, say nothing. When the other party speaks, they will start making concessions.'

I got 'Ado' to negotiate with the auctioneer for the jewellery shop and moved quickly on all other fronts, so we were ready to open by July. Willie had a sister, Breda, who had worked in the betting industry before and lived nearby in Arklow. Helen Boyd, who had worked in the Dáil as a TD's secretary, was now married to Deirdre's brother Roger and had moved to Wicklow. Both agreed to work in the new Wicklow Celtic Bookmakers shop. Despite its small size, I felt it had even greater potential than our first shop. I wanted to be more aggressive with our bonus terms to drive forward local market share and betting revenue.

My business model was a direct copy of Ryanair's principle: 'Pile 'em high, sell 'em cheap.' Celtic was to be the discount operator of the betting business. The mantra 'No one beats our bonuses!' adorned our logo and marketing material. We delivered tens of thousands of leaflets to households, highlighting our terms: the double result – if your horse finished first past the post or won the race on a stewards' inquiry, we paid on both winners; we paid each-way place odds of 1/4 in all races, unlike other bookmakers who paid 1/5. In the event of a dead heat, we paid to the full stake, rather than half the stake on both winners.

But our biggest bonus of all was that if you took a price for a horse live from the track and it drifted out to a bigger starting price, then we paid out at the greater odds for all single bets. It was a no-lose proposition for the customer. This cost us 1.2 per cent in gross margins. The key point for me was that the punter had to stay in our shop to keep taking the live relayed odds from the track. Therefore you got all their business for that day and provided a unique selling point.

This hawkish trading with ultra-competitive offers, which reduced our gross margin by three per cent overall, did not go unnoticed. Nineteen eighty-eight was the year that a big beast was born in the bookmaking jungle: Paddy Power. Newly formed, it was a merger between R. Power, P. Corcoran and Kenny O'Reilly bookmakers, with an initial network of forty betting shops. The mastermind behind the business was Stewart Kenny, who had sold ten shops to Coral only to reopen with their money in competition against them. He was a marketing genius and an awesomely ruthless adversary. John Corcoran, who was chairman of the board of Paddy Power for many years, not only brought his own shops into the merger but had an exceptional talent and flair for commercial property development, separately heading up Green Property plc. David Power was the biggest on-course bookie in Ireland. His son,

Paddy Power, was the face and name of the brand.

This spelled double trouble for me. The R. Power shop in Tramore was refurbished as a Paddy Power shop. The day before we opened in Wicklow, my main competitor there was also Paddy Power: they confronted our bonuses head on by introducing a knockout offer of 'All bets tax-free'. The company would subsidise all punters' betting duty – but only in Wicklow town, forcing us to follow suit. This was guaranteed to lose me money. Paddy Power's objective was plain: to put me out of business. Pat, for once, had no answers for me. He had never heard of this happening anywhere else.

Power's pockets were infinitely deeper than mine and they knew I could not afford to sustain such a tax war indefinitely. Sleeplessness took over: I had a family to support. I couldn't understand why such a small gnat in the industry as me should warrant such an outright assault. I was facing financial ruin.

In the following weeks, we broke even when the results were good. This was a great shop site, with excellent trading margins. After a number of months, the strain of losses became too much for Carty's, the other independent in Wicklow town, which closed. Within days of this happening, Power's restored the full 10 per cent tax charge on all bets, which resulted in Carty's reopening. The merry-go-round started all over again. Power's maintained that as long as there were three shops in Wicklow town the tax war would continue. The Irish National Bookmakers Association (INBA) lobbied the government to introduce legislation to prohibit this predatory practice, but to no avail.

In the autumn of 1988, I was appointed Fine Gael front-bench spokesperson on health. This was my big breakthrough in developing a national political career. I gave it my undivided attention, treating the business as a hobby. My focus had to be on politics in 1989 with the upcoming general election campaign. Meanwhile, Celtic Bookmakers' two shops were ticking over. Comparing the relative performance of Wicklow and Tramore, I learned that the latter had its limitations. Monday to Friday, it had little footfall as people commuted to work in Waterford city. Tourism seemed in long-term decline, people preferring guaranteed sun abroad. Average turnover in Tramore was only £3,000 per week, compared to £5,000 in Wicklow.

I sought and obtained a rent reduction for the six winter months. Willie tried to boost turnover by getting some telephone clients from outside the area to bet with us regularly. My assumptions and projections from the initial eighteen weeks, when we'd had an exceptional period of 18 per cent profit, proved to be grossly over-optimistic, not least because that period covered the peak betting spring season of festivals at Cheltenham, Aintree, Fairyhouse and Punchestown, and was unrepresentative of a full year.

My day-to-day role was to be around to receive two kinds of distress phone calls about bets. First, there was bet acceptance/authorisation, which usually went, 'We have a customer here who wants two hundred pounds on a horse at odds of twelve to one. Can we take it?' If the liability exceeded five hundred pounds, they had to get my approval. I would enquire who the punter was (a regular or a stranger) and, critically, who had trained the horse. A winner was far more likely from a top trainer, while smaller trainers thought all their geese were swans.

The other calls were about potential pay outs of several thousand pounds running on a multiple bet. A first or second horse had won, resulting in serious losses if the remaining horses in the combination came through. I had to decide whether to lay off with another bookie or not. I was generally reluctant to hedge, taking the chance that the punter would lose. They usually did.

This system, whereby I made decisions in critical situations, was haphazard and unprofessional. Sometimes I was not available on my mobile phone. We could not afford a proper race room, which routinely deals with these bets and comprehensively responds to all trading issues. An accident was waiting to happen. Disaster struck on a Friday in October at a big Newmarket flat meeting. While attending a factory opening in Enniscorthy, I left my phone in the car, unanswered. Around 5 p.m., I saw several missed calls from the Tramore shop and my bookmaker friend Pete Lennon. They had been trying to get me about a monster bet liability. A punter had a ten-pound Lucky 15 bet on four horses. Three of them had won at respective odds of 40/1, 8/1 and 6/1. The total pay out came to £34,800. We had not properly clarified the maximum pay out situation for this phone client.

When Willie could not reach me, he had rung Pete. Mercifully, Pete had bet back in doubles and singles with two other large bookmakers, with whom he had a regular client phone account. He had never encountered such a difficult bet: if all four horses had won, we would have had to pay out a six-figure sum. He won back approximately £18,000. One of the bookies closed his account. I did not have sufficient funds to cover the rest of the bet due to the punter. I met him that weekend and arranged to pay him in instalments. I had to borrow around £3,000 each month to clear the debt. It was a complete nightmare – and the last straw as far as the Tramore shop was concerned.

The business was continually losing money, and unlike Wicklow, there was never a bonanza day when we won a pile of money. After agonising for a few weeks, I determined that Willie would have to be let go and I told him that I couldn't afford to keep him on as manager. Deirdre would take over his role. I had consulted a lawyer on employment legislation and been told that you could replace an employee with a family member. I felt that I had no other option, but of course Willie was upset, as were other staff.

We somehow got through the next few months, into 1990. My accountant came up with an ingenious response to my indebtedness. He explained that under income tax law, if you're in employment and have losses from your own business, you can offset them by adding them to your personal annual tax-free allowance. This applied to Deirdre as a teacher and me as a Dáil deputy. Over a two-year period we obtained £7,989 in tax rebates, which I gave to my mother. It made the difference between going bust and staying in business. Taxpayers got a reasonable return on their investment because we generated more than €20 million for the Revenue Commissioners over the next two decades.

My next big break was the ending of the tax war in Wicklow town. When the third independent bookmaker closed, Power's relented. We co-existed for many years and Wicklow turned into a gold mine in margin and profitable turnover. Perhaps because the town was not directly visible on the N11 route, many potential competitors seemed to bypass and ignore it.

The business was helped by terrific results, like the 100/1 shock winner of the 1990 Cheltenham Gold Cup, Norton's Coin. Cash started to roll into the bank accounts. At this time, revolutionary change was taking place in betting shops. Instead of an audio-only commentary service, a new televised broadcast of live horse and greyhound races was introduced in Britain by Satellite Information Services (SIS). This impelled enthusiasts to spend more time in betting shops, watching their animals win and lose. The atmosphere came alive. We had to erect satellite dishes on the roofs of our shops.

By summer, I was keen for growth and another shop. Having passed Waterford travelling to and from Tramore, I knew the landscape and activity levels of every betting shop in the city. I observed this amazing shop run by a local guy called Davey Savage. During the hours of racing, he would conduct a floor show of calling out bonus odds and special offers as each race was being run. I was told by a reliable source that this heaving shop was one of the busiest in the country outside Dublin. My test docketing indicated multiple tills taking in more than five thousand slips per week. Savage was pumping up the turnover in order to sell it on to the UK bookmaker Mecca, and duly sold to them for a large sum. I wanted to attack this business by setting up right beside it in Ballybricken.

My plan was to be super-aggressive on our bonus terms in order to act as a magnet for bigger punters across the entire city, while having much lower overheads than Mecca. A former butcher's shop stood beside the corner pub twenty yards from the Mecca shop. I took a long-term lease on the property, rapidly obtained planning permission plus the betting licence, refitted the shop and opened in September 1990.

I recruited Caroline from R. Power's small shop in O'Connell Street; she went on to be one of our most successful ever employees. My favourite story about her relates to a robbery. A constant hazard of the betting business is men in balaclavas or motorcycle helmets bursting into the shop with a knife or gun demanding cash, despite CCTV and panic alarms.

One day in Waterford, a man appeared in the shop, dressed as a woman, with a scarf on his head and a wig. At the counter, he handed in a betting slip, then pulled out a large carving knife and menacingly demanded cash from Caroline.

'For fuck's sake, Pat!' she said. 'I know who you are. Get out before I call the guards.'

He did.

Whenever we opened another shop, I would tell new recruits of Caroline's heroics.

'Our standard policy with robberies is that you take a bullet on behalf of the company rather than pay out my money,' I would add, deadpan.

By the end of 1990, I had repaid my mother the money I had borrowed from her. The business was profitable. Deirdre was in position to oversee personnel and administrative issues, everything except the betting side of the business. We paid dearly for our mistakes, but because we were not drawing any salary from the business, we survived the toughest of times. Each year my objective was to add one more shop, preferably during the summer Dáil recess. In 1991 we opened a fourth 'virgin' shop (meaning the property was not previously a licensed betting office) in the heart of Carlow town.

Each new venture generated different, previously unmet problems and allowed me to make new and innovative errors. Short-term credit to a customer, who might have been a loyal regular and run out of cash, completely backfired. When they had cash a few days later, they would go elsewhere to bet, rather than repay me. I had given them a reason to move away. Bounced cheques were never recoverable. I had an implacable outright-refusal rule on these issues, telling staff, 'You can give them credit only from your purse.' I had a short fuse with errors such as over-payment of a bet or taking a bet without appropriate authorisation, and would phone Pat to moan about all my setbacks. He would mock my greed, perfectionism and impatience.

By November 1994, Deirdre and I had built Celtic Bookmakers from nothing into a chain of six betting shops. Tumultuous political events then catapulted me into the cabinet. From having a part-time passing role in the leadership of the business, with minimal day-to-day operational input, I had to forget about Celtic. My ministerial diary and political commitments were more than enough to absorb 100 per cent of my attention and focus. My instructions were for the business to cover its bills and not disturb me.

Pat Boland kept a watching brief. He and I had daily chats about the teething problems of my new venture. Even when he had no personal experience of a particular problem, Pat would find some contact who had, and was always in my corner against competitors or in customer disputes over a dubious bet. He taught me to accept the bad days and to keep moving.

When Pat lost heavily, he could lose his temper uncontrollably. I would bring a calculator to reconcile the records of transactions in the ledger and final cash on the way home, and whenever I found a shortfall, he would stop the car, search his pockets and feign outrage at me, as if I was accusing him of theft.

I was so appreciative of what Pat had done for me that when, on 12 May 2000, we moved from sole-trader status to an incorporated limited company, I gave him a one per cent share in the company and made him a non-executive director, albeit unpaid. At the height of the boom, when the company was flying high, he would regularly enquire what his one per cent was worth and mildly encourage me to buy it back from him.

While I was a minister, Deirdre and my sister Val managed the business. Any ambitions for growth were put on hold. There was no further development of the business until after the summer of 1997, when I was back in opposition. My sister Val had her second child and left the business in October 1995 to be a full-time mum. She recommended an experienced bookkeeper, Winnie Doyle, to do the weekly shop and overall business accounts. Winnie started working two days a week from her own home. By March 1996, she was working in the dining room of *our* home. By April 1997, we had converted a farmhouse loft into an office where Winnie worked, initially on her own, later to be joined by Mary Atkinson. Between themselves and Deirdre, they managed the daily and weekly cash records, bank account reconciliation and payroll administration. We installed computerised systems, including Turfsoft, a specialist software programme for the betting industry.

During my time in government, I couldn't help but notice on my travels criss-crossing the country the emergence of more and more new high-quality betting shops. Paddy Power had more than a hundred; John Boyle, from Newry, had a network of luxurious shops, especially in the north-east; Bruce Betting had a strong foothold in the midlands; and UK firms Ladbrokes and Stanley were consolidating nationwide operations in Ireland. Celtic, on the other hand, was at a standstill. Sooner or later, I would have to choose between politics and bookmaking. Business as a hobby was neither credible nor sustainable.

13: Building a Brand

I got out of politics in 2002 to concentrate on Celtic Bookmakers. Just one month into the following year, however, my gallop was brought to an abrupt halt. I was scouting potential offices in Galway, Sligo, Tuam and Ballina. Heading home, my lower back was in acute pain. I pulled in at Athlone and got some paracetamol from a chemist. When I woke up the next morning, I couldn't move. My left leg was paralysed, my toes numb. Deirdre had to help me hobble to the bathroom. I made various visits to my doctor in Gorey, Michael O'Doherty, who specialised in back problems. I went for physiotherapy but to no effect. An X-ray revealed nothing amiss.

At this stage, on good days I was on crutches, but mostly confined to lying flat in bed. This went on for several weeks. Later I went for an MRI scan, which revealed extensive wear and tear damage to two lower discs. My consultant suggested surgery, which I wasn't up for, or a course of injections. They were extremely painful and didn't work. Over many months I tried various alternative medicines, homeopathy, chiropractic and massage. None brought about any improvement.

To function at all, I had to live on a diet of anti-inflammatory and analgesic pills. I had two options. I could sprawl on the floor or I could stand up. That was it. Sorry. That's *still* it, even though I had surgery in June 2011, with two rods inserted to fuse my lower spine. I try not to aggravate it. Upside? Medicinal alcohol alleviates the pain.

My determination to propel Celtic Bookmakers forward was not going to be diluted by my dodgy back. I bought a second-hand Scudo white van with no windows in the rear compartment, and installed a mattress in the back. I would then drive the vehicle, pull in, take my tablets and lie down until the pain had eased, then drive off again, repeating the procedure every hour. On longer journeys Deirdre had to drive as I lay in the back. These journeys resulted in us opening six further shops in 2003.

The prospect of opening new shops had become a lot less daunting through my growing business relationship with Pat Crowe. Pat changed my life. A real Dub, from Crumlin, he always wore runners, was as thin as a whippet and had his hair tied in a small ponytail at the back of his head. Pat was at heart a carpenter, but could turn his hand to all jobs. He knew how to take short-cuts, cut corners and costs, and would work long hours to meet a deadline. I came to rely on him utterly.

Once I'd done a deal on a property and sorted out the regulatory issues, Pat could convert it into a Celtic betting shop to my specifications. We would agree the broad layout of where the counter, TV screens and seating would go, and around three weeks later I could walk into a finished betting shop.

A large map of Ireland hung on my wall. Each time I opened a new shop, I placed a red dot on it to indicate the new Celtic office. My ambition was to have a nationwide network of at least fifty shops and I would happily work sixteen hours a day to drive the business forward. Between 1998 and 2000, I added four shops, in Wexford, Dublin 6, Kilkenny and Athlone, which meant that by 2000 I had ten shops and an annual turnover of £12.9 million, with a net profit in excess of £300,000. The scale of the business dictated that we could no longer operate as sole traders, so in May 2000 Celtic Bookmakers was incorporated as an unlimited company.

In 1999 the reduction of the betting tax to five per cent had given a tremendous boost to our business. The government went further and introduced reforms to the 1931 Betting Act, extending opening hours to cover evening and Sunday racing. By then, every race meeting in Ireland and the UK was televised in shops. Betting on all kinds of different sports was growing, partly driven by the arrival of Sky Sports. Betting was now seen as part of the modern leisure industry.

I wanted to open flagship shops in the regional capitals of Cork and Limerick, preferably in the city centre, acting as a magnet for the wider urban area. A man named Richie Lonergan found me suitable properties for a fee. He had an in-depth knowledge of the off-course betting industry and had procured sites for Ladbrokes and Hacketts, the largest indigenous traditional family bookmaking firm owned and run by Cyril and Monica Hackett. It wasn't long before he was introducing me to potential landlords, such as a chemist in Upper William Street, Limerick, Jim McCormick, and a large split-level shop unit in Coburg Street, Cork. Next door was a funeral parlour, but we were the only betting shop on the north side of St Patrick's Bridge in the central city area.

Business was booming. We added shops in Gorey, Dun Laoghaire and Blackrock, and by the end of 2002 our turnover had climbed to almost €27 million, with a profit of €479,000. The changeover to the euro at the start of that year mirrored a pivotal growth period for the Irish economy. My plan in 2001 had been to get to twenty shops over a three-year period by opening at least three new shops per year. I submitted a development plan to Frank Casey, my local AIB branch manager and ally, which required an increase of our total borrowing facility from £138,000 to £350,000 with a continuing daily overdraft of £50,000. At this stage, we had thirteen years of trading behind us, building up a credible track record. The finance was approved.

Low inflation and an effective devaluation of the Irish pound by Ireland's having locked onto the euro at 78 pence had given a competitiveness boost to exports. The macro-economic conditions of low interest rates and access to vast new international credit were extremely favourable and buoyant. Even more significant was the reduction of the betting tax from five per cent to two per cent in the 2002 budget. The only cloud on the horizon was the British Horseracing Board (BHB) seeking to extract data charges for the text information in betting shops on runners and riders in British horse races. Concessionary terms were available in 2003, but each bookmaker must have a BHB licence in order to continue to receive pictures and text.

By the end of 2003 company turnover exceeded €41 million, with a profit of €223,000. I wanted to keep my corporation tax liability down each year, so we did the maximum reinvestment possible. The following year, we entered into commitments to operate thirty-five betting shops by the start of 2005. I took a chance at the start of the year, moving into a vacated small unit in Naas town centre, previously operated by Power's. But it was too small and didn't ultimately succeed. Most of the new shops were viable, including virgin shops such as Ballina, Roscommon, Portlaoise, Tuam, Mallow and Ennis. I bought Pat Boland's Metro betting shop and relocated it in new retail premises on the opposite side of Rush Street in Castlebar. We relocated the existing shops at Lombard Street, Dublin, in Wicklow town (again) and Carlow to new, bigger, more prominently positioned premises.

My biggest ever rent commitment (€92,000 per annum) occurred in taking over the ACC Bank building off Eyre Square in Galway. The busiest betting shops of Power's, Boylesports, Ladbrokes and local bookmaker John Mulholland were all situated in the same area. I wanted to go where the action was. We sublet the upstairs part of the property with a separate access. We also acquired as a going concern a betting shop in Crowe Street, Dundalk, from Terry Boyle (brother of John) for €120,000, on the basis that he had expended that level of investment to kit out the shop to a high standard. The pace of expansion was hectic.

By the end of 2004 certified turnover for the company was €69.1 million, with a profit of €359,000. The scale of the business required constantly higher standards of management and greater professionalism. We rolled out an expensive EPOS computerised system for bet acceptance and settlement. This provided a digitised copy of every bet, which could be downloaded to head office in Enniscorthy overnight. This transformed security systems, removing errors, revealing fraud and improving margins. We increased our marketing budget, prioritising large racecourse signage, with the Celtic Bookmakers name and logo close to the finish line. This was cheaper than race sponsorship and highly visible on the Racing Channel/SIS television coverage.

I was intolerant of sloppy or poor customer service, believing that a friendly smile, pleasant banter and an efficient service were essential to building customer loyalty. In order to get to know the punters' names, we introduced on the counter a blank sheet numbered 1 to 42. This corresponded to the number of lotto balls on the twice-weekly draws. Customers put their name against a number and were given a free bet if their number corresponded with the bonus-ball numbers.

My son Andrew was old enough to spend the summer holidays helping out with race-room work, learning the ropes the hard way – by making mistakes. Once he took a five-grand bet on Ernie Els in a US golf major at 10/1. When Andrew told me, I said, 'It was a brave bet to lay.' He started to panic when Els was in a two-way play-off for the trophy against some rookie. Fortunately for Andrew, Els ultimately lost. I didn't mind letting him sweat a bit.

For all this progress, I was becoming more concerned and anxious about the future of the business. Many towns that I scouted with a view to opening shops had more new betting offices each year. In towns where we had great shops, two or three outlets had sprung up around us. This increased capacity is not subject to verifiable statistics, but I sensed that the total national betting-shop estate increased from around nine hundred shops to more than 1,300. Excess capacity was apparent in many areas. I just couldn't convince myself that I should bet a hundred thousand euro in a capital outlay on each new shop.

Darker clouds were gathering. The betting tax was payable by the customer at two per cent, but many bookmakers decided to absorb this liability. Additionally, the BHB charge was now amounting to the equivalent cost of almost one per cent of total turnover. I'd had to write a painful cheque for €270,000 in early 2003. These 'tax wars' and additional data charges were making marginal shops unviable. Some indigenous competitors and family firms such as Bruce Betting were even more aggressive on bonuses than we were. Our once unique special offers were now commonplace. Ladbrokes and Boylesports became even more expansionary, often paying premiums of up to €500,000 for an individual shop purchase from an independent. Both had deeper pockets than mine. I decided to pull in my horns and focus on consolidating and improving our operational performance. Expansion could wait. Except, perhaps, in Britain.

The notion of opening betting shops in Britain started to form in my mind in late 2003. The logic was simple: the high-street betting industry was completely dominated by William Hill, Ladbrokes and Coral; they offered none of the competitive bonus terms that Celtic offered. In Ireland every betting shop provided the double-result terms of payment (first past the post and an amended result), but the chains didn't even do that. Running a betting shop was identical between the two countries. Gordon Brown, Britain's Chancellor of the Exchequer had introduced tax-free betting and replaced it with a 15 per cent gross profits tax a couple of years earlier and this regime was beneficial to my lower gross margin business model. What could be so difficult about setting up a handful of betting shops in the UK? The British spoke the same language and drove on the same side of the road.

I travelled regularly through South Wales, then along the M4 to London, and started to suss out Swansea. I located a 2,000 square-foot unit on the Kingsway. We were obliged to take all three floors of the building. It had a front and rear entrance, was really spacious and had once housed the *Western Mail* newspaper.

A fifteen-year lease was available. I reckoned I could use the second floor as a head office and storage facility, and the upper floor as a cheap and cheerful crash pad. I did the deal through a local estate agent, E. J. Hales, who acted on behalf of two elderly brothers living in London, who were to be my landlords. Now I had to obtain a betting-shop licence by appearing in front of three magistrates, laypeople who seemed never to have been inside a betting shop in their lives. The market was tightly regulated, and all three of the existing bookmakers had a legal army ready to go into battle to prevent newcomers providing them with competition. It was a scam of no benefit to anybody other than the lawyers involved.

I was determined not to be beaten. I found three local witnesses in adjoining pubs and paid them fifty quid apiece to testify that another betting shop was desperately needed. While I was pleased to have some locals on my side (albeit bought), I felt this aspect of the hearing was farcical. I explained our bonuses and how they were not available anywhere in Swansea, then spent a day and a half being cross-examined by three lawyers representing the bookmaker-objectors.

They made their submissions, explaining how poor business levels were. They omitted salient facts, like their profits from Fixed Odds Betting Terminals. (FOBTs operate gaming products, primarily roulette, poker and virtual sporting events, such as greyhound racing and penalty shoot-outs, and are the economic mainstay of the business model for high-street betting shops in the UK. They are controversial in that their critics have dubbed them the 'crack cocaine' of gambling addicts. They have never been legalised in Ireland.) My London barrister, Stephen Walsh QC, did a superb summing up: he ridiculed the vested interests, who were against real competition from a credible established Irish operator yet were pretending to have a civic agenda. The magistrates retired for three hours to consider their verdict. I was shitting a brick. My costs for this entire licensing process were enormous. If I lost, it was all wasted, flushed down the toilet. Worst-case scenario: I might even have to pay my opponents' legal costs.

We won. A betting permit was issued for our proposed property. Pat Crowe and his crew brought their van over and worked on site for four weeks. Early on, one of Pat's Welsh lads drilled through a concrete floor and cut into the mains electricity wire. It should have been laid three feet deep. He would have been killed but for the fact that he was standing on a wooden plank. The drill melted. He had to be rushed to hospital. Once they had discharged him, Pat got him as drunk as a skunk so he could laugh about it later, rather than make a claim. This was one of many teething problems: operating in sterling; registering with Her Majesty's Revenue & Customs (HMRC) for VAT, as an employer and for the gross profits tax; recruiting shop staff; and compliance with endless red tape.

One day a guy left a message in the shop for me to contact him. His name was Michael Legge. He had worked for thirty years in the South Wales betting business as an employee of Jack Brown bookmakers, the largest indigenous independent chain across Wales.

In July 2005 they had sold their 141 shops for £76 million to Ladbrokes, an incredible price of around £500,000 per shop, some of which were mere holes in the wall. I rang him. He explained that, as part of the former head-office staff, he was going to be made redundant and was currently on gardening leave. He would work for nothing.

'What? For nothing?' I asked incredulously.

'Just my verified expenses for a trial period until you get started.'

This was too good an offer for a cheapskate like me to turn down. I met Michael the following week. He provided a one-stop shop solution and stayed with us throughout our entire trading period there.

Celtic Bookmakers opened in Swansea on 25 July 2005. I bought the local Swans (Swansea City Football Club) and Ospreys (the local rugby team) sports kits to put in the front window – the generic Celtic name is, of course, every bit as Welsh as it is Irish. The brand (colours of red and green) resonated with the locals, in contrast to the 'English'-based multiple competition. Despite logistical and staffing problems, we were operationally functional. It was not easy running a business by remote control, but this was a minor financial element of our overall business and cash flow.

As always, it wasn't long before I was scratching around to expand. I arranged for Michael to do test docketing and scouting in Cardiff and Bristol. My plan was to create a small number of flagship shops, offering exceptional value in city centres, areas to which people in all the surrounding suburbs would gravitate.

We went for another magistrates' licensing hearing in Bristol on 25 January 2006. All the usual suspects turned up to object, not only the bookmakers' personnel but their army of lawyers. They bamboozled the magistrates, who had no clue about betting. They didn't much like me either. This time we were refused. Instead of backing off, I appealed to the Crown Court. The case dragged on for months, because we had to pick a suitable date for our competitors' legal representatives' diaries. To me, it was a sick, expensive joke. This time the hearing would be conducted by a professional judge, who could see through the self-serving arguments of the incumbent operators. I was stubbornly determined not to back down. Legal costs went through the roof. We won on appeal. I wish we had not.

Of all the Celtic shops I ever opened, Bristol was my worst mistake and biggest regret. Our reception from residents in the west of England was completely different from that in Wales. I had the impression we were perceived as Irish Paddies who mightn't honour a bet. Although we had successfully teamed up with the local *Evening Post* newspaper to offer £10 free bets, weekly shop turnover struggled to exceed £12,000.

I eventually offloaded the shop for ten grand to independent local bookmaker Roy Holbrook of the *Winning Post*, who traded for two years before he pressed the exit button. Much to my disappointment, and despite umpteen trekking sessions around the city centre, we were unable to procure a shop unit in Cardiff. We did find an available property in a side street off the main drag in Newport, about fifteen minutes east of Cardiff, situated midway between Swansea and Bristol.

Michael Legge identified Carmarthen as a potentially lucrative location for a new shop. It was the county town and busy capital of West Wales. In March 2006, we did a deal on a property in Lammas Street for a ten-year lease. I was properly prepared for the local magistrates' hearing this time, and our established operation in Swansea greatly enhanced credibility. We gained early approval and opened a lovely shop in August. Carmarthen proved our most successful British outlet, making profits of £50,000 annually. Our competitors, Coral and Ladbrokes, failed to upgrade their offices or to match our bonuses, which reinforced our image of quality and value.

Company turnover in Wales built up to almost €10 million annually, which was respectable by their standards. The British betting culture is far less mainstream than Ireland's. When the annual Cheltenham Festival is on, it's always front-page news in Ireland, but it's restricted to the sports pages in British papers. The critical comparative statistic is that in Ireland 17 per cent of all adults have more than one bet per week, against three per cent in Britain. The second difficulty is the profile dominance of the big multiple chains with their huge national marketing budgets. Regular punters sleepwalk into their shops despite unfavourable betting terms. It is hard to penetrate this fog. The big UK positives were FOBTs, few sharp punters and longer opening hours.

An unexpected feature of our UK venture was that Swansea became a second home to me. Deirdre made the top-floor apartment habitable, with a new fitted kitchen, two bedrooms and a sitting room. My son Andrew lived there while he was doing a commerce degree at Swansea University. I'm not sure what he learned about business, but he obtained a master's in gambling and a PhD in poker.

Our kids, as they moved through their teens, would listen cynically to my stories of brilliant new contacts made. Our elder daughter, Ciara, used to term them 'Dad's latest catch of the day'. Dad's catch of the day was always going to solve all problems. One such catch of the day, John Morse, had represented Coral at my original Swansea permit hearing. Having done a lot of work for Paddy Power's licensing applications in London, he had sympathy for my plight and we subsequently became good friends. In 2008, I transferred all my legal business in the UK to his office in Swansea.

Back home, 2005 was a tough year in the business, despite Ireland's Celtic Tiger economy roaring ahead. If more 4/6 favourites than 33/1 outsiders win races, the bookies' margins suffer. That year the sporting results favoured the punters. Even more difficult was the external environment: the smoking ban in March 2004 meant building alcoves outside the shops.

Our tax costs in the business were now considerable: about two million euro per year. We had to register to pay 21 per cent VAT on all imports and services, but were 'exempt' when it came to claiming any refund. Commercial property rates on each shop were soaring. PAYE/PRSI liabilities had to be met every two months. Notionally, of course, the customer was due to pay betting tax, but competitive pressures led to more and more localised tax discount wars, whereby the bookmaker absorbed the liability.

Celtic's business model was based on a gross margin of 10 or 12 per cent and net profit of 1.5–2 per cent. Paying the tax wiped out our profitability. From 1 May 2002, the British Horseracing Board introduced a licensing regime whereby it had to be paid for in addition to a tariff on live televised pictures. By 2005 our auditors reckoned this was costing us 0.91–0.95 per cent of turnover, plus 21 per cent VAT on top. This total cost (betting duty plus BHB) on turnover was turning heretofore viable shops into loss-makers.

I felt the BHB charge to be extortionist, excessive and illegal. William Hill had taken a case to the European Court of Justice against this data charge for their online business. They won in November 2004. Under the EU data directive, this information must be freely available (at no charge) to print and broadcast media throughout the world.

I was active in the Independent Bookmakers Association (IBA), established on 12 April 2005, through which we issued 'without prejudice' notice to the BHB that we were terminating the licence in six months' time, as provided under the contract terms as of 24 January 2005. The BHB hired Goodbody's solicitors and Paul Gallagher, SC. This revenue was worth approximately €18 million per year to them from Ireland. Celtic made a preliminary legal payment of €17,000 as its *pro rata* share. It was estimated that the legal costs for a full court hearing could exceed €400,000. We aimed to get the matter determined expeditiously in the Commercial

Court, a fast-track division of the High Court. We got a preliminary hearing in May, which led to a full trial in early November. Our goal was simply to void the contracts. The preparations for the case were voluminous, with umpteen boxes of evidence. It was agreed that I would be the first bookmaker to give evidence, so a detailed witness statement was prepared in mid-October.

A war of words erupted in the media between me and an abrasive Aussie, Greg Nichols, who was CEO of the BHB. SIS was a monopoly provider to all betting shops of basic data text and live pictures. Their legal advice was that they were obliged to cut off service to any bookmaker who had not paid in full to the BHB. Both refused all attempts at any negotiation. I accused the BHB of gross intimidation and said that all payments should be paid into an escrow account pending the judicial outcome. Nichols accused me of 'more bluster than reality' and 'using the case as a promotional vehicle'. I replied that if we won, we would be seeking a refund of payments made after our proceedings had been issued and would hold the directors of the BHB personally liable if they couldn't pay us. Heavy stuff. I loved the conflict.

The general speculation was that our prospects of success were limited. Many within the industry doubted our credibility. I was gung-ho.

Justice Peter Kelly heard the case. I was in the witness box for almost a full day. Our own barrister Brian Murray, SC, was superb with his opening statements and in privately cross-questioning me as part of our preparations. Because of my back problem, I asked the judge to let me stand in the box, almost cheek by jowl with him. He kindly agreed. My main argument was that the BHB had unlawfully imposed themselves on our commercial arrangements with SIS; every other organisation, such as newspapers, could obtain this written data of runners and riders in British horse races for free. This was a trumped-up way of blackmailing bookies. Dan O'Mahony (of Boylesports) was the second witness and well able to fight his corner.

However, none of the other independent bookmakers were eager to testify, fearing a mauling from Paul Gallagher. Terry Rogers, Barney O'Hare (Bar One Bookmakers), Dara Fitzpatrick and Pat Toolan also attended. It was a proper courtroom drama with the Irish BHB representative, Brian O'Farrell, formerly boss of Molloy's bookmakers, leading the charge for them and at all times being inflexible. As the case progressed, the word in the corridors (always critical in hearings) was that the judge was leaning in our favour. At the end of the first day, he suggested that both parties might profit from negotiating a settlement. Side talks continued into the night.

Eventually we were offered the ending of contracts in 2005 on the basis of no refund for past payments. Power's contacted some of our team to encourage agreement if terms seemed favourable, implying they would assist with the legal costs. We reached a settlement, but Celtic and Boylesports had to make specific payments for 2005. It was a major victory for the industry, but each side had to pay their own legal costs. All bookmakers benefited by not having to pay any further BHB liabilities for text services. Game, set and match. I reckoned, starting from Celtic's Irish turnover of €86.5 million in 2005, only yielding a net profit of €133,000, with projected growth, that this would be worth a million euro a year of savings to us.

The elation was short-lived. The total legal bill exceeded €1.5 million. At the next IBA meeting, we requested financial assistance from the multiples. William Hill said they would pay fifty thousand euro, but explained that nobody had assisted them with their European Court of Justice case. Ladbrokes promised to contribute, but Power's baulked. I was furious: they had requested our permission, on the day of the settlement, to access our in-house copies of Cox's legal papers, to which we had agreed. It was rumoured that settlement was worth €500,000 a month to Power's. Eventually they paid a miserly fifty thousand euro. In fairness to John Boyle, he agreed to underwrite the final legal bill; many smaller independents never stumped up and got a free ride.

Soon Power's left the IBA and opposed every lobbying measure we pursued. A further bitter row emerged in 2008, when SIS lost exclusivity for televising British race meetings. Approximately half the racecourses signed up with Turf TV and a subscription channel, RUK. Two sets of televised costs and contractors strategically shifted economic power from bookmakers to racecourses. It was important that the bookmaking industry stand united. Later, Power's unilaterally agreed to sign up to this televised racing service (with favourable concessionary terms for breaking the line). So we all had to follow suit. Power's logic seemed to be that the greater the weekly costs per shop, the less likely more new shops would open. While Stewart Kenny was no longer CEO, my relations with him and Power's were at an all-time low.

In reality, bookmakers with an Internet business were operating on a distorted playing field. While we were paying up to two per cent on all bets, they were making no contribution to the exchequer because of offshore rerouting of bets to the Isle of Man or Gibraltar. They only paid a fixed licence fee to the local tax authorities there, escaping significant turnover liabilities. Similarly Betfair, the mammoth online betting exchange, made little or no obligatory comparative tax payments on their gross revenue. The regulatory regime became even more favourable when Charlie McCreevy decided to reduce the betting tax further from two per cent to one per cent on 1 July 2006. Tax-free betting for punters was a boon to turnover. Along with the gigantic forward thrust each year of increased disposable income from the Tiger economy, everything seemed set fair for Celtic Bookmakers to resume rapid expansion back home.

In 2006 Celtic Bookmakers achieved a milestone turnover target of €101.7 million and a net profit of €300,000. Clearly, it was time to consider a significant acquisition. Consolidation was surely inevitable rather than endless extra capacity. It was time to talk to my bank about another significant development phase for the company; our brand had been built. A satisfactory intersection between the vanities of enormous turnover and the sanity of proper profitability had been attained because of court and government taxation decisions.

My dream of owning at least fifty Celtic Bookmakers shops was now an attainable goal. I set about plotting the most daring stage of our expansion.

14: 'All in on the river card'

My dream was to set up a family business that would be passed on to future generations as my great-grandfather had done.

By early 2006, we had progressively built up the business, from a dozen to twenty, then to thirty-five shops, an annual turnover of €100 million and fifteen consecutive years of net profitability, despite aggressive – and costly – capital expenditure programmes. We could not finance our business's move to the next tier from cash flow and profits. It would simply take too long. All the books I had read about corporate history suggested that I had to take on a significant loan or get an equity investment injection into the company. Different company executives and business leaders had told me that a reasonable approach to borrowing levels within a company was a debt to equity ratio of 1:1. I didn't know the equity value of the company, perhaps €6–8 million, but we had zero debt.

The most significant development in Ireland and the UK on the betting high street in 2005 was the acquisition of the entire Stanley Racing business of 624 shops by William Hill, making it – temporarily – the largest bookmaker in the world. This mega deal for £504 million included shops not only in the UK but also in Northern Ireland, the Isle of Man, Jersey and forty-five shops in the Republic of Ireland.

'We have parked a tank on the front lawn of Paddy Power,' was how the CEO of William Hill, David Harding, put it. It seemed to me that one day William Hill and Celtic Bookmakers could be a perfect fit. I made it my business to meet Ian Spearing, Hill's number two, who had responsibility for acquisitions and development strategy.

'Hill's doesn't do number six in any market,' he told me. That focused me on a merger between Celtic and Hills. But I did have another focus in the early months of 2006. Conversations at that time with business associates, economic experts and politicians, however, were all about one thing. Again and again, I was asked the same question: 'Ivan, why are you working so hard at the betting game when you could be making a fortune, with little or no work, in property development?'

Although returns on property over the previous decade had been spectacular, I found the area boring. However, housing development around my home town, Enniscorthy, was extraordinarily rapid, several new housing estates going up on the outskirts. These new homes were being snapped up as quickly as they were built. The commuter belt for Dublin, where prices had gone beyond the reach of ordinary working families, was now extending down the M11 beyond Gorey towards Enniscorthy.

I was told by experts that the 150 acres around Blackstoops had potential for decades of house construction with up to 2,000 houses possible. The farm could therefore be worth at least €25 million. I was advised that, such was the scale of development, this was the only remaining single large parcel of land on the northern side of the town that could support a sewage treatment plant.

My local AIB branch manager, Frank Casey, suggested I prepare a written Celtic Bookmakers development plan and he would arrange for someone from Business Banking in AIB head office to meet jointly to approve it. In May 2006, I submitted a proposal to obtain a capital credit line of €10 million to finance shop acquisition and expansion. This would be an interest-only loan, which Celtic would repay quarterly. After five years, the capital would be repaid by either a trade sale/merger of the business or the first phases of housing development and land sales at Blackstoops. I provided back-up documentation of the 2001 Enniscorthy development plan and a breakdown of six land parcels of the farm for phased development. Douglas Newman Good valued the farm at €26 million. At this stage Celtic Bookmakers was generating €80,000 per week in profit. We had taken in €4 million during Cheltenham week. Our management accounts were up-to-the-minute, indicating that 2006 would be our best-ever year. Frank Casey asked me to meet John Reynolds from Bank Centre in Ballsbridge to prepare a war chest of finance. They were enthusiastic to support us, liked our track record and believed it all made sense.

John was a great go-ahead young guy who knew about the betting/gambling sector, understood the need for ultimate consolidation and accepted the potential of our land asset. Instead of focusing on the net profitability of Celtic, he advised us to base everything on Earnings Before Interest and Taxation, Depreciation Allowed (EBITDA). While our EBITDA for the year ending July 2006 was €750,000, our projections for the year up to July 2007 and 2008 were for €4 million in EBITDA. Their rule of thumb was that valuations for companies could be assessed at a multiple of eight times the EBITDA.

A few weeks later, on a beautiful sunny May day, my mobile rang. 'Hello. Is that Mr Ivan Yates? Martin Honeywell here. I represent Sheila Pomeroy, the owner of Joe Molloy's bookmakers. I know you've expressed an interest in purchasing Molloy's in the past. I wanted to inform you that the business is about to be sold. We have provisionally negotiated heads of terms with a British bookmaker and it is at the legal stage. However, Sheila is the granddaughter of Joe Molloy, who set up the business in 1913. She wants to honour a pledge made to her parents, Kevin and Molly Pomeroy, that if the business was ever sold, it would be to another Irish independent bookmaker, to continue the tradition of a family indigenous business.'

I could feel my heart pumping as if it were a photo finish to a race with maximum liabilities: a combination of fear and elation. Elation at the chance to buy this established business. Fear that this might be a manoeuvre to engineer a Dutch auction.

'Martin, I'm familiar with the Molloy's shops and have been interested in buying them over several years. But maybe I can't afford to match the big boys. What's the price?'

Explaining the confidentiality terms they had agreed, he nonetheless indicated that €4 million would be required to outbid the provisional deal. He suggested I meet with Dermot Ryan, the financial controller of the company, to obtain information about the twelve shops and telebetting service.

After the meeting, Deirdre and I immediately carried out an unofficial inspection of all twelve shops and pored over the figures. The annual turnover was €20.6 million. The company was suffering from chronic underinvestment, leaving it vulnerable to predatory competitors. If the business wasn't sold soon, it would die.

We arranged a meeting with Sheila Pomeroy. I told her we were seriously interested, but had never undertaken such an enormous investment. She didn't want to lose the deal with Ladbrokes and would require a non-refundable deposit upfront. We agreed to buy nine shops – the other three were too dilapidated: €2 million, payable in June 2006, followed by €1.2 million in June 2007 and another €1.2 million in 2008.

The advantages for us were straightforward: no other compatible group of betting shops was actually for sale to give us our leap forward towards fifty shops; the geographic fit of the shops was excellent (giving us an enhanced position in the greater Dublin region, four more shops in County Tipperary, dual complementary shops in Bray and Kilkenny). Critically, it would allow us to set up a telebetting service by availing ourselves of Molloy's existing infrastructure. Because the shops were run down, I felt we could at least double turnover to €40,000 per week.

I still hesitated, doing the rounds of every expert whose brains I could legitimately pick. Nobody said 'Don't do the deal.' Ireland's economic growth rate was predicted to expand by at least five per cent per annum until 2015. We had fabulous demographics: the fastest-growing population in Europe, immigration of 70,000 annually, record employment levels.

Deirdre would go along with whatever I decided. AIB would definitely lend the money. I rang Andrew in Swansea him to explain my quandary.

'Dad, when I'm playing poker in the casino, sometimes you have to go all in on the river card.'

The river card is the last card facing up. I had to have the bottle to do it. At current levels of profitability, I could finance two of the annual payments out of cash flow. We did it, and announced it, signalling our intention to grow by acquisition. This brought our total staff to more than two hundred and sixty people, so we had to take on a full-time human resources person at head office. Brigid Rossiter left Irish Pride Bakery in Taghmon, a village in Co. Wexford, to join us.

Within a year we had fully assimilated the nine shops. Dunboyne suffered a serious setback with the opening of a new Power's shop in prime position in the town. Some shops increased turnover fivefold. Gross revenue objectives for the next three years were: 2008 €160 million; 2009 €200 million; 2010 €250 million. In 2007, we were well on target to achieve our best year ever with an EBITDA of more than €3 million and a net profit of €2 million, despite maximising reinvestment. My theory was that if we were going to compete in the Formula One arena of the Irish betting industry, we had to have a top-class engine, and that required constant reinvestment.

I perceived us to be the equivalent of the Lidl or Aldi supermarkets; not as ubiquitous as Dunnes or Tesco, but a competitive threat. A critical growth component was the telebetting facility; our target was to generate €20 million per year turnover. Twenty per cent of all Irish bets were placed at that time over the phone. We organised in-shop promotions to encourage regular customers to open accounts. The Cheltenham Festival had been an outstanding success in procuring new business, with €50 free bets for all new accounts opened then. I participated in several Cheltenham previews.

Deirdre was the glue holding the company together as a family business. She recruited and got to know every member of staff, always enquiring about the big events in their lives – births, bereavements and marriages – which were properly acknowledged. Deirdre does not do head-on conflict, but still manages to get her way. When she was interviewing potential employees, Pat Crowe's lads used to bet on the chances of the best lookers among the female candidates. They decided Deirdre must have a prejudice against pretty women. She fiercely denies this.

My big PR project for 2007 was to maximise my and Celtic Bookmakers' profile during the general election on every media platform, as well as generate €500,000 in betting revenue.

In the early summer of 2007, I received a fascinating call to arrange a meeting. It was from two guys in their early thirties, who had been schoolmates and were employed with sizeable separate corporates, one running the online division of a really successful bookmaker, the other in an indigenous stockbroking/corporate finance firm. They wanted to work for themselves and be equity owners in a new Internet bookmaking business. I met them in my home and they gave me a glossy thirty-page presentation, really slick and exceptionally professional. The lads had serious street credibility in terms of what it took to build an online gambling business and structure a corporate deal. They had done considerable research into Celtic: its turnover, brand image, shop-network profile. They had an equally impressive analysis of the overall betting sector.

In a nutshell, they were proposing to leverage off our brand and create a significant online operation. They were keen to access the Irish betting industry, viewing Celtic as an ideal platform to build a strong number four in the market. They had ambitious plans to attain €300 million in turnover by 2010. They argued that the revenue growth and net profit margins online would greatly exceed that of retail betting. They viewed Celtic as a bird with one wing: now was the time to create a Celtic Bookmakers online business. Specifically, they were offering to leave their jobs and set up a new joint-venture company. This would be a merger between our parent company and their proposed management buy-in. They provided detailed projections and draft contract terms. They would establish a new Dublin-based office to run the venture, which would merge with our existing race room. It would operate on a 24/7 basis. I was impressed.

Being a technophobe, I wasn't in any position to second-guess the practicalities of the proposition. I had listened to Stewart Kenny repeat to me since 2000 that online gambling and gaming were where the future lay. He visualised guys on their 3G mobile phones having a bet on their Internet account several years before it became reality. However, I had read lots about the dotcom bubble and mega investors' wipe-outs. I was aware from Power's accounts of significant initial losses and that it had taken their online division five years to start paying its way. The two lads explained that gaming products, such as casino roulette, poker and other games, offered the potential for significantly higher net margins, with relatively low levels of investment. They had the experience and relationships to add these in a cost-effective manner.

I had no spare capital and was concerned not to overstretch myself with borrowings beyond €5–6 million. I asked the lads to come back with a detailed business plan and proposed capital investment costings. I was genuinely interested and excited at the prospect of the company making a leap in a direction that I was too terrified to engage in myself.

They submitted a detailed indicative proposal, which set out how Celtic.com would grow: year one would generate €10 million; year two would deliver €30 million; year three €75 million, with respective operating loss/profit projections of €2.7 million (loss), €1.3 million and €2 million. They provided detailed projections for the number of active customers, total bets, and an average bet stake. They estimated the marketing budget of €3 million in year one, rising to €4.5 million in year three. It seemed that the cost of marketing the brand and client acquisition was anything up to €100 per customer. Additional costs related to IT hardware, software, and employees' wages.

The funding plan was to borrow €3.5 million from the bank, with €1 million investment each from Celtic and their management buy-in team. This was a high level of gearing. I reckoned if it was a disaster, there would be a loss of around €6 million, with me carrying the can. The package also involved a remuneration package of €300,000 for them, a valuation multiple of twenty times their investment within the overall Celtic company valuation, and a 15 per cent equity share in Celtic, to be awarded to them in the form of new ordinary shares, plus various future incentive share issues based on performance.

I felt that this was my last chance to get into the online betting market, as the sector was starting to mature and latecomers would struggle to establish a presence. I thought the guys were typical of the breed who would bring us from a family organisation to a proper corporate structure. I found it impossible to attract such personnel to work in Enniscorthy. A Dublin base would overcome this problem. They could remodel the geographic perception of Celtic.

Despite all this, I turned them down. My instinct was that fixed-odds online bookmakers would struggle to compete with the betting exchanges, which provided much better odds to punters through, mostly, Betfair's layers. My other fear was that customers online were not mugs: they had multiple Internet accounts and bet with you only when you were going the wrong price.

The train was leaving the station and I wasn't on it. I got this badly wrong, although other independents lost millions in the attempt to gain market penetration. In retrospect, the dominance of the cyber platform relative to retail bookmaking was inevitable, with total dominance online in every facet of gaming and gambling. The younger generation live entirely online. My reasoning was that I should stick to what I knew best, the high street, and not take on a further mountain of debt in a sphere that I was not comfortable with. My clinching and decisive internal argument was that in any prospective deal with William Hill, this Internet joint venture would be surplus to requirements. They wouldn't want to use anything other than their own facilities. I did not want to mess the guys around and couldn't reveal my medium-term intention to flip my business.

The previous year, I had had a few meetings with two lads from Limerick, John Lyons and Pat Murray. They were partners as commercial property developers with other careers. They had developed a retail unit in Dooradoyle, Limerick (opposite the regional hospital), for letting as a betting shop. When the deal had fallen through, they had decided to open the shop themselves, calling it U Bet. They went on to open seven further shops in the mid-west region. I had a few meetings with them and was tepid about acquiring them. I knew they had been trying to sell to Ladbrokes, Boylesports and Hill's without any success. They were looking for more than €1 million to offload as a going concern.

By the summer of 2007, John and Pat renewed their dialogue with me. I was indifferent. They had fitted out all the shops with the latest technology, but their management systems were dire. The business was haemorrhaging cash and served as a distraction from their core enterprise of property. They owned the freehold property of all the outlets, except one. They desperately needed a credible tenant. They started to lower the price. I met them in Clonmel and offered them €500,000 on the basis that there would be a one-year break clause on all the leases so that I could exit any site I chose. If I got three or four good shops out of it, it would be a reasonable deal.

Having been through the Molloy's experience of taking over a number of shops, we knew how to implement a simultaneous shop transformation to our livery and brand. On 8 August, we issued a joint press release announcing the acquisition for an undisclosed sum. This would bring us up to sixty-two shops, with more than three hundred staff. It made us the largest bookmaker in County Tipperary, with seven shops in total. It greatly intensified our presence in the larger County Limerick area, renowned for gambling.

We made an offer, which they accepted. I was amused to read the related newspaper coverage, which indicated that the price was between €2.5 and €8 million. We spent an additional €300,000 upgrading and marketing the chain, achieving an average turnover of €40,000 per week per shop.

By January 2008, we had opened our sixty-sixth shop, in Cashel, and relocated to fabulous new premises in Wexford town during the following month. Celtic's turnover in Ireland exceeded €180 million, with an EBITDA of around €1.4 million. We were servicing the interest-only AIB repayments of €355,000 annually.

At this stage we had four shops in the UK and had climbed the learning curve there. I had in place a team that was much more proficient and professionally trained at all management functions than I ever was. We had achieved my target positioning to leverage a significant merger, under which we could be the smaller party. If a suitable exit door presented itself, I would take it. What could go wrong?

15: Lights, Camera – Reinvention

'Linda Sherlock here, Ivan. Voice from the past? I used to be on the Oireachtas gallery. I was there with RTÉ.'

'Ah, Linda. How are you?'

'Well, I now work as producer on a programme called *The Week in Politics*.'

'Oh, yeah, seen that.'

'As you know, 2007 is a big election year and we're doing some forward planning. You may not have heard of this American guy named Frank Luntz. He has this special focus-group kind of technology whereby he ascertains opinions in a kind of specific setting and we were looking for Irish pundits to appraise what he's doing and give an insight into what is an American technology. Would you be interested? It involves maybe three or four shows, going around the country. We're talking to other people as well, someone with a Fianna Fáil background and other communications experts and so on. How would you feel about that?'

'Grand . . .' Hmm. No mention of money. Still . . . 'Look, I have great regard for Seán O'Rourke. Don't know the first thing about what you're talking about.' But, methinks, Celtic Bookmakers will be taking bets in every constituency. This could be a wonderful opportunity for Celtic to get our brand out there. 'I'll tell you what, Linda, I'd be very interested in doing that. You just let me know when and where I'm going to turn up – I may need some training or whatever. Do put me on your shortlist and call me back.'

Time went by. Then came another phone call. Would I turn up to Collins Barracks in Dublin on such-and-such a night? Seán O'Rourke would be there. Right. When I arrived, Terry Prone was there. I'd been on one of her courses with Tom Savage and really enjoyed it. They're searingly blunt, the two of them: 'Get to the point. Be prepared. Stop faffing around and don't be taken off your agenda. This is your air time as a politician. It's up to you to be interesting, understandable and memorable.'

So Terry was there, as was *Irish Times* columnist Noel Whelan. I knew Noel's father, Seamie Whelan, from Ballycullane in New Ross. Noel had run in Dublin for Fianna Fáil and not quite made it before going to work in Fianna Fáil head office. And then my old pal Seán O'Rourke – the first big interview I'd done after quitting politics had been with him. All good, so far.

The briefing was complicated. There was going to be this and then that and, after Makeup, there would be the other, and we needed to know about this department, and that camera trains would be here and moving slowly to there. Frank Luntz was clearly going to be the star of the show, with us commentators as bit players. There was so much production in advance, it was like a kind of circus. I was circling a table, which was scattered with sandwiches, notes and cups of coffee, when Terry Prone looked at me with extreme irritation. 'Ivan, do me a favour. Sit down. You're a total distraction walking around like that.'

I explained that I couldn't sit down because of my back, and offered to lie down instead. She immediately apologised, not having known about my problem, and I lay on the floor. A few minutes later, I hauled out a vial of tablets and washed a couple of them down with some red wine. She looked a question. 'Morphine,' I said truthfully. Her eyes closed while she absorbed that. It was pretty obvious she thought I was going to be a liability to the show. Just then, I was summoned to Makeup, and ten minutes later, it was lights, camera and countdown.

Frank Luntz was a bit like a college lecturer: he put up and postulated certain ideas, then asked the audience questions. They were to press keypads 'Yes' or 'No'. They could also use their handsets to indicate, when they were listening to one of the political party leaders, whether they liked or hated what was being said. Luntz then went away, measured it and came up with his analysis of who was going to win the election.

Then Seán would come to me, Noel and Terry for comments on what Luntz had said. It seemed to me very like *The X Factor*: Simon Cowell, Sharon Osbourne and Louis Walsh. Terry was Sharon Osbourne. I thought she would fight with me, but I think she was so relieved that I could speak without slurring that she left me alone. However, I quickly picked up that Terry did not like Frank Luntz and that it was mutual. She thought he was a fraud. I decided to stay out of that and stick to what I knew. Cut away all the analysis and Noel Whelan was role-playing the unreconstructed Fianna Fáiler to my ex-insider cynic. I had jettisoned Fine Gael, they hadn't jettisoned me, and I had no reason to be bitter about politics and politicians. On the other hand, I had no particular interest in espousing the Fine Gael side of any argument.

Celtic Bookmakers was my first and only priority in the series. I'm sure Terry would have wanted to plug the Communications Clinic, but she couldn't possibly do it with the ease and fluency I could: with every fourth sentence I threw in some gambling analogy, talk about odds or something like that. I was using the thing as a vehicle, as I did all subsequent interviews in that 2007 election. I would give the odds on Kenny to be Taoiseach, Bertie to be Taoiseach. I would predict the odds on the Progressive

Democrats getting ten seats or the odds on them to get no seats at all. I was a version of John McCririck. To treat politics, this revered profession, as if it was a horse race was bold, but nobody else talked about politics like that, so people loved it.

I had done a few celebrity-based TV programmes, including *The Panel* a couple of times, *Celebrity Bainisteoir* and *Wild Trials*, but the Frank Luntz programme moved me into a whole new space. My public persona changed. People who remembered me as a minister began to see me in a new way, and younger people who didn't know me at all developed an understanding of me as someone irreverent and chronically disrespectful.

My attitude on the show was a combination of not taking it too seriously and seeing it as light entertainment. It was blissfully different from the days when I was a po-faced politician making a pronouncement on the Fine Gael position on A, B or C, avoiding mistakes and getting my sound-bites in. I now had the freedom to be a vagabond, while promoting Celtic Bookmakers.

'And I'm betting on that too,' I would say, or 'The odds are shortening on candidates who do X.' And 'Anyone who wants to make money on this election should bet on Y.'

The programme opened up for me the possibility of becoming the Eamon Dunphy of politics. I could be a pundit. Halfway through the first programme, I actually thought, Snap! I'm home. It was such a thrill, talking about politics and politicians in the way I would talk to Phil Hogan. Down and dirty. The freedom of not being obligated to the Fine Gael party, not being part of the team game of politics. I could talk in a kind of crude way about the naked ambition of politicians, that the national interest was their career interest, and doing it in a kind of boldly cynical, naughty way that effectively said, 'Never mind all that respectable veneer stuff. This is what it's *really* all about.'

The series ran for three or four programmes in urban and rural locations. We went to Boyle, we went to Clonmel, we went to different places to sample a range of opinion. The groups were chosen from various segments of society, based on demographics, age and gender. Essentially, what Luntz was doing was using a slice of Irish opinion to predict what would happen in the general election. Actually, he got it all arseways. He predicted that Pat Rabbitte would be Taoiseach, which was never going to happen to the Labour Party leader. That was just crazy. Bertie Ahern won the 2007 election pretty convincingly.

Afterwards Seán O'Rourke used Noel and me regularly on his lunchtime programme as a Punch and Judy. An opinion poll came out: good for Fianna Fáil? Bad for Fine Gael? The leadership debate. Then *Morning Ireland* took it up: here's the Fianna Fáil gene-pool pundit response; here's the Fine Gael gene-pool response. You know what baggage each of them carries. This is their spin on it.

On the day of the count, the three of us were in a cast of thousands in one of RTÉ radio's biggest studios for a programme presented by Seán O'Rourke and Rachael English which involved a constantly changing roster of candidates, successful and unsuccessful, and major figures like Garret FitzGerald. At one point, Seán went right around the studio asking who would be the outstanding winner of the election. Various people named candidates from different parties and said why they thought they were the stand-out of the campaign. Some people dithered, either because their favoured person had already been picked or because they were having difficulty choosing a candidate, but when he went to Terry, she didn't hesitate for a second.

'The outstanding winner of the election was Ivan Yates,' she said. 'He came out of nowhere, or at least out of being half-remembered, and in a matter of weeks he became a media star. He should abandon that betting stuff and move into media.'

The people in the studio laughed. But I was surprised to notice how many of them, including Garret FitzGerald, nodded at Terry's judgement. The programmes had been great fun – watching Terry's dislike of Luntz develop into full-blown loathing had given each edition an extra frisson, but that was it.

The first time it dawned on me that the election had had some impact on my persona, as opposed to me trying to promote Celtic Bookmakers, was about a month after the election when I met Mark FitzGerald, Garret's son. 'You do know that the 2007 election was the best election you ever had? And you weren't a candidate,' he told me. 'You were the most interesting thing in that election. You have a real opportunity in media.'

Terry had been telling me this all along, every time I met her, and I had ignored her. I thought it was just flattery. I realised it hadn't been when Newstalk said they wanted me to present *Breakfast*. I couldn't get my head around what was different. I had done a great deal of broadcasting down the years, and a pretty mixed bag it had been. Some of it was enjoyable, some horrific – like the time I had a brain freeze on the old *Questions and Answers* – and some disappointing, like when I had subbed for George Hook on *The Right Hook* at the request of his producer, Mark Simpson. Mark was a really strong supporter of mine, who stood by me when I made a hames of it, which several people told me I had. They were right. First, I was not at home in the studio environment. I used to get quite tense and nervous when the red light came on: I was afraid I'd lose my concentration or train of thought in the interview. The interviews were very long and I found it difficult to talk to anybody for twelve minutes, whereas George had this meandering style. It really did not matter if there was a guest there at all. He could just talk and talk and talk.

But I was beginning to see a downturn in the economy and a downturn in our business, so I was not going to brush away any possibility of earning a bit of extra money. So, instead of seeing media as transient and a bit of a laugh, if I got a second opportunity I was going to take it mighty seriously. I met Frank Cronin, the Newstalk CEO, and Garrett Harte, the editor, in the Schoolhouse restaurant on Northumberland Road. They were enthusiastic about putting me on *Breakfast*. I thought they were out of their latitude, I genuinely did. How could it work to put me alongside Claire Byrne, a BBC-trained journalist? Everyone on the show knew the etiquette of journalism, what questions to ask. I just nattered away and had proven on *The Right Hook* that I was a head wreck for everybody. I could not get my arse in or out of an ad break. I had no sense of timing. I would let items run over. They still wanted me.

I decided to go back to Terry Prone, who had already turned me into a newspaper columnist, whether I liked it or not. I had done a chapter on Celtic Bookmakers for a book KPMG had produced about entrepreneurs. The Communications Clinic does consultancy and training for KPMG, so Terry saw the chapter and decided I should talk to Tim Vaughan, editor of the *Irish Examiner*, about a column. He said yes. In the beginning, I would send my first draft to Terry for her to sub-edit and tidy up, but after a few weeks she told me I didn't need her any more. The *Examiner* and Tim Vaughan were brilliant to me for almost three years, me writing a weekly column on whatever topic I chose, submitting copy weekly to assistant editor Jack Power, an absolute gentleman to deal with. So when Terry ordered me into doing some run-throughs in their offices, I said, 'Yes, ma'am.'

That provided me with the humbling opportunity to cock up in private – several times, as I tried to come to terms with the multi-tasking involved in a radio show. You have to focus on an interview, listen to the producer's instructions in your ear, read listeners' texts, lead into traffic reports, ad breaks and news bulletins, often simultaneously. Terry pushed me relentlessly, tolerating no excuses.

It was tough, but had the side-effect of making me believe her when she kept telling me I had the personality, voice and intelligence to make it in radio. I had disbelieved her up to that point. The training sessions changed that because she drove me so hard and also because she had nothing to gain. I kept offering to pay her. She kept telling me to shut up and make notes. She seemed in charge of basic skills while Anton Savage, managing director of their company, put a useful frame around the programme for me.

'In the morning,' he said, 'as your listener, I do not want you having a long conversation with a wine waiter, a discussion about the red, the white, the older of the two Bordeaux, as you would do with an evening meal, a dinner. In the evening, you're out to relax and enjoy yourself. In the morning, it's porridge or cornflakes time – I just want my news information so I can get on with the rest of the day. In the evening, my top shirt button's undone and I want to relax – yeah, that's interesting. Never thought of that angle. I want a more relaxed conversational pace, whereas in the morning it's bam-bam-bam, get on with it.'

It took a while, after I went on the air, to match that advice with what was happening on the programme. At the beginning, Claire Byrne was concentrating on giving people the information they needed for the day and I was a loose boot with an undefined kicking role. Claire wasn't comfortable giving her opinions because in her view it was her job to ask questions and be fair. I had no interest in delivering news, all solemn and uniformed like a postal worker. I had even less interest in news-gathering. Almost everybody in any newsroom wants to come first with stories. The urgent takes precedence over the important. Newstalk were interested in getting an interview before RTÉ or Today FM got it. I wanted to tell people what I thought about things, especially if someone in authority was spouting a load of cobblers. Every time I sensed a moral consensus building, I wanted to kick it in the balls. I wanted to be outrageous, not an earnest, worthy, *nice* broadcaster, but it took me a while to get past expectations.

Then Claire moved on and a young lad named Chris Donoghue came along. He'd been around the station for ages, and if anybody ever sponsored an eager beaver award, Chris would win it, hands down. He'd get up at two in the morning; he'd do any outside broadcasts; he would record interviews all day, undertake endless research, Twitter away; he'd do the work of a producer, edit tapes and take charge of everything I was incapable of doing. A totally admirable professional.

On air, however, I didn't treat him as a totally admirable professional. I treated him as if he was an intern, there for work experience. I took the position of a raddled old roué, scoffing at the innocence of this personification of the younger generation. I rubbished his legitimate conclusions and proposed unacceptable ones instead. I lectured him on the realities of politics and business. I laughed at his rectitude.

Nobody had ever broadcast a radio news programme where one presenter humiliated the other but Chris was clever enough to realise that, bizarre as it was, it worked for both sides. Deirdre and I had dinner one night at Claire Byrne's house. 'I really don't get your on-air relationship with Chris,' she told me.

She meant that she thought it was appalling. It was bullying. And she was absolutely right, but it was beginning to work in a way nobody had expected. On one side of the studio was this news-hungry eager beaver and on the other was a big old dog raising his head now and again. Listeners told each other about this odd programme – 'Couldn't be less like *Morning Ireland*' – and our ratings began to climb. I became surer of my radio persona, helped by a note I'd made when Anton Savage had trained me. 'Don't set out to be likeable,' he'd said. 'If you try to win all the people all the time, you'll be so bland and so boring you'll have nobody listening to you.'

That gave me the courage to cope when the texts came in, saying, 'Ivan, I now know you're the greatest wanker of all time.'

'What a discerning listener,' I would say.

I wouldn't read out the complimentary texts, only the critical ones. I would deliberately look for the ones that were shitting on me, read them aloud and attribute fantastic insight to their writers. In no time, listeners began to see that as part of the programme and enjoy someone who didn't take themselves too seriously. That said, my new job was a culture shock in every respect. I was used to getting up early in the morning, but not in the middle of the night. I couldn't go to sleep on time, and walking into the place in the pre-dawn dark, looking at all these kids who were half my age, I would wonder what the hell I thought I was doing.

My biggest ally was Garrett Harte. I had known his father, Paddy Harte, a Fine Gael TD from Donegal. He became a more hands-on producer of *Breakfast* when the previous producer emigrated to Canada, having delivered a farewell speech stating that the final trigger for his departure had been my arrival. Garrett was infinitely patient when I got hand signals wrong and made dozens of mistakes that would drive the entire production team scatty.

My back pain meant that the microphone had to be mobile so I could sit, stand or kneel, depending on how bad it was. Towards the end of the programme, I might even have to lie down on the floor. Interviewees found it astonishing, but only Senator David Norris ever complained.

Whatever else I was, I was not a prima donna. At the beginning, even the guys making the coffee were telling me how to do my job. 'Okay,' I would say. 'Tell me more.'

Garrett Harte was the person who believed in me, believed in the show and believed in the station. About twenty minutes before air, in the early days, I'd be listening to reverential discussion of something and I would lose it. 'For fuck's sake, does anybody believe this shit? You're completely missing the main point! Do you not see how this is going to play out?'

This diatribe would come up at them from the floor and some of them would be wearing an expression that said, 'God love him, he didn't get much sleep last night,' or 'Manchester City obviously lost yesterday – he's like a bull that swallowed a wasp.' They probably would not get what I was on about. Then Garrett would pipe up: 'Go for it,' he'd say. 'Just exactly as you said. Don't change a word of it. Say it at five past seven and at five past eight, just a stream of consciousness.'

I tried to build a radio persona that was a hybrid: former politico, with insider knowledge, businessman with experience, good and bad, resident cynic and wind-up merchant. I would recklessly make predictions and forecasts, and carry on regardless if I was proved wrong. I wanted to say what no one dared say but many were thinking. My core values were pro-taxpayer and against all vested interests.

My demeanour was that of a world-weary curmudgeonly Victor Meldrew. I could do without sex but not glasses. Bed was merely for sleeping comfortably, sex just a memory. I portrayed myself as a submissive husband, an outdated technophobe, a balding has-been, a tiresome old fart of limitless self-confidence. Sport was as serious as economics, the way I saw it; I hated Manchester United and loved Manchester City. I claimed every passing prejudice as my own, which on one occasion caused former Manchester United footballer Paddy Crerand to slam down the phone, live on air. I was all the time on the lookout for elephants in the room and emperors with no clothes.

I could not have had a better time between 2009 and 2012 to be presenting a national radio show each weekday morning. Some of the political and commercial dramas of those days will never be repeated. While people were switched off by the negativity of endless bad news, they needed to know what would happen next, and I had to develop the ability to eschew scripted questions and engage with curiosity and spontaneity.

All media shows live or die by two factors: ratings and sponsorship. *Breakfast* was sponsored first by Siemens and then Aer Lingus. Advertising was also strong. The JNLRs, surveys conducted every quarter, give two measurements of listenership: a 'reach figure' of people who listened to the programme at any single point the previous day, and an average quarter-hour (AQH) figure of listeners during the programme. From April 2009 onwards we hovered between 53,000 and 63,000 for a 'reach figure'. By the time I left in April 2012, we broke a new record, winning a figure of 138,000 under this heading.

This generated other kinds of work for me, all of it welcome for reasons that will soon become clear. I presented a dozen programmes in a TV3 series entitled *Business Matters* for David Harvey and filled in for Vincent Browne over a number of years. Sebastian Hamilton, now group editor of the *Irish Mail* newspapers, took me to lunch.

'Ivan, I'm listening to you in the morning waxing lyrical on daily sports controversies,' he told me. 'You seem full of partisan opinions – just the guy we're looking for to write on the back page of our sports supplement *The Title* in the *Mail on Sunday*.'

Charmed by Seb's persuasiveness, I agreed to do it for a short period. My first offering led to litigation against the paper, but soon a greater problem arose: I quickly ran out of opinions and forecasts on sport, exhausting my limited repertoire. They kindly released me when I realised I did not have it in me to be a full-time sports writer.

Often when one door closes, another opens, and that was what happened in May 2010 when I was contacted by Ger Walsh, an old friend from my Wexford political days. Ger was then group editor with the *People* papers and he wanted me to write a weekly page for syndication in all their publications, including the *Kerryman*, the *Donegal Democrat*, the *Roscommon Herald* and the *Wexford People*. I agreed and enjoyed writing about politics, current affairs and sporting events, especially since I had free rein to comment on any controversy of the moment.

Because I had done a chapter in KPMG's entrepreneurial book, the accountancy firm asked me to speak at a series of corporate breakfast events they were hosting for clients in Dublin, Cork and Galway. The audience maintained their attention and laughed occasionally. Economist Jim Power, seeing me in action, advised me to get in touch with Frances Keane of Personally Speaking. She turned out to be a highly professional operator, who, like me, didn't speak Latin so didn't understand the concept of *pro bono*. Originally from Tipperary, she is a practical, no-nonsense, common-sense agent. She has developed a lengthy list of corporate clients, who hold annual and special events, and all the top high-profile speakers. They include David McWilliams, Eddie Hobbs, George Hook, Mark Little, John Bowman, Alan Dukes and other household names from the worlds of sport, celebrity, commerce and media, plus former politicians.

'Ivan, there are some golden rules,' she told me, when she took me on. 'Don't ever speak drunk. No cursing, swearing, no filthy jokes. Treat all clients with respect and be punctual.'

She put my biographical details on her website and soon the diary started to fill with keynote speeches at seminars, after dinners and at conferences. To handle this revenue and my related costs of living in Dublin in order to fulfil my media and other commitments, I set up a company for full effective corporate-tax compliance, called Platinum Presentations. Deirdre acted as my secretary, doing invoices, accounts and bank reconciliation. This company directorship added to my list of non-executive directorships.

I had received invitations to join the board of a handful of companies. I became a director of Chevron Training in County Wexford, One51, and I was appointed to the board of Geothermal Energy. I was also chairman of Irish Radio Sales, which gave me a keen insight into local independent radio. To me, none of these was a sinecure. They were not money for old rope. I took the non-executive director role very seriously and enrolled on a chartered director programme run by the Institute of Directors in the Irish Management Institute.

What neither listeners nor readers nor audiences in hotel ballrooms knew was that I was living, if not a lie, then a serious contradiction. On the one hand, I was popular, well paid and successful in a new career that had presented itself to me, thanks to a breakthrough TV programme to which I had paid less respect than it deserved, and to some good friends, who had more faith in me than I had. On the other, Celtic Bookmakers was moving into serious financial trouble. As one aspect of my life took off and soared, another was heading for a catastrophic crash.

16: Celtic Crash

As a pundit in the 2007 general election and thereafter in economic commentary, I was constantly accused of being excessively negative and pessimistic. But even I had not begun to fathom the degree or duration of the downturn. The recession – or depression – between 2008 and 2013 was the worst in Irish history. It was the only recession in which the indigenous Irish banking industry collapsed. It was a cataclysmic event, with which the fortunes of Celtic Bookmakers and the Celtic Tiger were inextricably linked. None of the surrounding circumstances reduce my culpability and responsibility for what was to ensue, but they were without precedent and brought down large numbers of businesses, which, like mine, had been significantly successful for more than a decade.

Celtic Bookmakers' accounting year ended in July annually. On Holy Thursday, 20 March 2008, Padraig Hall, our chief finance officer, completed the half-year management accounts from August 2007. I had started to notice, since the builders' two-week holidays, that many of our most successful shops were not showing the same buoyancy during and since the critical week of the Galway and Glorious Goodwood racing festivals. Nothing to be too alarmed about, just no further forward bounce on our rapid trajectory of revenue growth. Or so I thought until Padraig showed me figures that revealed a six-month loss of more than €726,000, a huge amount of money that could not be explained away by winter factors of shorter days and fewer betting opportunities on racing and sports events. That whole Easter weekend I thought of nothing other than how to rectify this haemorrhaging of losses. Over the past year, we had spent more than €1.6 million on expansion. Now everything stopped. Dead.

Once I had stabilised the cash flow situation, it was time to pursue my main goal of a sale to William Hill. For an asking price of €18 million, we would give them, in one leap, the critical mass they required to be a serious player in the Irish market. I was happy to act as a consultant or marketing person to provide an Irish shamrock for a British company – or disappear altogether.

Deirdre, two guys from AIBCF and I trooped into Hill's boardroom in north London for a 9 a.m. two-hour meeting on Wednesday, 8 October. I wanted to exit before the market declined further. To sweeten any deal, I was happy to be paid in William Hill shares, rather than cash, on the basis that they would take over the AIB debt and all existing contractual liabilities.

The top executives listened carefully, asking probing questions. They accepted the broad analysis that they could not stay in the Republic of Ireland with just forty-eight shops, languishing as an also-ran in the overall market. Their board would have to make a long-term strategic decision to get serious or get out. Their dozen shops in Northern Ireland were performing well. They agreed that the geographic spread of both our estates could provide a single credible national footprint. They could use their resources of technology and shop systems to improve margins. A critical issue for them as regards high-street shop viability was whether FOBTs would be legalised in Irish betting shops. They were aware of the Independent Bookmakers Association's (IBA) lobbying to get them licensed, with two per shop being sought. The meeting went well. They would reflect on it and consider preparing a recommendation for their CEO, Ralph Topping, and board. They proposed to get back to us in a few weeks.

The following Tuesday, 14 October, Brian Lenihan, as minister for finance, rose to his feet in the Dáil chamber to deliver an emergency budget in the aftermath of the government bank guarantee and collapse of the public finances. I was due to provide media analysis of the budget across various radio stations, so I was listening and making notes. To my utter consternation, Lenihan announced the doubling of betting duty from one to two per cent in 2009. I knew instantly this would torpedo any prospect of a deal. My dream evaporated. In subsequent conference calls, the William Hill people politely explained they wished to 'park' the dialogue until they had clarification on the regulatory environment. They could not understand how the tax could be arbitrarily doubled. It wiped out profit margins at the stroke of a pen. William Hill subsequently lost faith in the Irish market when the licensing of FOBTs was rejected. They closed fourteen of their forty-eight shops in September 2009, a further twenty in December 2010, and exited Ireland altogether by selling their remaining shops to Boylesports in 2011.

I contacted Brian Lenihan directly because I had always got on well with him. For a number of years I had tipped him for promotion in reshuffle speculation and as a future party leader. We met one December morning in the Department of Finance. He was accompanied by a senior civil servant, who had initiated the betting duty increase. I explained the unfair reality of online betting and phone betting by multiples being completely tax-free since it was notionally transacted abroad. This measure would destroy indigenous Irish bookmakers and retail betting, and drive more revenue abroad. We didn't have a net margin of two per cent, so if they proceeded with this tax hike, it would close three hundred betting shops.

I was alarmed at the lack of understanding on the part of the official, who seemed impervious to all arguments or the loss of 1,500 jobs. His was secure. The atmosphere was so bad, Lenihan asked the guy to leave. We chatted for an hour and he could not have been more pleasant, accepting my points. Instead of being overawed by the depth of the fiscal and banking crisis, he seemed filled with energy. I had the impression that he was up for the challenge of perhaps the toughest ever period for a finance minister, but he was naïve and over-confident of the banks' solvency, too quick to believe that Anglo-Irish and Irish Nationwide were systemic to the Irish economy. He did a U-turn on the betting tax decision in 2009, but too late for me to sell to William Hill.

In the autumn of 2008, I had to reassess the cost structure of the business. Our total overheads on our profit and loss account were €17 million. The largest single component was wages: €140,000 a week for 330 staff. Deirdre and I started to lead by example: as directors, we took no salary. The maximum we ever paid ourselves was €25,992 per annum. We reduced manning levels in the shops, so one person worked behind the counter alone in the less busy morning and evening periods.

The key gatekeepers to cost control were the supervisors who drew up the weekly staff rosters. They ensured that the more senior staff were not working together, effecting savings. In the past we had paid a double week's bonus at Christmas and Cheltenham: this was abolished, as was all overtime pay. At head office and supervisor level, we introduced a three- and four-day week, which increased productivity and allowed some employees to receive welfare payments. I reckoned we were paying €5,000 per week on shop cleaners: the staff agreed to do this work themselves in many places. All management personnel took a pay cut. There was no company pension scheme, no fringe benefits, no pay scale increments. Overall, we reduced our wages bill from €7 million to under €5 million.

We started to renegotiate with our suppliers to seek a 10 per cent discount across the board. For electricity and telecommunications, we regularly changed from the ESB and Eircom to various centralised suppliers on special terms, sometimes returning on more favourable conditions. All bills were haggled over prior to payment, but we always paid promptly.

Then we bit the bullet and closed shops. In April 2001 I had sold our first shop in Tramore as a going concern because we could not obtain a long-term lease and saw it as having limited potential. Other than that, and various relocations, I had never accepted defeat by closing any shop. In early 2009 we began to acknowledge site failure by closing shops in Navan and Bristol. It felt like an amputation of a limb to safeguard the body.

Other than payroll costs, my biggest other overhead was property rent, at more than €2 million annually. In the poor-performing shops I would ring up landlords and explain that the unit was losing money because of the downturn and reduced revenue. The landlords were superficially sympathetic. When I met a number of them face to face, it was a dialogue of the deaf, with no resulting discounts or break clauses. I kept chasing them, but they would not reply. In March 2009 I wrote a letter to every landlord, explaining our plight and stating that we would pay 50 per cent of the rent as it fell due. I was trying to create an arrears situation, which I could do a deal on at the end of the year. They were now contacting me, instead of ignoring my pleas, which was a good start. Quickly, these became disputes and got tied up in solicitors' correspondence. The law was completely on the landlord's side. The company was liable for the cost of the rent, irrespective of whether the shop was viable or not.

They knew their legal strengths and were impervious to our losses. Very occasionally, some landlords would take a common-sense approach. They were usually single-property owners. The multiple-property players were complete bastards. Their stubborn refusal to face reality, sometimes understandable in the context of their own debt situation, hastened many retail closures. The High Court ruling in relation to abandoned leases meant tenants had to pay up to two and a half years' rent as a surrender premium. In our case, this could amount to €100,000 per shop.

In my constant dialogue with John Reynolds and Frank Casey of AIB, I outlined in detail the work we had done to stabilise our profit and loss account. They were impressed, stating that they would cite us as an example to other clients who were in denial about the need to take an axe to their cost base. The Celtic Bookmakers accounts for 2009 showed a decline in turnover: €152 million from €189.5 million (including Celtic in the UK) in 2008. This 20 per cent fall was in line with the rest of the industry and generated a loss of €1.3 million. But it was not as disastrous as it seemed: at least half of it was a paper loss, the result of depreciation.

No strikes or industrial-relations disharmony ensued. Deirdre and I were transparent about every facet of the finances of each shop and the overall business. I repeatedly explained the risks I had taken with the bank debt to finance expansion. We were all in this together. Marketing, advertising, charitable donations and sponsorship expenditure were slashed. I knew there was a limit to what we could achieve in terms of cutting any further. Having reduced costs by €6 million annually, all the fat was gone. We were down to the bare bones.

While the recession deepened throughout 2009, I decided that my overall priority was to shift my focus from our profit and loss account towards our balance sheet. We needed to restructure the company by getting an injection of equity capital from an outside investor. Deirdre and I had a relaxed attitude to parting with a significant stake in Celtic. We would welcome any new shareholder. My day-to-day role in the business had changed. The professional team in the race room handled virtually all betting-related issues without me. The cost-cutting decisions were completed. While the notion of my taking no salary was good for Celtic Bookmakers, it was unsustainable for a family man with four children embarking on university education. In the early summer of 2009 Deirdre and I moved to a rented house in Sandymount, a lovely part of Dublin, to take up the media and other work.

I stepped down as managing director of Celtic Bookmakers and appointed Padraig Hall as acting Managing Director. My son Andrew came home, having completed his degree in Swansea, to work full-time in the business. He had specific responsibility for the race room and marketing issues, as well as being a director. John Lynch, my long-standing friend and mentor, now executive chairman of CIÉ, agreed to be non-executive chairman of Celtic Bookmakers. My hope was that if we got to the heads of agreement on a restructuring deal, John's experience and credibility would give a more corporate than family image to the business. A precondition of any refinancing was that the company would have to switch from its unlimited status to being a limited liability company. This was done with the Companies Registration Office in February 2009.

In 2009 I had conversations with Justin Carthy of Chronicle bookmakers, which was part-owned by Dermot Desmond, through a mutual friend Kevin Murphy, who supplied our football coupons. This resulted in a meeting with Dermot himself, who was one of the shrewdest cookies I'd ever met, with an exceptionally brilliant mind and business acumen. Sadly, the talks came to nothing.

I approached the main corporate finance firms in Dublin, AIBCF, Davys and NCB, to try to raise €1 million in equity finance in exchange for a quarter-share of Celtic. They drew up lists of potential investors, including overseas hedge funds, venture capital providers and private wealth clients. Nothing much materialised.

I generated my own discussions with Victor Chandler over a very pleasant dinner in Shanahan's restaurant on St Stephen's Green, having got to know one of his key Irish guys. He had only three shops in Ireland and a few in the UK, as his main business was based in Gibraltar, providing global online and telephone gambling services. He laid bets on behalf of many of the high-rollers from his racecourse bookmaker days and had pioneered online poker. Nothing materialised from our discussion.

I met Steve Fisher of Stan James in the Conrad Hilton Hotel. He was interested in developing or acquiring an Irish retail estate in February 2009. They opened a few virgin shops in Munster and Dublin, in a joint venture with some Cork operators, but again their principal business was as an odds provider and an international online/telephone bookmaker, so nothing materialised. In April 2009 I met David Archer from the north of England, who had sold out his betting chain to a larger player. He was restricted from re-entering bookmaking in that part of the UK but was considering an Irish acquisition or taking a stake in Celtic. Much later, in July 2010, Sun Capital contacted me out of the blue and came over from London to do due diligence on Celtic Bookmakers.

All these conversations ran into the sand. Nobody was explicit as to why, but a combination of concerns about Celtic's legacy bank debt, the future of retail betting shops relative to the Internet and the unrelenting downward spiral of the recession all prevented meaningful progress. Meanwhile, every set of management accounts revealed an ever gloomier picture of declining revenue. Some excellent shops had gone from taking in €80,000 per week to only €45,000. It seemed that while the total number of bets hadn't significantly dropped, average stake sizes had plummeted. Other bookmakers assured me that they were going through the same torment. Managing cash flow became critical, especially around the quarterly liability that had to be paid by cheque to the Revenue Commissioners, almost €400,000 for betting duty.

The kernel of the problem was that guys from building sites, regularly punting €100 per race, were now betting €20. Some of the heaviest gamblers disappeared entirely, presumably going bust or emigrating. Annual turnover dropped to €122 million (down some 35 per cent from the peak). Although its cost base was down to €11.9 million, the company incurred an EBITDA loss of €335,000 and net loss of €1.5 million up to the end of July 2010. Each week started with the cold, harsh reality that we had to win more than €300,000 from punters to cover our costs.

It was just as well that I was not in Enniscorthy head office every day: I was becoming increasingly abrasive, irritable and fearful at the thought of losing twenty grand per week. Our bank overdraft was rising steadily. In February 2010 AIB changed the personnel who dealt with us from Frank Casey at local level (he moved to the Wexford town branch) to Philip McDermott in the regional Kilkenny office, and Barry Tiernan instead of John Reynolds in head office. We converted a revolving fund of €300,000 into additional overdraft facilities. We were asked to sign a new personal guarantee. I gave a specific secured charge on eighty-three acres of land and a house. The bank was continually supportive and did not appear to be as alarmed as I was about the precarious nature of the business and its survival. We were in this together, was the impression it gave.

The only remaining option was to try to sell the best shops, on a piecemeal basis, to raise sufficient capital to clear the debt. I did a geographic assessment of each shop in the context of the areas where Ladbrokes and Paddy Power did not have an outlet. Thirty shops would strategically enhance Ladbrokes' nationwide network and twelve separate shops were most compatible with Power's estate. NCB prepared a prospectus for each company, called 'Project Yankee', highlighting the profitability and established market strength of each. The plan for the remainder of the shops was to try to sell them to individual independents or even offload them for nothing to procure an orderly wind-down of the business. Top shops were still commanding a premium price of up to €500,000. My hope was that we would raise €6 million in separate deals to clear the debt. Any prospect of Deirdre and me getting any return on our hard work over more than twenty years was down the drain. If we could get out, move on with our lives and repay the AIB debts, we would be relieved.

Celtic's management team advanced a plan to close twelve of the worst-performing shops. We had walked away from the short-term lease in one of the U Bet shops in Henry Street, Limerick, without any hassle. Chapelizod was a disaster, with several months of road works making it inaccessible: they had shut it and were being sued by the landlord. They were now ready to close Dundalk, Dunboyne, Tallaght, Carlow and Athlone, and wanted to close Sligo, Raheny, Ballina, Carrick-on-Suir, New Ross, Tuam and Newport in Wales. I stalled some of these because of the potential for resale. I could not reveal my exit plans to anyone for fear that reputational damage would impair the goodwill value of all the shops. I was distressed by the job losses. New competitor outlets opening around them, disappearing punters and Celtic Tiger peak rents created a perfect storm of commercial destruction. The tale of woe and bad news was unrelenting. I was deeply depressed, often unable to sleep.

I was determined to press on with my plans for filleting the business by presenting the best shops to the biggest players in the industry. I rang Joe Lewins, the Irish boss of Ladbrokes, whom I knew well from IBA meetings. He seemed keen and understood the critical confidential nature of the sale proposition. He said that such an acquisition would have to be dealt with by Terry Leon in Britain, their overall development and acquisition executive. NCB forwarded a confidentiality agreement and the turnover details on the thirty shops that were not directly competing toe-to-toe with theirs. A meeting was arranged with Andrew and myself at a restaurant in York – we were there for a few days at the York Ebor Festival in mid-August. I was deeply concerned to ensure the anonymity and secrecy that could not be guaranteed in Ireland if we were spotted together.

Both men were extremely cordial and expressed a desire to enlarge their estate in Ireland. Most of the shops were an excellent fit for them. They wanted to consolidate their position as Ireland's largest and most prolific high-street bookmaker. I explained that they were getting first refusal and favourable positive consideration by Celtic as the buyer of choice. Heretofore, they had the largest cheque book and had successfully consummated many similar acquisitions, although not as numerous as thirty shops in a single purchase. They did ask for more detailed three-year management accounts for each shop. I naïvely acquiesced.

Meanwhile, I telephoned Patrick Kennedy, the CEO of Power's, to invite him to lunch on a Friday afternoon in Shanahan's restaurant. He was extremely kind and supportive, obviously grasping the extent of Celtic's difficulties if I was selling the best shops in an asset-stripping exercise. His track record of increasing share value was becoming the most formidable of any company quoted on the ISEQ, with considerable appreciation in share values. Their online performance was legendary, their acquisition in Australia highly profitable, and their joint venture in France bearing fruit. He also was a non-executive director of the Bank of Ireland and Elan, the pharmaceutical giant. He was excellent company, a family man and modest about his achievements. I liked him and wanted to sell Power's many of my best shops, despite past rows with them. NCB had prepared its own glossy brochure with all the key information. He said he would arrange for his commercial manager, Andrew Algeo, to liaise with NCB and hoped we could do business.

Over the following weeks, I eagerly awaited their response. Even in the most favourable circumstances, I couldn't see Celtic surviving under my stewardship. Back in August, I had attended a meeting in Wexford with my solicitor, Tony Ensor. When I outlined the impossibility of trading out of our difficulties, he had one succinct piece of advice: 'Whatever you do, Ivan, don't put any more of your money into this business.' It was a wake-up call: it indicated that Celtic Bookmakers and Ivan Yates were not the entity I had always considered us to be. I also met Pat Boland, my founding mentor and close friend, in the Sligo Park Hotel. I wanted to ensure that he escaped from Celtic as a director and shareholder before things got too difficult. I paid him €10,000 to transfer his one per cent share in Celtic back to Deirdre, even though I knew it was worthless. It was the least I could do for all his years of patient support and understanding. It was sad that past dreams of success had utterly vanished.

Patrick Kennedy rang me back to say that they were very interested in acquiring the Lombard Street shop in Dublin. This was our best shop, taking in more than six thousand slips per week and highly profitable. I was surprised and disappointed that they wanted only the single shop, but he signified further interest in due course for a handful more. Shane Lawlor, of NCB stockbrokers, quickly arranged a contract for an initial purchase price of €450,000, with additional earn-out payments if the shop performed to a certain level in the first year under their ownership, which could amount to a further €450,000. Two weeks later they abruptly reduced the upfront price to €350,000, citing the downturn. Tough poker, but we accepted it and signed the contract.

Some weeks later, Joe Lewins asked to meet me in a private room in the Westbury Hotel. To my surprise Terry Leon had flown in for the meeting. They requested even more data on all the shops. I gave them everything, despite strong advice from NCB not to do so. The tentative indications seemed to be that they were preparing to make a serious offer for a number of shops. Around mid-morning on 10 November 2010 I was walking from the DART station in Sandymount to our house when Shane Lawlor rang to say he'd received a call from Terry Leon that they had made a blanket decision not to acquire any further shops in the Republic of Ireland, owing to the prevailing economic climate. I thanked Shane for all his endeavours, my voice calm. I rang off. Then I stood there, as winded as if I'd been kicked in the solar plexus. The game was up. I had no buyer for any of the shops, except one. Landlords from the closed shops were screaming for surrender premium payments, which I didn't have. I walked on, knowing that Celtic Bookmakers had just died. The company's assets were illiquid. The previous weeks and months had been like trying to catch a falling knife.

I was entering the biggest crisis of my life. The death of a family business is akin to a personal bereavement. Deirdre and I felt shock and extreme disappointment that twenty-three years of such hard work by so many people would come to nothing but tears and grief. I had to set aside our emotions and take full responsibility to ensure that the wind-up of Celtic's affairs was carried out in as orderly a fashion as possible in the weeks ahead. I saw no point in delaying matters or denying the inevitable, since losses would only intensify. Every facet of the collapse would be in a goldfish bowl of publicity.

I convened a meeting of the board of Celtic Bookmakers on 16 November to clear the decks so that I could resume total responsibility for the company. At my suggestion, John Lynch resigned as chairman and director, along with Andrew. I was appointed executive chairman and Deirdre company secretary and sole member. At this stage Deirdre and I were the only directors and she the only shareholder. I outlined the legal definition of the precise point of acknowledging company insolvency: when our liabilities exceeded our assets and when we envisaged we would not be able to meet our bills as they fell due for payment. Until now that point had not been reached. Paul Kelly, of Mason Owen

Lyons auctioneers, had prepared a memo in relation to creditor liabilities on shops that we had closed, subsequent to his direct negotiation on our behalf with landlords. We faced walkaway costs of €500,000, which the company didn't have. Bill O'Connor, of Ensor O'Connor solicitors, had taken over my case from Tony Ensor and was now navigating me through company law. I devoured a book on the obligations of directors.

We had three insolvency options: liquidation, receivership or examinership. Padraig Hall had juggled deteriorating cash flow, difficult landlords, an escalating overdraft, worsening losses and my failure to restructure the company with total secrecy and professionalism. He suggested I contact a former schoolmate of his, Neil Hughes of Hughes Blake chartered accountants, who had offices in Dublin and Enniscorthy, to pursue the question of examinership, based on retaining the thirty-five A-list stores identified by NCB. I learned from him that this was a ninety-day court process, which would give protection against all creditors and allow for outside investment and the negotiation of new contracts, including lower rent terms and property leases. It would allow Celtic to make a fresh start, by ditching the poor shops and obtaining a lower cost base.

Deirdre and I met Neil in his office, beside Holles Street Hospital. He was a shrewd operator, specialising as an insolvency practitioner (a polite term for financial undertakers). He had survived the boom. Hungry for cases, especially a high-profile one, he explained his recent role as examiner in other retail chains, such as Four Star Pizza and Zumo Juice Bars, outlining his success at renegotiating leases down to market rents. The likely cost would be €50,000–70,000. While I could see the upsides of the examiner process, my fears focused on the downside risks if the judge deemed that the plan wasn't viable and just an attempt to dry-clean debts and liabilities.

I realised that I couldn't refinance Celtic because we had never reached first base on developing the lands on the home farm at Blackstoops, Enniscorthy: my mother had not agreed to release her life interest in the property. Valuations of green-field development sites had been in free-fall since 2007 anyway. The construction and development train had left the station without us on it. My concern, therefore, was that, having beaten the bushes for a new investor for more than a year, we would end up with no white knight and crash into involuntary court liquidation, which would be an unmitigated disaster for everybody.

I had chaired and acted as MC for a number of speaking events for Grant Thornton accountants. I rang the managing partner to get personal advice for Deirdre and myself, separate to that of Celtic. We met Paul McCann, a senior partner for insolvency cases, and outlined the full dire situation.

'Ivan, you have to accept that it is what it is and just deal with it,' he said. 'Life is life.' His strong advice was to go for the receivership option in conjunction with the agreement of the bank, exercising their secured charge on the fixed and floating assets of the company. No solution was perfect, but if AIB provided working capital for the period of the receivership, the best shops could be sold as a going concern. I explained that all bets would have to be honoured or there would be no goodwill value in any shop. There seemed to be no precedent for a bookmaker to go into receivership. We concluded that a receiver who was prepared to work like an examiner could save significant jobs and recoup substantial cash. Grant Thornton weren't able to take the job.

I reverted to Neil Hughes to see if he would act as receiver. He agreed on the basis that AIB supported his nomination. He prepared a plan outlining all issues to be resolved and initially the need to establish legal certainty that a bookmaker could continue to trade while in receivership. There were enormous risks, such as key suppliers withdrawing services. He itemised critical factors relating to preferential creditors, landlords, a communications plan and timetable. Then we met Barry Tiernan in BankCentre on 2 December, accompanied by Paul McCann. He was initially taken aback by the prospect of our imminent insolvency. He said Celtic was barely on their 'credit watch' list of companies. He explained that he would have to make a proposal for the appointment of receiver to their business credit committee within AIB's higher echelons. He required a paper from Paul McCann outlining the reasons for same. AIB seemed to be in similar turmoil to ourselves.

Our regular suppliers and punters would be at the end of any queue to get paid. I was among those who would go unpaid. The company owed me personally €160,998 from cash support I had paid in over the years since 1987 from savings. At any stage during the distress period, I could have paid this off, but was concerned to keep the company afloat. The likelihood was that the bank would get all shop-sale proceeds after the receivers' expenses were paid, with all others getting little or nothing.

My biggest concern was the €60,000-plus of clients' deposits in our telebetting accounts. This was their money and they had been happy to leave it with Celtic, as they bet out of it. An unmitigated mess would result if it was not dealt with prior to a receivership. I imagined irate calls to Joe Duffy's *Liveline*. I arranged to close the telebetting operation in early December and repay all clients' funds. The staff in the phone centre were shocked and incredulous that I would close a seemingly viable business, but I couldn't tell them what lay ahead. It was the beginning of a living nightmare.

Eventually after a few weeks, we got the green light for Neil Hughes to be appointed as receiver by AIB, at our invitation. The delay meant that we were approaching the Christmas period. I convened a Celtic management meeting on 15 December in our home at Sandymount. Up to early December, we were fairly up to date with most creditors who presented bills, other than our landlords, especially where we had closed shops. By this stage I had privately contacted John Boyle by phone and explained that I wanted to offer him the sale of our prime Enniscorthy betting shop. It was a busy, highly profitable shop. Within ten days, we had agreed a purchase price of €300,000, got the landlord's consent and wrapped up the deal legally. I took responsibility for notifying key senior staff, who in turn would call each employee. Draft letters were prepared for all staff members, landlords and long-standing suppliers to issue simultaneously on the appointment of the receiver.

Some €650,000 of payments from Boylesports and Power's (from the Lombard Street sale) were about to come into Celtic's bank account. This would provide the cash flow to cover the trading period of the receivership, presumably no more than several weeks, before every shop was either sold or closed, with the receiver operating as a bookmaker under Deirdre's licence. Neil prepared advertisements in the *Racing Post* to sell as many of the forty-seven shops as possible, in an attempt to save up to 237 jobs. Celtic in the UK was not affected by the receivership. However, without a head office and race-room facility, we would be unable to run the shops, so we would undertake a separate wind-down operation, rather than the receiver, in Wales.

On 22 December the following resolution was adopted by the directors of Celtic Bookmakers: 'It was resolved that by reason of financial constraints and with a view to preserving the Company's business in protecting its assets that the Company do hereby request Allied Irish Banks to appoint a Receiver over all the undertaking property and assets of the Company pursuant to the provisions of the Debenture dated 15 January 2008 issued by the Company to the Bank.'

Complete secrecy over the next week was essential so we could choreograph and control events without the company's affairs falling apart. I was doing media work right up to Christmas Eve and took the train home to Wexford, knowing nothing lay ahead but bad news and misery. Deirdre and I felt awful for the staff who would lose their jobs.

Meetings were held with Neil Hughes and his general office manager, Joe Walsh, in Dublin on Friday, 31 December, and in Enniscorthy on the bank holiday Monday, 3 January. Angela Donnelly, our operations manager, attended all meetings. We finalised arrangements to issue a letter to each employee and an email for each shop, explaining the announcement. A general staff meeting was set up for the night of the appointment in the Red Cow Inn Hotel for the receiver to meet all staff to answer questions about redundancy entitlements, employment contracts, job prospects and character references. Each shop had to prepare detailed cash-handling records and arrange to replace existing new cheque-book/bank accounts. Even the ESB meter had to be read. The entire operation of all Celtic's finances was set to move out of our hands at twelve noon on 4 January. We had an afternoon scare when an *Irish Independent* journalist rang to confirm a rumour she had heard of our receivership. I got Andrew to deny it and no story broke. Thirty people, comprising long-standing and valuable employees, close associates over the years in the business, family members and friends needed to hear the bad news from myself, rather than from a third party or the media. I started calling at about 6 p.m. on Monday. It took more than three hours. People were shocked, taking time to absorb the information, never having believed my continual forebodings of doom within the company. Others were kind, sensitive and supportive. It was a black day of unremitting gloom. The next morning I spoke to our head-office staff around 9 a.m. with an impromptu gathering. I had kept my composure up to that point. Faced with my closest and longest-suffering core head office staff and explaining Celtic's demise, I broke down.

Then Deirdre and I drove to Dublin to face the media storm. By arrangement with Nigel Heneghan, a personal friend who owns and runs his own PR company in Dublin, after the twelve o'clock embargo I did interviews with Newstalk's lunchtime news and Seán O'Rourke live in studio at RTÉ for the one o'clock news. This was quickly followed by pre-recorded television news interviews with RTÉ and TV3. I spent a few hours in Nigel's offices talking to print journalists and local radio stations. I was determined to answer each and every question for a twenty-four-hour period to get it over with. Finally I did the Six One news, in studio with Bryan Dobson, where I openly confessed that I had 'lost my mojo'. All the queries were along predictable lines: job losses, reasons for failure, my indebtedness, risks to our home ownership, unpaid bets, my culpability, future and emotions. I tried to be completely honest and open in all respects. I wrote a lengthy article in my *Examiner* column that week, outlining the inner details of the business collapse and my feelings of 'demoralisation, dejection and sadness'.

We then attended the general staff meeting, held by invitation of the receiver at the Red Cow Inn. Many of those present were deeply upset. We assisted the receiver in answering any questions about day-to-day trading. Neil and his staff had no clue about betting issues, much to the amusement and light-hearted relief of the staff, despite the grim circumstances. Myriads of practical problems remained to be resolved. These were now the responsibility of the receiver. Our role was to provide a support act to maintain trading until shops were sold or closed. Neil wasted no time in getting to grips with the landlords, offering them a blunt choice of closure or significantly reduced rents in an attempt to sell the shops as a going concern. They quickly acquiesced to 'market rents', in some cases less than 50 per cent of what they had insisted I had to stump up.

A couple of weeks later, in mid-January, the receiver closed sixteen shops with the loss of fifty-six jobs, but concluded a satisfactory sale of seventeen of the best shops to Boylesports for €2 million. Further individual shops were sold to independent bookmakers in each locality. In total, he sold twenty-nine shops for €2.54 million.

The week after the Cheltenham Festival in late March, the last unsold shops were closed, and the remainder of the staff made redundant. Head-office staff found it most difficult to secure alternative employment in the recession-ravaged Enniscorthy and County Wexford area. An interim dividend of €1.5 million was paid to AIB. In early 2012 the Lombard Street shop qualified for the additional trigger payment of €450,000. This completed all the outstanding operational issues of Celtic in Ireland as the processing of staff redundancy, welfare claims and legal property transfers with landlords were completed. We sold the Celtic shops in Swansea and Carmarthen to Roy Holbrook of the *Winning Post*, while closing the Newport shop. All creditors were paid from the proceeds.

While the insolvency practitioner deals with the affairs of the company, it reverts to the directors to actually wind it up. Neil put me in touch with a colleague, Alan McLean of Whiteside Cullinan chartered accountants, who would act as a cost-effective liquidator of the company. After preliminary meetings, preparations were made to hold a formal meeting of creditors in the Pearse Hotel on Friday, 16 March, under Section 266 of the Companies Act. I knew there would be further publicity because a legal notice of the meeting had to be printed in two national newspapers ten days in advance.

My chairman's statement explained the sectoral decline in betting revenue from €3.6 billion in 2007 to €2.7 billion in 2010. I took full responsibility for the rapid expansion, under-capitalisation and failure of the company. I expressed deep regret to the unpaid creditors and explained all the gross proceeds of €3.2 million had to be paid to AIB ahead of them. About a dozen people attended in a small room at the back of the hotel. The mood of the meeting was business-like and sympathetic to our plight, notwithstanding their losses. They realised there had been no crazy diversification or property play, that no assets had been transferred out of the company, that there had been no reckless trading and that we had shown no preference to individual creditors. Complaints mostly related to the receiver's rigid refusal to pay anything to creditors other than those service suppliers he needed to maintain the shops for several weeks.

The media weren't allowed to attend, but I held an informal press briefing with Donal O'Donovan (*Irish Independent*) and Seán MacCarthaigh (*Irish Examiner*) afterwards. The media, generally, were kind to me.

We were inundated with kind and sensitive texts, emails, letters and calls – even from people we didn't know. It is a particularly nice trait of Irish people that they support individuals in crisis. 'Ivan, you'll look back at this in a year's time and laugh about it,' some well-meaning people said. Although sincere, they could not have been more wrong. I will never, ever laugh about any aspect of this painful, costly humiliation. I felt a deep sense of responsibility for those who became unemployed or were unpaid. The wind-up phases of Celtic, receivership and liquidation, were harrowing, but what was to follow in terms of personal bankruptcy was to be even more so. In business, we were all in this together: management, shareholders, employees, suppliers, banks, creditors and customers. The business had a life, passion and identity of its own.

After the corporate death came the consequences of the personal guarantee. I had no concept of the aggression and strife that lay ahead. AIB were determined to make an example of me.

17: Bankruptcy

The death of Celtic Bookmakers in early 2011 meant facing up to the residual debt Deirdre and I owed AIB on the company loans that remained unpaid after the receiver had realised all the assets from shop sales.

I asked Mon O'Driscoll, who had helped me when he was head of AIB Corporate Finance, many years earlier when I was looking at a merger with Stanley Racing, to give me a read on our situation. He was exceptionally sharp and unsentimental, leaving me in no doubt that we were shockingly vulnerable. We had signed away everything in the small print of a personal guarantee on 23 November 2010, as part of the annual bank's renewal of Celtic's term loan and working capital facilities. I knew they had a stated secured charge on my eighty-three acres of land at Blackstoops and a dwelling on 1.1 acres also at Blackstoops. I believed that this related to our dormer bungalow, our first marital home on a one-acre plot, built in 1985. Instead, it was Plant's House, another bungalow on a one-acre plot, which we had bought for €700,000 in 2006. I suddenly realised that all my income since I had set up Platinum Presentations in 2008 had gone to repay more than €800,000 and clear this mortgage, a futile exercise. I had paid all my earnings from broadcasting and speechmaking to the bank and none of it served us.

AIB procured a secured charge on it under the terms of the

personal guarantee. I previously presumed I would have this as a negotiating asset to sell. Not so: it was theirs, despite being debt-free. In 2009, as I was paying down the mortgage, I tried to stop the bank obtaining any secured charge on that separate loan before it was all repaid. I didn't appreciate that this charge was registered on the house deeds. I was livid with myself at how casual I had been in my dealings with the bank. Whenever these topics had been referred to, in the local branch with Frank Casey, it had been light-hearted banter about an abstract concept. Now this small print would govern the rest of my life.

Worse news emerged. The bank could grab the remainder of our family assets that were never covered by way of secured bank charge, namely the main house and eighty-three acres. The direst possibility we faced was that AIB could also obtain from the High Court power of attachment against any future earnings to recover cash on an ongoing basis. It could continue to charge interest indefinitely, even though the company for which the loan had been provided no longer traded.

It was game, set and match to the bank. While my mother's life interest could delay matters, the doomsday scenario was that we would lose our family home. That was the stark contrast between corporate and personal insolvency. Companies can literally walk away from bad debts, trade liabilities and owners' contracts through examinership, receivership or liquidation. Family businesses don't have that crucial 'non-recourse' escape clause. Different rules apply to an individual entrepreneur versus a corporate entity. One rule for big business and another set of punishment beatings to be administered for owner/manager businesses. We clearly had to reach a negotiated settlement with the bank and avoid legal confrontation at all costs.

One friend suggested we ask the bank to look at the original capital sums borrowed. 'In a perfect world,' he said, 'banks get repaid capital plus interest; perhaps if just the capital was repaid, then the interest you have already paid could be credited against the principal sum.'

I checked the company accounts and found that between 2006 and 2010, we had repaid €1,106,377 in quarterly interest payments. Despite this, even though we were now under receivership, AIB continued to charge interest.

Everyone I spoke to, with and without expertise, felt that the banks would eventually agree to some level of debt forgiveness, if they understood that my total assets amounted to less than the outstanding debt. They felt my high profile could work to my advantage, allowing me some sympathetic consideration, which might be helped by the fact that I had gone out of my way not to attribute any blame to AIB for Celtic's collapse, taking full personal responsibility. While other bust-business debtors were busy shifting assets beyond the reach of creditors, I wanted to repay what I could afford, do a fair deal and move on with my life.

My chief bank negotiator was Bernard Somers, who had done valiant work as a senior financier, in the 1980s, as receiver to the insolvent Dublin Gas Company. He was at the top of the profession as an accountant, insolvency practitioner, non-executive director and debt negotiator for three decades. 'You couldn't get any person more respected in relation to debt settlement,' everybody I asked told me. Bernard knew from thirty years' experience in dealing with bad debts that debt write-offs were nothing new, although, owing to the insolvency of the Irish banks and their subsequent nationalisation, some age-old practices of debt settlement were now in suspended animation.

A meeting was arranged with AIB for 6 May in our rented home at Sandymount, so I could lie on a couch as my back was really bad, keeping me out of radio work since Easter. I presented a comprehensive summary document of our assets, earnings, Celtic's fallout liabilities and proposed sale of property. Bernard Somers, Deirdre and I articulated a desire to reach a full and final settlement.

We reckoned the bank had received more than €4.5 million of their original loan of €6.7 million. We proposed to sell my eighty-three acres plus house on the land in return for a full and final settlement. We hoped that these assets would realise in excess of €800,000, which would represent a total repayment of 82–86 cent per euro of what we had borrowed back in 2006, disregarding interest. Our argument, in the prevailing circumstances of Ireland's economic catastrophe, was that such a debt discount represented a reasonable and fair outcome for the risks the bank had taken. They asked us to put the proposal into a formal written offer through Bernard, which they would submit to their credit executives. Because I was due to have a major back operation on 13 June, I said they could proceed directly with Bernard in the coming weeks.

Bernard submitted a six-page document on 26 May. In my absence, as agreed, a meeting was held in AIB BankCentre with him on 22 June. David Renwick and Paul Dowling were announced as the new team dealing with our case. Bernard intimated that this could be a positive development: they were senior guys, so more likely to make a decision, rather than procrastinate. He had worked with Renwick before, as his boss. I was dismayed that any credits I had built up of continual co-operation with Frank Casey, John Reynolds and Barry Tiernan at various stages of Celtic's relationship with AIB were being flushed down the toilet. The new personnel would merely look at the facts in front of them, rather than previous contexts or background.

'AIB face challenges in writing off debt and are also obliged to seek to recover outstanding loans,' Bernard wrote in a later note to me. 'AIB would write a loan for the balance, which would not be repayable except in circumstances where the fortunes of Ivan Yates improved dramatically or maybe never.'

I attended further meetings in BankCentre on 5 October and 17 November. Although civil, these guys were clearly AIB's toughest corporate recovery officers. They wouldn't table any written counter-proposals. On 1 December, I accompanied Paul Dowling on an inspection of all the family properties in Enniscorthy. I explained each folio map, right of way and access point, parcels that were readily saleable and others that were not, my mother's life interest in eighty-three acres of land and a ten-metre right-of-way with road access. We spent three hours walking the land.

He drove from Dublin to Enniscorthy and back again, during which we had a bizarre discussion. On the way down, we chatted about his own banking background and career. He had worked with David Drumm in Anglo Irish Bank at a senior level, and described the dramatic descent from hectic loan growth into insolvent disaster. That was before he moved to AIB. He expressed regret about the lack of public and media understanding of Anglo's achievements, and added that Drumm and the bank's executives had good qualities, then outlined the impact of the US sub-prime market implosion and the collapse of Lehman Brothers. I listened with fascination to an insider's viewpoint and vivid recall of key meetings.

On the return journey, I explained the era during which Celtic Bookmakers had borrowed the money in 2006 to grow the business, with the enthusiastic support of AIB. They were eager to grow their loan book, not to 'let Anglo eat our lunch'. I told him how AIB said I should use bank debt to develop the business through acquisitions; up to €16 million could be lent. He didn't seem to connect his sympathetic perception of Anglo's situation with my request that a similar sensitivity now be shown to me. His one focus was on securing all the property assets of my family for AIB. The conversation remained civil but I left him in no doubt that I would not meekly accept whatever the bank wanted to dish out to us.

By year end, though, I found myself with no cards to play. The bank was content to sit tight. This was still a performing loan. Not only were they not prepared to offset previous interest payments, they refused to stop the interest clock.

I couldn't relate my experience with AIB to what I observed, working in the media, all around me. The extent of the catastrophic economic meltdown was apparent to all. New realities meant that asset values had halved, but green-field potential development land in rural areas like Enniscorthy had declined by up to 90 per cent. Corporate debt levels, resulting from acquisitions in 2002 to 2007, were unsustainable. Businesses that were 'too big to fail' were taken over, with debt write-offs. The developer elite class were being allowed salaries of €200,000 a year by NAMA. Toxic property bank loans were transferred to NAMA with gigantic write-downs to market values. Yet AIB refused to countenance any debt discount to the likes of me.

When I stated publicly that I expected to be declared bankrupt in 2012, whether in Ireland or another European jurisdiction, there was a flurry of follow-up articles across the print media. By threatening personal bankruptcy abroad, I hoped to focus AIB's mind. All the advice I received came to the same conclusion: the best option was a negotiated settlement with the bank. The downside risks of UK bankruptcy were deeply problematic and uncertain.

My motivation in publicly contemplating British bankruptcy was to focus AIB on the consequences to them if I ceased earning and caused a disorderly fire sale of saleable assets. Our next meeting, due to be held in January 2012, was postponed until 7 March. As usual, Bernard Somers and Deirdre accompanied me. At this stage all the cards were face up on the table. They knew every aspect of my assets and the impediments to selling them.

Paul Dowling initially suggested that we consider letting Platinum Presentations acquire Celtic. He suggested my Platinum revenue could repay Celtic's debt to the bank. I totally rejected this crazy proposition. There was no valid connection between the two companies other than that we owned both. The other creditors of Celtic Bookmakers would be left hanging indefinitely with nothing, while AIB took everything. David Renwick indicated that the land assets would have to be sold along with two houses, even though they held absolutely no security over most of these. They would create a new mortgage of €500,000 for the main house, adjoining access and garden, so we could retain it. They also proposed to take a significant but unspecified share of our income for up to the next ten years.

They proposed to park some of the debt, called the 'rump debt'. It could ultimately be written off or pursued if my earnings increased. I asked what would happen if I did well. This would provide more resources to repay AIB, they agreed. 'What happens to the rump debt if I die before it's dealt with?'

They looked at each other hesitantly. 'We would have to reserve our position after the grave'. I recoiled at the prospect of my children having eternally to face my problems with AIB. I then enquired if they would sell my debt to a third party. I had no specific person in mind, but others had suggested to me that if the debts could be sold at a discount, it would be in my interest to do so, with me repaying that party. 'Ivan, we buy and sell debts all the time. But I don't envisage us selling your debt.'

I explained to them that a residual mortgage on my family home was extremely costly and inefficient from a taxation perspective for me. They shrugged their shoulders. That was my problem. I reiterated that all my assets were debt-free. The sole basis of my indebtedness to them arose from company rather than personal loans, from which I derived no personal benefit. I was being asked to take full responsibility for lending decisions that they had been as enthusiastic about at the time as I had. I had drawn down only a minority of the cash they were prepared to offer to Celtic. As the exchanges became more heated and tense, I pressed them to give a commitment to reverse the interest clock since the company receivership. I pleaded with them to realise that if the interest kept rising by more than €4,000 a week, my indebtedness would be worsening, even if I gave them all my net income. They wouldn't give any commitment on even this most modest issue.

It became obvious to me that what I'd thought was a genuine mutual risk relationship between AIB and Celtic for loan finance meant that I took on all the downsides. It was also clear that what they meant by a personal guarantee was an open-ended commitment by us to mortgage our future lives to them. Specified secured assets meant nothing, since they would reach for any other assets they wanted. My non-executive directorship fees, media and public-speaking income and Platinum Presentations had not existed in 2006 when these loans had been issued. They could keep rewriting the rules based on any good fortune I might have in my life or create by hard work. And yet this same bank was more insolvent than I was, requiring a taxpayer bailout of €20.7 billion.

Property lending was a priority with the executives in AIB head office through the boom years. What price had been paid by them for calamitous lending decisions? 'If I'd wanted a job with the bank, I would have applied for it,' I said. 'I don't see that any part of what you are suggesting gives me any incentive to go along with it. These hazy proposals may overcome today's issues but only by creating long-term hazards. I can't even get from you any specific written figures of what you require. You give me no certainty, no finality – only endless distress and anguish. I am prepared to offer you in excess of eighty cent per euro as a full and final settlement, if I'm given enough time, say three years, to obtain it one way or the other.'

'Ivan, you don't seem to realise where the bank and its shareholder is coming from. If you offered us ninety-nine cent per euro, we could not accept it,' Renwick said. 'We don't and won't do debt forgiveness. If we were to apply that approach to our entire loan book, Ireland would close down overnight.'

We left the meeting in despair. I told Deirdre I'd made up my mind to quit my work commitments and leave the country. I couldn't cope with the harassment. I wasn't going to let the legacy problems of Celtic, above all else, run into the next generation. I didn't care about the reputational issues and the damage I would suffer about being perceived as a poster boy for UK bankruptcy tourism. I just didn't care. Bernard and my solicitor Bill O'Connor advised me that it was highly unlikely that AIB would take bankruptcy proceedings against us for two reasons: the net amount of our debt after they had realised their secured assets was around €2 million, which wouldn't justify the heavy costs of litigation; second, AIB had no record of bankrupting the property developers who owed them hundreds of millions of euro – why would they take such draconian action against such a small entity as us? They could not have been more wrong.

On 13 March AIB issued me and Deirdre with a letter stating that as Celtic Bookmakers was going into liquidation, this constituted a default event under the terms of Celtic's loans and guarantee. Therefore they required us to pay €3.68 million by 13 May 2012. Dowling rang me in advance of receipt of this letter to explain that I should not be concerned because it was merely 'good procedure'. After the Celtic liquidation meeting in the Pearse Hotel on 16 March, I spoke to Donal O'Donovan of the *Irish Independent* and Seán MacCarthaigh of the *Irish Examiner*. I lashed out at the bank continuing to charge interest and accused them of adopting an 'impossible position' in terms of debt resolution.

The following day both papers ran front-page lead stories of my comments. The *Irish Examiner* carried the headline 'Yates to move to Britain as the debts mount'. I hadn't said anything about going to the UK, but some weeks earlier I had notified their editor that I would not be able to continue my column in that newspaper. When pressed to reconsider, I had privately explained my proposed exit to South Wales and termination of all my earnings. Bernard rang me to express alarm. The bank might react negatively to this full-frontal, high-profile attack.

The atmosphere at the next meeting was even more difficult than previously. Paul Dowling commenced by reading out a list of written questions that had to be answered, before there was any further dialogue:

Did I intend to quit my media employment?

Did I intend to go to the UK? If so, why?

I replied in the affirmative and explained that my motivation to do so was not, as publicly speculated, in order to go bankrupt, but rather to escape the debt distress in the public spotlight. I wanted to continue to negotiate further with them and return in September. I reiterated that a negotiated settlement was always my optimal aim.

'Ah, you intend to hold a sword of Damocles to dangle over us in the autumn, having established your UK COMI [centre of main interest]. We won't tolerate that'.

They then produced a Particulars of Demand seeking payment of €3.69 million within four days. If unpaid, they would commence bankruptcy proceedings against us. We were taken completely by surprise. Bernard was aghast. In his thirty years of dealing with banks on behalf of clients, he had never seen anything like it. Outwardly, I kept my composure. 'Well, lads, I too would like to serve a document on you,' I said. 'We have prepared a revised offer. On top of our previous willingness to sell the lands in my name and the house on the land, we are now prepared to sell the rest of the farm after the lifetime of my mother. We also commit to pay ten per cent of after-tax income during the lifetime of my mother.'

I gave them a copy of the data prepared in advance of the meeting. They asked to leave the room so that they could confer. They returned after five minutes and agreed to withdraw the legal bankruptcy summons threat, pending consideration of our new proposal. Next morning I completed my Thursday early stint in Newstalk, but told them it would be my last show. I broke down saying goodbye to some of my friends there; I had no idea if I would ever return to Ireland, let alone the radio station.

Deirdre had booked tickets for us to leave at 9 a.m. on Easter Monday, 9 April, on the ferry from Rosslare to Fishguard. She would come with me to settle me into the flat – with my back, I couldn't have managed it on my own. On Good Friday, callers came to our door in Sandymount and to that of my mother in Blackstoops: representatives of AIB and their solicitors to re-serve the summons and a letter from the two corporate recovery men: 'Regrettably, and following careful consideration, we must advise you that this proposal falls substantially short of what the Bank considers to be a satisfactory proposal,' it said. 'The Bank has instructed its legal advisers to prepare and issue a Bankruptcy Summons for service upon you.'

They served the envelope on my elderly, bewildered mother as she returned from a Good Friday church service. They didn't care what trauma or anxiety they inflicted before they enjoyed their long holiday weekend. I knew we could offer no more. If they wanted all-out warfare, they had picked the wrong person.

Over the Easter weekend, I composed a detailed letter to Dowling and Renwick, setting out my overall position. I set out my record of co-operation with AIB, the attempts to stem the losses in Celtic, restructure the company, inviting in the receiver at the earliest possible date, ensuring the successful sale of a majority of the shops with the receiver, hiring Bernard Somers to see how I could repay them the maximum amount possible, submitting two written offers to sell my current and future assets and explaining that over thirty years I had always discharged all my personal debts with the bank.

I reassured them that in my absence, Bernard Somers and my solicitor Bill O'Connor would continue to seek to negotiate an agreed solution with them. I pleaded that they would stop pursuing my wife since she had no assets other than a half-share in a bungalow, for which my mother had a right of residence, and her only salary was that of a teacher. The legal pursuit of her would not realise any material cash. It was just harassment. I repeated that I would not be able to pay the full amount owed by Celtic Bookmakers and had been open with them about the prospect of personal insolvency at all times. The bank at no stage had put forward any compromise proposal other than demands that I work for an unspecified period for the benefit of AIB and liquidate all assets for the bank's coffers. The bank was not prepared to take any culpability for their original lending decisions. I added:

My life since late 2010 has been a living hell. The pressure of working in a high-profile media role on a daily basis, while trying to deal responsibly and fairly with my financial affairs, has been extremely stressful. Over recent months this has become distress, which I cannot sustain. The incessant public probing of my affairs and the intransigence of AIB has forced me to escape to anonymity. This has caused enormous dislocation and upset to me and my family. My elderly mother and children find it extremely difficult to cope. I found the hostility displayed by you both personally at last week's meeting to be quite shocking in all the above circumstances, but we will positively participate in the next meeting in a month's time as agreed at the conclusion of the last meeting.

On that misty spring morning, as the ferry pulled farther and farther away from Ireland, I stood alone on the top deck looking back until the Wexford coastline became first indistinct then disappeared. This was the first time I had left the country for more than a few days at a time. I was always naturally a home bird, with little interest in travel. Neither had I lived on my own, at home or abroad, before – Deirdre was adamant that she would not give up her teaching post and, in any case, our youngest child, John, was still in full-time education; she needed to be around to look after him. I had no idea whether I was embarking on an adventure or on the road to nowhere. To emigrate in your twenties, thirties or even forties can be an exciting chapter of new situations and opportunities – but not in your fifties, happily married for almost thirty years, with four children.

My new home was to be Apartment 25, Meridian Wharf, Trawler Road, Swansea. Ironically, it was part of a new complex developed by Irish builders who had gone bust. I was the first tenant. Dawson's letting agency in the marina was responsible for everything: lease/rent for a minimum of a year, maintenance, refuse collection, security and furniture. We moved all my clothes and gear into the two-bedroom flat, which had a small balcony overlooking boats in the marina. It was adjacent to ten kilometres of a beautiful sandy beach. I had always wanted to live beside the sea, but had never known that this was Hurricane Central: the howling wind and rain didn't seem to stop for the next fourteen months.

I applied for a unique tax reference number (UTN) and notified the Irish Revenue Commissioners of my change of residency. I joined the local library, which was a fantastic free service, and for the first time in my life read a book per week. I learned to do my own shopping in Tesco, laundry, ironing, hoovering and household cleaning. My radio attitude to housework had always been 'It may not kill you, but why risk it?' Doing it now proved I was a meticulously tidy person. Who knew?

The brilliant thing about living in Wales was total anonymity. No one had a clue who I was. The worst thing was the loneliness. Time drags in exile. There are 168 hours in a week, and if you count down the minutes, it's a long time. I found this solitary existence utterly depressing. Some days were so long and empty I would simply kill them off by getting drunk. Drink was cheap – the price of a pint as low as £2.30. My favourite pub was Walkabout in Wind Street: it had the biggest screen displays of televised sport. Two working men's clubs had cheap booze and racing on the TV. Swansea, and particularly this street, are known as the 'piss pot' of Britain because they teem and throb with hen and stag parties every weekend. I was too old for that night-time rowdy social scene.

Strangely, I wanted to be alone, despite hating my loneliness. I felt humiliated, like a fugitive, and didn't want to talk about my circumstances to anybody. I wanted to endure my penance and culpability for my failings on my own.

Any menial, ordinary task I had to do was planned as if it was a major event. I would think, I could do this tomorrow or be really bold and do it next week. In the adjacent convenience shop to the apartment building, I bought the *Racing Post* every day to study all the horseracing and sports betting/form/results. I joined the swimming pool beside Swansea University, a wonderful 50-metre pool, where I swam sixty-four lengths (two miles) over more than two hours in a session without stopping. My other main preoccupation was walking miles each day along the bay.

My daily high point was chatting to Deirdre on the phone and eventually on Skype each evening. She would fly over to me through Cardiff or Bristol airports every third weekend. My life revolved around those forty-eight hours of reunion with my soul mate. Each time she arrived, I was full of expectant delight. I'd sink into despair when she left. The worst of the winter weather came in January. Cardiff airport was shut, so Deirdre was unable to come over to me. I was desolate.

The state health system, the NHS, although much derided, worked brilliantly for me. I went to the nearby Kingsway surgery, applied for and obtained a medical card. I made an appointment to see Dr Evans to procure my back tablets. He duly prescribed them each month and explained they would be entirely free. 'And how much do I owe you, Doctor?' I enquired, expecting it to be the usual fifty euro or the equivalent, as it was in Ireland.

'Oh, my services are free also.'

The Welsh people are lovely – friendly, modest and polite. I had only to open my mouth and utter any sentence for people to respond, 'What part of Ireland are you from?'

Because of my previous early-morning radio routine, I still woke up at five most mornings. I would start each day by listening to Irish radio via Sky TV, with an hour of Newstalk *Breakfast*, followed by an hour of *Morning Ireland*. In bad weather, I was cooped up between the sitting room and the bedroom in the flat, with no one to talk to and only my own moody company. No pictures, posters or photos could be affixed to the plain bare walls. I went weeks without having a face-to-face conversation with anyone. The most famous Swansea son is the poet Dylan Thomas. In the railway station, there is a plaque with his words 'He who seeks work finds rest. He who seeks rest finds boredom'. Boy, could I relate to that.

AIB, meanwhile, was determined to make me bankrupt in Ireland at the earliest possible date. Having given me until 13 May 2012 to repay them €3.69 million, they proceeded into the High Court on 14 May seeking a bankruptcy summons to be issued by Justice Elizabeth Dunne. When a person resides outside the jurisdiction, the legal procedure is to get court approval for one month's notice by post, in lieu of direct summons service on a resident. She duly granted this summons dispatch. A full urgent hearing of the case was sought by AIB at the earliest possible date after 14 June.

I was almost ready to keel over and accept twelve years of Irish bankruptcy. However, my Wexford solicitor Bill O'Connor enlisted the help of a specialist barrister, Brian Conroy, who convinced me I was obliged to resist. The hearing of the case was due for mention as early as 9 July, so I had urgently to prepare a lengthy affidavit of response. I lost interest in explaining publicly or privately that under the law I had done nothing wrong. No misrepresentation, no false accounting, no transfer of assets, no statutory breaches of tax compliance, no wrongdoing under any section of the Companies Act as a director, no reckless trading, no fraudulent practice, no preferential treatment of creditors, no misconduct, no financial irresponsibility, no neglect of financial affairs, no failure to keep records, no reluctance to co-operate. The Office of the Director of Corporate Enforcement (ODCE) made no finding under Section 56 or Section 150 of the Companies Act against me. I had no holiday home, yacht or opulent lifestyle.

Further to a lengthy conference call in the third week of June, I explained to my legal team that I disputed the amount owing on two grounds: that it was unfair to continue to charge me approximately €240,000 in interest after they had exercised their fixed and floating charge on the assets of Celtic through the receivership on 4 January 2011; that the total professional fees of the receiver and his legal team, which exceeded €306,000, were way too high. We also disputed bank charges for items such as night safes, which continued long after shops had been closed. We highlighted that their grounding affidavit against Deirdre had been placed in my envelope and wrongly served. This was all contained in my affidavit, which was sworn in John Morse's office on Saturday, 24 June, and submitted to the High Court by Bill the following Monday morning, as part of my application to dismiss the bankruptcy summons.

The bank responded with a submission to the court, producing a certificate invoking Clause 5 of the guarantee we had signed. This said:

> A certificate by any officer of the Bank as to the amount for the time being due from the Borrower to the Bank or where the amount so due exceeds the amount up to which the Guarantee may be enforced by a certificate to that effect but without specifying the amount so due by the Borrower and as to interest after demand from time to time payable hereunder shall be conclusive evidence for purposes against the Guarantor.

This standard provision in all personal guarantees apparently stated that it did not matter what the actual amount owing was: as long as two authorised officers of AIB certified it was a stated amount, then that was what was owed. They tried to pole-vault over the issues we had raised, disputing the amount of the liability through this certificate. According to this, they claimed I had no right to challenge any sum they sought as a consequence of the explicit terms of the guarantee. I had never seen this certificate before. It had no date on it. The two signatures were not accompanied by any typed names or titles of people in the bank. It did not have the bank's seal. My response was that this was worse than the most draconian powers of the Revenue Commissioners. It did not matter what anyone owed AIB, as long as AIB certified that they owed it. How could this be fair or proper procedure?

At the hearing on 22 July, Justice Elizabeth Dunne said she would be on holiday for the next three weeks and would give a reserved judgement on 21 August.

That evening Brian Conroy rang to explain that, even if we won on the legal and procedural points, AIB could obtain a judgement for a reduced amount and proceed back to the High Court. He indicated it was only a matter of time before I was compelled into bankruptcy. From that point on, I had to work on establishing a COMI, providing bank accounts, utility bills and other evidence to prove I had been a habitual resident in Swansea for the better part of six months. On Monday, 20 August, I registered my bankruptcy petition in Wales and paid the £700 fee. An appointment was made for a district judge to hear the petition at 10 a.m. on Friday, 31 August.

One week before that, Justice Dunne gave her verdict. She found that the bank were wrong to proceed without a judgement to establish definitively the precise amount owing prior to bankruptcy proceedings. She issued a warning of sorts to the banks, about relying on their own certification. In this regard, I believe it was a landmark judgement, whereby financial institutions would be unable to try to bulldoze debtors with the small print of a guarantee in relation to such certificates. She stated she wouldn't hear any more about the case until 8 October and we were allowed to apply for our costs. The result was entirely due to the exemplary quality of my legal team, who kept battling on even after I had given up hope.

The media reported the case as a victory for us over AIB. I knew it was nothing of the sort. It was a temporary reprieve from bankruptcy, which I expected to happen on 31 August, ten days ahead. As part of our submissions to the Swansea court service, we had made reference to the ongoing proceedings in the Dublin High Court. This judgement, terminating Irish bankruptcy proceedings against me, greatly simplified arguments in favour of our own petition in the UK. There was now no parallel process.

While the British were enjoying a summer of celebrations with the Queen's Diamond Jubilee and the spectacular London Olympics, I spent those wet months (the coldest and wettest summer on record in the UK) agonising over every legal strategy of bankruptcy. I had no certainty as to whether I would get a bankruptcy order or what life in bankruptcy would entail. I concluded to myself: even if I win, I lose. Prospects of a negotiated settlement with AIB had evaporated; they were determined on the legal route. Either they would bankrupt me for a long, long time in Ireland, or I could go bankrupt in Wales for a year. I chose the latter.

The British have been at this since 1986. Their system, unlike the Irish regime, works. They understand that getting people through a financial crisis and out the other end is more important than indefinite damnation. It's better for the economy and society to give people a fresh start, rather than paralysing them while they can still make a contribution to society. I was under strict orders to keep my mouth shut to anyone back home. I kept my sisters Christine and Val apprised of developments, so they could filter news to my mother. I didn't want to cause her any added stress.

By Friday morning, 31 August, Deirdre had returned to teaching in Dublin. John Morse and I rocked up to courtroom number four, waiting in the antechamber.

'I don't think His Honour will keep you too long. He's due on the first tee for his round of golf at noon,' the porter quipped to me. We fidgeted nervously on observing another man in the same waiting room. Was he there on behalf of the media or AIB? Relief. Apparently, he was totally unconnected with our case. District Judge Peter Llewellyn was wearing a three-piece navy pinstriped suit, with a pink silk handkerchief in his top pocket.

'Oh, Mr Morse, who are you representing?'

'Your Honour, Mr Yates is a long-standing valued client,' John replied.

The judge asked me to remain standing. 'Are you Ivan Alfred Yates?'

'Yes, Your Honour.'

'Are you, Mr Yates, residing at apartment 25, Meridian Wharf, Swansea?'

'Yes, Your Honour.'

'I have read through the files of this case and am satisfied under the 1986 Act and European rules that you are entitled to create your COMI here and have successfully done so. At 10.07 a.m. on this day I declare you bankrupt. If there are any further issues, it will be a matter for the official receiver's office.'

'Get out quickly. This is what we came for,' John muttered.

It was all over in a matter of ninety seconds. I was bankrupt – an indelible stain on my CV and a nasty stigma. Instead of being introduced as 'former minister, bookmaker and broadcaster', I knew that, after I was discharged, I would be 'former bankrupt'. A low point in my self-image, integrity and life. We made arrangements to call back later in the day to collect a copy of the bankruptcy order. I thanked John for all his efforts over the previous three weeks in preparing the mountain of paperwork. He had no experience in dealing with insolvency cases. But I wanted a local guy to handle the case and he had done me proud. It was a rare sunny morning as I walked alone by the river Tawe, on my way back to my apartment.

But I had a more immediate problem. I realised that, by the following Tuesday, the UK insolvency service website and the Swansea court register online would reveal that Ivan Yates had become bankrupt on the previous Friday. At all stages I'd briefed Nigel Heneghan of developments, as my close friend and unofficial link with the media. His office would send me copies of all press clippings relating to myself. We hadn't come to a conclusion as to how, when and where to issue the news of my bankruptcy. While I had imposed a news blackout about my circumstances to friends, I knew there would be a firestorm of publicity about my new status.

Having returned from the court, I pressed the fob key against the front-door panel of my apartment building, then spotted a photographer and another man in dark glasses about twenty yards away. The camera, with a really long lens, was aimed at me. Who could be photographing me? Maybe I was being paranoid. What further trouble was to befall me? It was around midday.

After I got in, the external doorbell to the flat rang a few times. I didn't answer it. I was trapped. The next five hours were among the most stressful of my time in the UK. There was a loud banging on my internal flat door, from which I assumed that the strangers had penetrated the building. In fact, it was staff belonging to the property complex, who had disapprovingly noticed them loitering around. The two men had been talking to kids and asking questions. Then a note was placed under my door from the concierge people, warning me that they might be bailiffs seeking to collect a debt. Jesus wept. I knew who they were, but I wasn't going to budge. Later on, I noticed across the marina, some ninety metres away, a man with a long lens focused on my balcony. Had I been photographed peering out?

This anxious stalemate went on for hours, until at 5.03 p.m. I received a text from John Drennan, political columnist with the *Sunday Independent* and long-standing friend: 'Hi Ivan. There's two fellas from the Sindo outside your Swansea residence today Friday. They are not unsympathetic and would owe you big time if you stepped out and said hello. Frankly, they are desperate. Regards, J Drennan.'

I rang Nigel, who spoke to their news editor, Liam Collins. The journalist in the dark glasses was Ronald Quinlan. He and his photographer were due to catch a flight back to Dublin from Bristol airport and had to leave. I was too upset to talk to them. Nigel agreed I would do a phone interview with John Drennan on Saturday morning at 9 a.m.

It seemed those guys had come over on a speculative investigation as to my circumstances. It was a complete coincidence that they had landed at my door within hours of my bankruptcy order. I turned a problem into a solution by announcing the full details of my bankruptcy exclusively in the *Sunday Independent*. I would have to live the next fifty-two weeks of my life in bankruptcy and in Wales. My economic liberty was gone. I was disbarred from being a company director. Any earnings could be subject to an income payments order or income payments agreement, whereby the UK's state insolvency service, called the official receiver (OR), would take for the benefit of AIB any income beyond what were deemed to be 'reasonable living expenses'. In my form-filling, I had declared that my pensions were worth £3,100 a month.

I stated that I needed all this to maintain myself and my family back in Ireland (they would have £1,000 per month). Basically my main aim was to keep my pension. I had no other source of income. By this stage all my savings had been exhausted on relocation costs and professional fees. My other objective was to be allowed to keep my car, a Volvo S80, purchased in 2006, with more than 220,000 kilometres on the clock; it had been valued at less than £2,500.

My overriding strategy was to do everything to co-operate with the OR's office in terms of information, transparency and local availability for interview. I knew that as long as I co-operated fully my discharge on 31 August 2013 would be automatic. My sole goal in life was to obtain my discharge on time, with the minimum level of impediments.

My life and livelihood for the next year would be conducted in the legal context of my being subject to control by the official receiver's office, which had the power to take over all my affairs. Bankruptcy anywhere in the world is the same. The deal is quite straightforward. On your discharge date, all your debts are wiped away. The flip-side is that all the assets you own on the day you are declared bankrupt become the property of the OR.

The first thing that would happen next was my formal interview with the OR case officer. My entire files presented to the court were transferred straight away to them at Langdon House in another part of the marina area of Swansea. This forensic event, lasting up to four hours, is usually organised within seven days of your bankruptcy order. I was braced for the scrutiny to which they would subject me. I also feared that my local bank account would be frozen, closed down indefinitely, and I would be unable to receive my pension payments. I was beginning a voyage of discovery into an unknown world. While I had studied all the legal ramifications of the 1986 Insolvency Act, I didn't really know how it would work in the practical sense. I faced an exceptionally bleak year as an economic zombie, with the ultimate loss of everything I had ever owned.

AIB issued a statement about me on 3 September. It said that they did not typically comment on individual customer cases and were working in good faith with customers to agree solutions based on consensus:

> AIB does not set out to target specific individuals in any circumstances and approaches each case on its own merits. AIB only pursues bankruptcy in a limited number of customer cases and for valid and considered reasons. These potentially include situations where a customer, in AIB's view, is no longer co-operating with the bank, or where a customer seeks to establish residency in another country which might result in a lower recovery for the bank and the Irish taxpayer.

I was utterly shocked to learn subsequently, by way of answer to a parliamentary question (ref: 50683/12 of 15 November), in correspondence from Minister of Finance Michael Noonan on 23

November 2012 to Eoghan Murphy TD, that only two persons had been subject to bankruptcy summonses and court proceedings by AIB since 2010. Those individuals were Ivan and Deirdre Yates.

My formal interview with the official receiver on 11 September lasted almost four hours and covered the minutiae of every aspect of my business, family, personal and banking life over the previous handful of years. Because of back pain, I had to lie on the floor for most of it. George Field, my case officer, was a senior civil servant, with thirty years' experience in the insolvency service. He took copious handwritten notes that he asked me to autograph, page by page, as a witness statement. He then informed me that because there were debt-free assets, with net cash realisable on my bankruptcy, he was going to refer my case to a trustee in bankruptcy (TIB). I asked who this would be and whether they would be chosen from a South Wales panel. He said that AIB would nominate its appointee. I felt as if I was starring in a film of a prison escape: digging an underground tunnel, climbing over barbed wire and now finding myself in the swamps, where the bloodhounds would be released on me.

I knew AIB would be relentless in selecting the most expensive, thorough, sharpest insolvency practitioner to grab and liquidate our home and farm, as well as seize every other asset they could. No taxpayer resources would be spared to continue their vindictive pursuit of me and my family. On 10 October, I received notice that Baker Tilly in London, one of the largest financial firms in the world, was to be my TIB. Joint trustees were appointed, from their London and Dublin offices.

Once they had assessed all my data, they arranged an interview in my solicitor's office in Swansea, which again took more than three hours of painstaking explanations about the history of our family property, my mother's life interest, the agricultural long-term leases and the potential sale of everything, sooner or later. It's amazing:

when you're asked to explain details on a bank account three years ago, you honestly can't remember the transaction. Although it could be entirely innocent, with an acceptable explanation, you suddenly feel trepidation that you may have committed some offence. I was nearly always able to retrace my steps and provide them with a comprehensive answer. Everything was done on the basis of 'to the best of your knowledge and belief', which was fair enough.

They seemed content for me to keep my pension income to live on. It later transpired that no legal basis existed for them to take money from a foreign superannuated group pension scheme.

I kept reading in the newspapers of this wonderful soft option of a more lenient UK bankruptcy. This was written and spoken about by people who had no clue what they were talking about and had had no direct or indirect experience of the process. A foreign bankrupt is a very wounded and vulnerable animal, without recourse to local pals for moral or technical support. During my year in UK bankruptcy, it seemed that the official climate for anyone with an Irish address was increasingly rigorous and worthy of extra pursuit as a deterrent to other Irish debtors. I suspected that the Irish government had made representations because between 2010 and 2012 the number of Irish people obtaining UK bankruptcy rose from 15 to 75.

Bernard Somers was a constant source of strength and wisdom. He had seen this tsunami of indebtedness before in various cycles.

It would be wrong to say that my sixteen months in South Wales was devoid of memorable high points. I really appreciated the individual visits and conversations of encouragement over a meal and a drink with old comrades Tom Tynan, Philip Lynch and Stewart Kenny. Nigel Heneghan was exceptionally kind to me and insisted that I come up to Elland Road to watch Leeds play Chelsea in the League Cup quarter-final with him. I hooked up with my old pal from AIB, London, Kevin Dever, at a few race meetings. He had taken early retirement from AIB GB. He was always in flying form, raising my spirits.

One London lawyer described my lifestyle as 'more brown ale than Bollinger'. I got ossified drunk the day my beloved Manchester City won the Premiership in May 2012, originally because I thought they were going to be pipped at the post – until the ecstasy of two late goals. My favourite moments were Friday nights going to the adjoining Grape and Olive restaurant on the top floor of the iconic Marina Tower (twenty-eight storeys high beside my flat) for a late-night meal with Deirdre. We became long-lost lovers again, cherishing moments together. She made life worthwhile, despite her dreary absences.

I won't pretend I was ever broke. Because of my pension, I didn't have to resort to selling the *Big Issue* on the streets, flog my organs for clinical trials or visit the gold-exchange shops to raise cash.

The biggest regret of my life, with the benefit of hindsight, was borrowing money from AIB and blithely signing personal guarantees, naïvely trusting in their decency and fairness. While Bernard Somers was negotiating on our behalf at various meetings, we would chat about each other's contemporary work at the time. I couldn't help but absorb details of his period as a non-executive director on the board of Eircom to aid in the restructuring of their enormous debts, further to five changes of ownership post-privatisation. He helped secure the write-down of €1.7 billion of corporate debt. No one there lost or will lose their home.

Would I advise any other Irish debtor, among the 18,000–40,000 potentially insolvent people, to follow in my footsteps and seek British bankruptcy? The public perception of UK insolvency is facile, and no two cases are the same in terms of age, family circumstances, income, creditor vindictiveness, personal health and, most importantly, temperament. I cannot deny that there were a few specific moments of black despair. However, this saga has taught me new survival skills of toughness. I intend to put it behind me, and will ultimately be better, rather than bitter.

Epilogue

If a week is a long time in politics, it's an even longer time in broadcasting. There's always someone younger, hungrier and potentially better than you are, ready, willing and able to take the microphone or talk to the camera.

When I parted company with Newstalk, that was it. I didn't ask Garrett Harte to consider re-employing me when I came back after the Swansea sojourn. In the nature of things, he would try out other talent. Nobody in his position could run the flagship morning programme of his station on a contingency basis: 'We quite liked yer man and he might come back . . .' I knew that was never going to happen.

Before I left, Denis O'Brien had met me, expressed concern about my situation, and offered to help. I don't know what he made of my reply, which was that I was probably the only person who'd ever visited his office and didn't want anything from him. I'd cocked up my finances all by myself, so it was up to me to deal with it. I was grateful for his kindness, but I preferred bankruptcy to begging. Now, when you've told a radio station that you're abandoning a programme you've helped to build up, failed to explain properly why you're doing what you're doing and closed down all contact with them for months, your chances of re-employment have to be limited.

But towards the end of the summer, Garrett persisted past my rude ignoring of his messages just enough for me to realise that I might have a life after bankruptcy. And it might, I discovered as the summer melted into autumn, be an interesting life. Pat Kenny was leaving RTÉ to join Newstalk. Tom Dunne was taking his light-hearted knowledge of everything musical to a night-time slot, so the morning would be solidly news and current affairs until Jonathan Healy's lunchtime was overtaken by Seán Moncrieff's highly successful idiosyncratic afternoon programme. Chris Donoghue and I would be handing over to Pat at the end of our show. And, just as I had studied and stolen from George Hook, I could now study and steal from Pat.

'Yes, please,' I said to Garrett. 'Yes, thank you.'

I was interviewed by Pat, then by Chris about the bankruptcy tourism. The reactions were mixed. Those who had debt or insolvency experience were extremely supportive, unlike those who did not.

No time, fortunately, for argument or self-pity. I was back in the saddle, talking to the microphone, slagging Chris (whose workaholism had gone up by several notches since I'd left). The city was peppered with vast posters of the two of us, carrying instructions on how to find us on your radio. Then Stephen Rae, the Editor in Chief of Independent Newspapers, rang and asked me to do a weekly column for the *Irish Independent*.

As a postscript to Swansea, I tidied up all my affairs there, insofar as there was no income payments order sought against me through Swansea Court. Neither was any bankruptcy restriction order placed on me, despite the most exhaustive investigations by the UK insolvency service into all my actions before I'd gone bankrupt. This gave me the opportunity of an entirely fresh start, which was all I wanted.

As of now, I have lost the farm and home property in Blackstoops, Enniscorthy. While my mother still resides there, a stay of execution postpones the final parting with it. Certain options remain open for a final negotiated settlement. Time will tell.

What's for sure is that my days of being a serial entrepreneur are over. I've learned hard lessons, and I'm far more risk-averse now than I was before. Including my year in Swansea, I lived through three years of self-recrimination, pain and anguish. Often I felt completely isolated. I didn't expect people to have sympathy with my situation – especially not in the grip of a very painful recession for the country, where the sins of big risk-takers were being paid for by the innocent masses – and this knowledge only added to a growing sense of isolation from those around me. But worse than that was the bitterness I felt – towards the situation I'd got myself in to and towards a bank who as I saw it had left me high and dry. I had made my bed, yes, and I was very much lying in it – a broken man.

When I returned from Swansea, I made a decision. On 23 October 2013, I finished my morning show and returned home. I sat myself down and had a good honest look at my life. I may have had very little left in the world, in terms of worldly goods, but then again, I had everything that mattered – my family, my loved ones, my loyal friends. I could fall into the trap of living in the past, going over my mistakes and regretting my choices. I could let bitterness dictate my future. Or I could decide to put the past where it belonged and look to that same future. Fuck it, Ivan, I told myself, it's time to let it all go. And there and then I resolved to remain positive and restore opportunity to my life.

In the months that followed, I slowly came back to myself. For the first time, I found myself living in the present, enjoying what I had in the moment, whether it be an outing to a movie and a bite to eat afterwards with Deirdre, or just a quiet walk along the strand. My focus switched from what I had lost to what I had found, including appreciating the simple pleasures that had always been right in front of me. And as my perspective shifted, so too did my mood. Happily, these days, I would describe myself as a busy fool, rather than a fool who dwells on the past.

The main thing I found is that the most important thing in life is your relationships. I am blessed to have a wonderful wife and life partner in Deirdre, a healthy family and extended family and friends that I have come to utterly rely on for unswerving loyalty. I may have lost a lot, but I wouldn't change what I have now for anything in the world.

Index

Acknowledgements

While this book is dedicated to my mother, Mrs Mary Yates, and my wife, Deirdre Yates, I am blessed to have had the ongoing support of my family through my sisters Christine and Val, and brother John, who have endured my successes and failures with forbearance and patience. Deirdre's extensive and extended family of the Boyd clan have been an equal source of continuing strength and happiness. Our four children, Andrew, Ciara, Sarah and John, have provided me with a source of inspiration and unceasing joy – they could not have been reared without their second mother, Josephine Fenlon.

I will be forever indebted to the volunteers and supporters in the Wexford constituency party organisation, who supported me in the early years – they know who they are. I always reflect on the wonderful life opportunities they opened up for me when taking a chance on a complete novice.

The task of putting together this book over the past three years has meant that I have had to rely on many friends in order to properly recollect distant events. I would like to thank in this regard especially Bernie Redmond and Breda Cleere, my foremost organisational lieutenants in local politics; recollecting ministerial moments with Tom Tynan and Dermot Murphy; former teachers Brian Studdert and John Fanagan; from my Dáil days Peter White and Geraldine Lannigan-Ryan; stalwarts of Celtic Bookmakers' endeavours Winnie Doyle and Pat Crowe; as well as my long-standing friends Adrian

Rothwell, Pat Boland, Phil Hogan, John Lynch, Jim and Jackie Bolger, Jim Furlong, Philip Lynch, Michael Sheil, Niall and Joyce Ashmore. I would like to acknowledge the excellent archive services of the National Library of Ireland, which I visited over many months to obtain print newspaper records.

If life is a series of temporary alliances, I continue to enormously benefit from so many rich friendships in Wexford and Dublin – while too numerous to mention here, they are invaluable to me. Their continuing reconnections have made my life fulfilling. As stated in this book, I live to work. I have greatly benefited throughout my adult working life from the dedication of so many superb colleagues in employment circumstances of farming, politics, Celtic Bookmakers and media. So many memorable people from whose efforts I gained are not listed herein, but mega thanks are due to you.

I could not have survived the intense stresses and distresses of the past four years without the personal warmth and skills of key individuals: Bill O'Connor, Sean Bates, Bernard Somers, Nigel Heneghan, Gavin Duffy, Paul McCann, John Murphy, John Morse and Cyril Barden, along with the specialist expertise they obtained on my behalf. I must record my deepest appreciation for those who have never ceased to believe in my limited talents: Garrett Harte, Denis O'Brien, Andrew Hanlon, John Baker and Frances Keane.

I have no experience of being an author, so this book project could never have been undertaken without the constant urgings, professional assistance and continuing encouragement of Terry (Tess) Prone, who has been a dear, loyal and indispensable friend for several years. The inimitable agent Jonathan Williams has guided me through the process of editing and publishing. Publishers Hachette Ireland and their entire senior management have consistently shown remarkable belief in me and commitments to making this book a success. I would like to particularly thank Ciara Considine for her professionalism, hard work and dedication to completing the process.